Prisons and Punishment

PRISONS AND PUNISHMENT

Reconsidering Global Penality

Edited by
Mechthild Nagel and Seth N. Asumah

Africa World Press, Inc.

| P.O. Box 1892 | | P.O. Box 48 |
| Trenton, NJ 08607 |  | Asmara, ERITREA |

Africa World Press, Inc.

P.O. Box 1892
Trenton, NJ 08607

P.O. Box 48
Asmara, ERITREA

Copyright © 2007 Mechthild Nagel and Seth N. Asumah
First Printing 2007

Book design: Saverance Publishing Services
Cover design: Ashraful Haque

Library of Congress Cataloging-in-Publication Data

Prisons and punishment : reconsidering global penality / edited by Mechthild Nagel and Seth N. Asumah.
    p. cm.
Includes bibliographical references and index.
ISBN 1-59221-480-0 (hard cover) -- ISBN 1-59221-481-9 (pbk.)
1. Prisons--Cross-cultural studies. 2. Punishment--Cross-cultural studies. I. Nagel, Mechthild. II. Asumah, Seth Nii, 1954-

HV9443.P758 2006
365--dc22
                        2006008513

It is not the prisoners who need reformation, it is the prisons.
-Oscar Wilde

*Men fight for freedom; then they begin to accumulate laws
to take it away from themselves.*
-Anonymous

To

Philip Otieno

To

Tosha Abiana Asumah

To

All those who have sacrificed their lives and those who are engaged
in the struggle to reform the distributive paradigms of justice
and prison systems in the world

Table of Contents

III. AFRICAN AND COMPARATIVE PERSPECTIVES ON PENAL LAW AND PRISONS

IV. ALTERNATIVE VISIONS ON PRISONS AND PUNISHMENT

Acknowledgements

We have been assisted by many people in our work on this project. It would have been impossible to produce this volume without the support of our families, colleagues and friends at the State University of New York College at Cortland. We appreciate the financial support of the office of the provost at SUNY Cortland and Dr. Elizabeth Davis-Russell, Provost and Vice President for Academic Affairs.

Our special thanks go to Ms. Sandra A. Long for a superb job in assisting us in putting together the manuscript; for layout, design, word processing, and technical assistance for this volume. Also, by posing challenging questions she enhanced our ability to produce a work of quality. To Debby Dintano, secretary, Political Science Department at SUNY Cortland, we express our appreciation for your assistance throughout the process.

We like to extend our sincere gratitude to Damola Ifaturoti, Kassahun Checole and the staff at Africa World Press for their patience and commitment in assisting us in bringing this project to fruition. Finally, for those we have forgotten to thank in this process, we humbly apologize.

The editors are grateful for permission to re-publish these articles:

Drew Leder's article The Life-World of the Incarcerated was previously published in *Social Justice*, 31, 2004, pp. 51-66. It was also published under the title "Imprisoned Bodies: The Life-World of the Incarcerated" in *The Phenomology of the Body: The 20th Annual Symposium of The Simon Silverman Phenomenology Center* (ed., Daniel J. Martino, 2003, pp. 1-18).

A different version of Tiyo Attallah Salah-El's article "A Call for the Abolition of Prisons" was previously published in *The New Abolitionists* (Joy James ed., SUNY Press, 2005, pp. 69-74).

John C. Mubangizi's article "Comparing Human Rights Protection for Prisoners: Which Way South Africa?" was previously published in *South African Yearbook of International Law*, 26, 2001, 87-113.

Foreword

It is a privilege to be asked to write a foreword to this extraordinary volume full of contributions from extraordinary people.

The contributors of this volume have ventured in a sphere of scholarship that most people will hesitate to engage in because of society's perception of prisons and the prevailing discourse over penality, especially after September 11, 2001. This volume, like the conference on prisons out of which it has emerged, represents a threefold scholarly synergy among the experience and understanding of those who have experienced imprisonment, of other scholars committed to learning from that experience, and of comparison of the evolution of penal practice and of its actual and potential transformation across continents, from Africa to Europe to North America. African penality has been especially neglected in criminological and criminal justice literature, and the wealth of pan-African material in this volume—closely integrated as it is with material on European-American penal systems which have been imposed on Africans—sets this volume apart from earlier cross-cultural compilations on the evolution of penal practices and of their alternatives.

This book represents the most comprehensive evidence I have yet seen on the global growth of the crime control-industrial complex. The explosion in use of imprisonment in my home country, the United States, is disturbing enough in itself. With 4 percent of the world's population, we now hold 25 percent of her prisoners. Contributors to this volume share my recognition of this distinct role of dubious leadership that the political culture of the United States plays in promoting incarceration and other forms of punishment.

The United States was constituted in genocide and conquest of its earlier inhabitants, and in enslavement of kidnapped Africans. The nation was constituted in war. Its politicians have since risen to and held onto power by mobilizing the populace to support war upon war against foreign and domestic enemies. By the last century a pattern had become established: Incarceration rates only leveled off or declined when the same class of young men who otherwise were the stereotypic "dangerous class" of those most imprisoned were sent abroad to fight overt wars against foreign enemies. Most recently, incarceration rates dropped during the Vietnam War, and rose back to unprecedented heights just as that war ended. The trend turned most sharply upward just as the Cold War ended. At the moment at which "economic conversion" of military industries was being widely advocated, an already established crime control industry proliferated. As many of the authors in this book describe, the crime control industry has expanded from building prison hardware to operating private juvenile detention facilities, jails, prisons and prison industries first in the United States, and now globally.

To me, the most insidious aspect of the growth of private prison industry is that it is not publicly accountable. A few years back a group of prisoners made national news by escaping from a private prison in Ohio. When Ohio legislators asked to inspect the prison, the private corporate owner refused permission, and the legislators were powerless to gain access to the grounds or to prison records even though the prison owner was paid by the state to do the public's business. Private prison activity, supposedly serving the public good, is publicly unaccountable. If imprisonment in itself is an abuse of the public good, private prison industry opens the door to abuse at a whole new invisible level—to absolute power with the potential to corrupt those who do and manage imprisonment absolutely. If privatization opens the door to abuse and exploitation for profit in Ohio, which at state roadside rest stops there is touted as the "heart of America," the harm privatization by multinational corporations causes as it expands in the so-called "third world" must almost be beyond comprehension. It is not news to me that this global expansion is happening, but the documentation of the extent to which contributors to this volume document that expansion, as in South Africa, takes my breath away.

Benito Mussolini as an Italian "duke" proclaimed that the greater good of the Italian people—as in making their trains run on time—lay in "fascism," which he defined as having the state serving private corporate interests. In *Prisons and Punishment* we see how strongly, at a global level, fascism has embraced and gripped the policy and practice of what some label "criminal justice." We see that prevailing penal policy and practice is a significant part of the global tendency of corporate power to make state actors serve corporate power's unquenchable thirst to rape, enslave, and potentially destroy the capacity of our mother earth to support and sustain, let alone nurture and care for, life in human and other forms. For anyone who values life over death and destruction in any form, *Prisons and Punishment* should be a wake-up call. If only we pay attention, the authors and editors of this volume offer us a major gift of understanding contemporary, global processes of exploitation and of paths to life-giving transformation of this process.

Co-editor Mecke Nagel is among the contributors of this book. Like me, she is a full-time employee of the state as an academic specializing in a field that since the 1960s has come to be known as "criminal justice." She, like other contributors to this volume, including co-editor Seth Asumah, a colleague at the State University of New York College at Cortland, was born in a country other than the United States (she from Germany, he from Ghana, but a naturalized citizen of the United States). Nagel, like Asumah, happens as an academic to be working on a faculty that is not explicitly criminological or criminal justicey—she in philosophy, he in political science and Africana Studies. She, like Asumah, has a record of research and personal experience across continents. Another contributor to this volume, Tiyo Attallah Salah-El, introduced Mecke and me to one another years ago. From inside prison in the United States in Pennsylvania where he is serving a sentence of life without the possibility of parole, Tiyo has become a Quaker with a compelling vision of how to respond to what we now call "crime" without prisons; he is a pioneering member of the penal abolition movement. Mecke has worked closely with him for years, illustrating the collaboration between activist academicians like the editors of this volume and those are now and who have in times past been in prison. While the European-American model of punishment separates those officially labeled offenders from the rest of us, the works in this book represent a commitment, as contributor Ishka JoJo Alpern puts it, to "Rebuilding Burnt Bridges between Prisoners and Communities." I thank them for the monumental contribution to my own, to say nothing of its potential contribution to other readers' understanding what this work represents.

Hal Pepinsky
Bloomington, Indiana, USA
January 2006

INTRODUCTION

Mechthild Nagel and Seth N. Asumah

It is not the prisoners who need reformation, it is the prisons.

-Oscar Wilde

Prison reform will not work until we start sending a better class of people there.

-Anonymous

Confinement within institutions, such as prisons, jails, reformatories, detention centers and reform schools, as a method of punishment has become a universally acceptable practice in recent times. Indubitably, the relatively modern use of institutions for the detention of lawbreakers in societies around the world has been predominantly shaped by the United States of America. Before the eighteenth century, the typical methods of punishing convicted offenders were through levies, public humiliations, corporal punishment, and executions. At that time, the confinement of people in public institutions for a relatively short period involved two categories; debtors who failed to pay their debts or accused persons pending trial. Yet, the euphoric prognosis in the twentieth century about the nature and function of prisons with respect to ideological justifications of incapacitation, deterrence, retribution and rehabilitation has since subsided. Many scholars and activists are therefore reexamining the essence of prisons as institutions of punishment in our societies in the 21st Century. While the United States has the dubious distinction of leading the world in incarceration rates, it has also exported its policies and thus globalized its punitive penal regime.

Some of the urgent issues to be tackled by critics of the modern penal apparatus are indefinite incarcerations in the United States and Iraq of "enemy combatants"; inhumanely run and overcrowded prisons all over the world; female prisoners' human rights violations; the establishments of secret CIA run "gulags" in Europe and the Middle East, and the demise of habeas corpus rights in the US military prison of Guantánamo Bay. In an era of globalization and post September 11 obsession with national security, where the authority of the nation state is being challenged amidst economic uncertainty and civil liberty crisis, prisoners of war are cavalierly labeled as 'enemy combatants' in order to evade protocols of standard treatments of such prisoners. Consequently, theorists and activists have to engage in novel praxis philosophy, such as attempting to join in peace, anti-racists, civil libertarian, and anti-globalization movements, in order to engage and confront authorities and proponents of cruel, inhumane, abusive, and degrading punishment of prisoners under the custody of the nation state and private security companies. This book challenges the status quo and accomplishes several objectives in response to the global discourse over prisons and punishment: the efficacy of imprisonment is scrutinized; the notion of crime is problematized in the accounts of former prisoners of conscience and social prisoners; and punishment itself is analyzed from a variety of philosophical perspectives.

While it has become fashionable to speak about the Prison Industrial Complex, echoing Eisenhower's Military Industrial Complex, to describe and critique the global prison crisis, one may have to add another complex to address the systematic deprivation of human rights to people targeted by the state as terrorists, enemies, or subversives: *The Torture Complex* is a fitting and troubling concept for the range of institutions, particularly in the United States, which are aiding and abetting torture practices, such as the executive branch of government, the law, media, medicine and the academy (*The Nation*, 2005). The US led War on Terror since September 11, 2001 has provided democratic governments a convenient carte blanche to engage in a discourse of torture openly and unabashedly. In fact, "the Bush administration's open embrace of torture is unprecedented—but what's unprecedented is not the torture, it's the openness" (Klein 2005, p. 12). The United States has trained for decades dictators, generals and other military cadre from Latin and South America in the School of the Americas, renamed by activists as the School of the Assassins; yet, the government previously engaged in plausible denial. Prior to this new development of declaring torture as a legal and legitimate weapon, the US public was incensed to hear about the human rights abuses at the Guantánamo Bay prison and the Abu Ghraib prison torture scandal. During Saddam Hussein's reign in Iraq, Abu Ghraib Prison reached the apogee for one of the world's notorious entities for confinement with frequent executions, tortures, and despicable living conditions. Abu Ghraib, now controlled by the United States military, has been resuscitated into a dehumanizing crucible especially for civilian prisoners, whose torture Major General Antonio Taguba (2004) graphically described as:

> Breaking chemical lights and pouring the phosphoric liquid on detainees; pouring cold water on the naked detainees; beating detainees with a broom handle and a chair; threatening male detainees with rape; allowing a military police guard to stitch the wound of a detainee who was injured after being slammed against the wall in his cell; sodomizing a detainee with a chemical light and perhaps a broom stick, and using military working dogs to frighten

and intimidate detainees with threats of attack, and in one instance
actually biting a detainee (Hersh, Sept. 13, 2004, p.2).

It is indubitable that such dehumanization is unacceptable in any nation state
or culture. Moreover, in the Arab world and Islamic culture homosexual acts
violate Islamic law. It should also be noted that the abysmal treatment of women
prisoners in Abu Ghraib has received no moral outcry from the media or Pentagon circles. The very fact that these actions were condoned under United
States' watch in Iraq invites questions and concerns about torture for other
unnamed prisoners and prisons in this country. Yet John McWethy's questions
on *Nightline*, May 13, 2004 about vanishing detainees were not too far fetched.
"Since when are people in American custody allowed simply to disappear into
a black hole?... Are they stateless?... Are they dead? Are they alive? What oversight does Congress give?" (McWethy, 2004). However, this moral indignation
seems somewhat misplaced given the sordid historical record. A United States
Supreme Court's *certiorari* hearing of a case in November 2004, which involves
the state of California's racial segregation practices in prison even though the
Court had ruled in 1968 that a similar practice was unconstitutional in Ala-
bama's prison system, gives critics reason to question fairness in the US criminal
justice system. Objectors may argue that in addition to incarcerations that occur
because of criminality or injustices either by design or accident, institutionalization has been reaccentuated in structural forms to define cultural, racial,
gender, socio-political power differentials. Nowhere did racist disappearance
and shameful neglect of criminalized, poor people become more evident than
during hurricane Katrina's downfall on New Orleans in August 2005. As prisoner Dan Bright told Human Rights Watch, "They left us to die there" (quoted
in Sothern, 2005, 18). Countless prisoners of the city's jail in fact died; several
detainees were gassed when trying to evade the rising waters, and they were kept
in locked cells while the warders absconded. The survivors' plight only worsened
when they were transported to other Louisiana jails, brutalized and continuing
to be locked up for months after their jail sentences expired. They indeed disappeared into an administrative abyss, and without a lawyer they continue to be
jailed without due process afforded to them.

As social philosophers, political scientists, and social commentators, we
write the essays in this volume from the premise that it is important to present
viewpoints on punishment and prisons, which differ from most mainstream
perspectives. Most of these essays were presented at the international conference "Thinking about Prisons: Theory and Practice," sponsored by the Social
Philosophy Department at the State University of New York College at Cortland in October 2001. SUNY Cortland is located in rural Central New York
and is surrounded by many medium, maximum, and some supermax prisons, as
well as minimum and shock treatment camps, in addition to county jails. Since
the 1980s we have witnessed a dramatic dismantling of vibrant industries in the
area. These industries first went to union-free South Carolina and later to the
global South. The prison boom, which also began in the 1980s under Governor

Cuomo of New York State, has replaced all non-agricultural industries in this area as the number one growth industry!

The conference brought hundreds of activists and scholars together from South Africa, Canada, and the United States. Prisoners (whose papers were read) and former political and social prisoners reported on prison conditions in the United States and some ventured to map out another future—without prisons! We are, of course, also reminded of Socrates, the market gadfly, who was our first prison intellectual, and of the many venerable philosophers who suffered the course of death, exile, or imprisonment. Philosophy, as a discipline, has dedicated and championed many studies to the theories of punishment, notably, retribution and deterrence. British 18th Century philosopher, Jeremy Bentham, also inspired prison architects in the US to construct a panopticon house of confinement—the birth of the modern prison. Yet, philosophers have been quite silent on the carceral society. French philosopher Michel Foucault's book, *Discipline and Punishment*, served as a watershed and opened a new field of study. Still, academics from other disciplines (e.g., sociology, cultural studies) have taken an interest in his theories, and philosophers of penality are still a small minority in the profession, such as Angela Y. Davis, Joy James, and Drew Leder (Davis 2003; James 2003 and 2005; Leder 2000). Thinking about reforms and possibilities of excarceration seems daunting in the United States where more people are incarcerated for nonviolent and petty crimes than in any other nation state of the world. Yet it is precisely what we must accomplish—to imagine the impossible. One hundred fifty years ago, a similar struggle was waged between those cautionary voices who only supported a gradual abolition of slavery and those militant activists who advocated for total abolition of the "peculiar institution." Precisely because we live with a grim overindulgence in a culture of incarceration, visions of alternatives to incarceration and articulation of abolitionist strategies are of utmost importance to social justice activists. Contributors explore the anti-globalization motto "another world is possible" refracted through the lens of abolishing penal regimes. At the same time, it is prudent to work on reform measures, which will affect a marked decline in use of imprisonment, such as abolishing the death penalty and life sentences; creating alternatives to incarceration programs; decriminalizing addictions; and abolishing minimum sentencing guidelines.

SYNOPSIS OF SECTIONS AND CHAPTERS:

Uniquely examining cross-national perspectives about penal theories and empirical studies, this book brings together African, European, and North American social philosophers and sociologists, political scientists, legal practitioners, prisoners, and abolitionist activists, to reflect not only on the carceral society, notably the United States, but also on the reconceptualization of punishment. Philosophers, such as Leder, Moses, Antonio and Morgareidge, reflect on the meaning of "doing time" in prison. Using different methodologies and theories, they give a nuanced critique of the callous saying "you did the crime, you must do the time." Michael Nieto Garcia weighs in on the meaning of the proverb from a literary perspective, while Ed Kinane gives a vivid account of personal experience as a conscientious objector being confined in a federal penitentiary and notes that indeed it is worth doing time as a political activist who struggles against injustice and in particular for a world freed from war, torture and prisons.

I. Theorizing Prison Experiences, Gender and Resistance

Sharing personal experiences of imprisonment in federal detention centers and in state jails ought to contribute to a richer understanding for those who may only have a mediated and romantic sense of being locked down—given by Hollywood movies or makers of the *Oz* show. A gendered experience of prisons is also highlighted to counter the tendency that female prisoners are only an afterthought in correctional policy. Such neglect is often justified by policy makers because women make up a small fraction of overall prison population. In the first section, most of the authors focus on the carceral apparatus in the United States, while Nagel also provides a cross-cultural analysis of prison regimes in Europe and Africa. Elijah and Kinane discuss the predicament of political imprisonment, and Elijah's article in particular will give us disturbing trends of further erosion of civil liberties in a post September 11 world. Nagel and Barr illustrate the gendered nature of violence fostered by the criminal justice system. Ex-prisoners Kinane and Barr also discuss how prisoners have resisted the dehumanization process that prison experience inevitably brings about.

Soffiyah Elijah, a lawyer and keynote speaker at the SUNY Cortland conference, gives a brief legal history of the emergence of political prisoners in the US. However, this is still a hidden aspect in American legal and political history, since the US government does not recognize the category of political prisoner. Elijah, who is one of the few lawyers representing these prisoners, notes that the vast majority of them faced trumped up criminal charges, in particular the leaders of the Black Panthers who were framed under the FBI's counterintelligence program (COINTELPRO). She highlights the political trial of the Cuban 5, imprisoned in US prisons on espionage charges. Ed Kinane also focuses on political imprisonment. He gives a detailed diary account of his experience in a federal minimum prison. He received a prison term for his non-violent protest of the School of the Americas in Fort Benning, Georgia. In his vivid description of the prison routine he reflects on the challenge of becoming a (male) prisoner of conscience. Kinane notes that prison conditions for women are far worse. In the aftermath of September 11, 2001, political activism against state violence has been singled out for harsher sentencing practices. Mary Barr's article echoes Kinane's concern that women's prisons are detrimental to a prisoner's personal health, safety, and security. Mary Barr's personal reflection on women's imprisonment in the United States focuses on the incessant victimization faced by women defendants and convicts. She gives a sobering account of police brutality and corruption in New York State. Barr highlights the effects that prisons have on families, and especially on children, and notes that the punitive nature of U.S. policies leaves ex-convicts with little options but to re-offend. Barr concludes with concrete proposals to change fiscal policies from a retributive paradigm to a rehabilitative model, in particular for non-violent drug users.

The world over women's imprisonment is not a central concern of policy makers. Instead, criminalized women who face incarceration are often considered as an afterthought. Mechthild Nagel's article discusses the perils of border crossing for women from the Global South to Northern countries, such as Great Britain, and Germany. Even as women are overcriminalized in the global War on Drugs, female prisoners are marginalized as a matter of public policy, public awareness and academic pursuit. Nagel emphasizes the need to address women's human rights, women's victimization, and the demonization of "fallen" women. The carceral complex perpetuates women's victimization; yet, at times, it can also foster a spirit of humanity, as exemplified by some of the rehabilitative measures in a German and a Malian prison.

Theorizing experiences of imprisonment from the perspectives of social and political prisoners are paramount to an understanding of the carceral society, yet, we still need to explore what ideological justifications of punishment are given by policy and law makers that reify and legitimate imprisonment as the state's main tool of meting out justice. The next section is therefore devoted to the theoretical underpinnings of the carceral complex.

II. Theories of Punishment and State Violence

In order to contextualize theories of punishment a critical look at the vindictive climate engendered by fear and moral panic is warranted. Fear engulfs politicians as they enact punitive sentencing practices and call for 'extra' punishment exerted in prisons, affecting, in particular incarcerated women, people of color, political prisoners, and other marginalized or scapegoated people. Trends towards retribution and revenge are observed even in juvenile courts the world over. Theorizing punishment and state violence from philosophical perspectives require an analysis of the meaning of "doing time" and of a "just desert" theory in punishment. Diane Antonio's article provides a novel perspective by probing the concept of "just mercy" from a feminist ethics of care. From their politics of location behind bars, students and practitioners of philosophy also unlock the spatial and embodied existence of the imprisoned self.

Drew Leder explores in a phenomenological narrative the spatial, temporal, and embodied sense of prisoners' perceptions of their existence. He draws on the illuminating dialogues of his students, incarcerated in Maryland, who are also featured in his acclaimed book *The Soul Knows no Bars* (2000). Greg Moses expands on Leder's analysis of what does it mean to "do time" in prison. Working with Pritchard and Dewey's conception that time cannot be isolated, he investigates the effects of time and punishment on prisoners, their families, guards, and the broader societal implications in a political climate, which favors retributive justice. Clayton Morgareidge discusses the merits of the "just desert" theory of punishment. He interrogates who is responsible for violent crime. He argues that if one gives a clear account of such responsibility, much popular support for prisons would wane. Diane Antonio pursues a discussion of "just mercy," drawing on Derrida's notion of justice, and on a feminist ethics of care. She analyses Sister Prejean's book (and film) *Dead Man Walking*. She notes how the state perpetuates violence when it denies "just mercy." Somjen Frazer reviews the Drug War which was waged against Chinese Americans during the Exclusion Era (1882-1943) and compares the social construction of Chinese immigrant gang activity to its latest victims: African American women and men. Opium meets crack cocaine in an age of moral panic. Frazer addresses racial and sexual stereotypes, which produce the convenient street villain and ultimately criminalizes them. Moral panic is also an issue explored in an article by Susan Terrio. The specter of US media and public policy looms large over Franco-American penal discourses. Susan Terrio's comparative study of French and American juvenile justice systems reports that there are overlapping concerns, in particular in the area of public opinion on youth violence. Terrio echoes a concern about moral panic addressed in Frazer's article. In her ethnographic fieldwork research within the minor court of the Paris Palace of Justice, she discovered that law, justice, and deviance are socially constructed, catering to the desires and fears of the public. In the United States, media exposure of juvenile criminality has made the retributive position palatable to try youth offenders as adults. Finally, Michael Nieto Garcia makes use of a literary work to discuss the state's desire to punish. He illustrates this notion of revenge with Jorge Luis Borges' allegorical short story "The Lottery of Babylon." Borges draws out the arbitrary and capricious character of the criminal justice system: one gets hit with a sentence, if one "loses" the lottery. If one wins, one remains free. Yet, the fates of the winners and the losers are intricately intertwined, which is often accentuated in the lives of the guards, who remain jailed for at least eight hours of their days.

III. African and Comparative Perspectives on Penal Law

Indubitably, the United States leads the world in mass incarceration. Apropos to this infamy, the U.S. is also exporting its retributivist and anti-terror ideologies overseas, feeding into nations' moral panic from France, through Malawi, to South Africa. While it is important to analyze the North American punishment industry, often called Prison Industrial Complex by prison critics, one can no longer afford to ignore global trends of punishment models. Therefore, contributors to this volume explain how the US prison complex has expanded globally, throughout many developing nation states, backed by private security companies and drug and juvenile justice legislation. In this section, contributors continue the global perspective on penality, which Nagel and Terrio's articles explore above focusing on gender and youth issues. Seth N. Asumah examines development theories and their complex interconnection with prison systems in Africa. He argues that governments and regimes in Africa, desirous of transcending development crises have capitalized on European models of prisons as institutions. He questions why freedom fighters, such as Kwame Nkrumah and

Jomo Kenyatta, emerged from prisons to assume the presidency subsequently incarcerated their opponents. It is to Nelson Mandela's credit that he did resign from the presidency after just one term in office. His resistance struggle is one of the topics in an article by Rashad Shabazz, whose article takes us back to the era of apartheid in South Africa, by focusing on the creative, literary works of resistance fighters who spent many years in the penal colony, Robben Island. Shabazz frames his analysis of racist practices endured by political prisoners in the context of the meaning of imprisonment in Africa, not just in the settler-nation of South Africa.

Mubangizi and Martin's articles focus on the contemporary, post-apartheid South African context and propound critiques with respect to prisoners' human rights which might worsen with the specter of privatization of prisons. John Mubangizi focuses on the human rights debate in South Africa. To what extent are prisoners protected by the UN Standard Minimum Rules for the Treatment of Prisoners in post-Apartheid South African prisons? In comparing United Nations and European Court reports and judgments, he notes that South Africa has adopted evolving standards for prisoners' rights in the Bill of Rights. Yet, given the reality of prison management among other issues, it is unclear to what extent prisoners are truly protected. While Mubangizi focuses on legal and human rights perspectives in South Africa, William Martin's article investigates the political effects of neoliberal policy on South Africa's prison system. US based security corporations are beginning to invest in establishing private prisons overseas, in particular in South Africa. Global Apartheid has married a Global Carceral Complex. Structural adjustment policies, popularized in the 1980s as a way to control Third World debt and to force Third World countries to privatize their means of production and educational systems, have reached the state security apparatus as well—a concept, still controversial in the Global North, in particular in the US, with the notable exception of the privately run federal detention centers for immigrants.

IV. Alternative Visions on Prisons and Punishment

In this section, activists and scholars, some of whom are imprisoned intellectuals, discuss the merits of higher education in prisons; community justice programs; and their perspectives on decarceration of criminalized poor communities.

Ishka "JoJo" Alpern, incarcerated at the time of the prison conference, relates his concerns about the personal and collective bonds between families, communities, and prisoners. Geographic distance between families and the incarcerated increases the difficulty of maintaining emotional ties over long "bids" (prison sentences). In New York State, most prisoners come from about seven neighborhoods of New York City, and a vast majority of them are transported to prisons located in Central and Northern New York. Alpern proposes a host of programs, including higher education, which ought to be instituted in prisons; at a minimum, they would facilitate integration of ex-convicts into their communities and curb violence and recidivism. Howard Davidson is critical of most higher education programs in prisons, which often amounts to correctional education, because teachers get co-opted in the process of delivering their courses. Davidson concurs with Alpern that outside activists should be working with prisoners, and he presents strategies how cooptation might be avoided. Tiyo Attallah Salah-El provides us with a strategic vision for abolishing prisons, suggesting decarcerating measures and novel functions for prison buildings once complete excarceration of prisoners takes place. Marsha Weissman and Alan Rosenthal give an account of a community empowerment model in a city in central New York, which focuses on curbing gun use among youth. They discuss the implementation of the program and give a cautionary tale of what happens when community organizers work with county officials.

We wish to close with prisoner activist Tiyo Attallah Salah-El's advocacy for change exemplified in this anthology:

> History is often seen through the eyes of kings and generals, queens and presidents. However, the real driving force of history is more often movements of ordinary people struggling to improve their lives. Where the language of liberty and justice did not exist in the Constitution, as in the cases of slavery and women's suffrage, social movements forced the document to be amended. Each movement has learned lessons from the movements that came before. I think it is important to keep this in mind when confronted with the 'hopelessness' of a situation. When discussing the lessons to be learned, it is important to note that many of the shortcomings of certain movements were not a result of incompetence or shortsightedness. Rather, many of them resulted from inevitable constraints on time, energy, knowledge, and entrenched interest. It might be useful to ask ourselves the following questions: (1) how can we apply these lessons to our current movement building? (2) How can we avoid the pitfalls of the past? And (3) how will these movements feed into our current efforts? (2003)

We believe that this book provides solutions to these questions by taking a salient look at carceral models from a global perspective. It compares historical and contemporary ideological formations that lead to a moral panic, resulting in more punitive measures to criminalize populations. Furthermore, it provides tools for beginning students of criminal justice as well as advanced social theorists for thinking critically about prisons and punishment.

References

Davis, Angela Y. 2003. *Are Prisons Obsolete?* Seven Stories Press.

Hersh, Seymour. May 10, 2004. Torture at Abu Ghraib. *The New Yorker.*

James, Joy (Ed.). 2003. *Imprisoned Intellectuals: America's Political Prisoners Write on Life, Liberation, and Rebellion.* Lanham, MD: Rowman and Littlefield.

James, Joy (Ed.). 2005. *The New Abolitionists: (Neo)slave Narratives and Contemporary Prison Writings*. Albany: SUNY Press.

Klein, Naomi. December 26, 2005. 'Never Before!' Our Amnesiac Torture Debate. *The Nation* Vol. 281(22).

Leder, Drew. 2000. *The Soul Knows No Bars. Inmates Reflect on Life, Death, and Hope*. Lanham, MD: Rowman and Littlefield.

McWethy, John. 2004. *Nightline Magazine* broadcast, May 15.

The Nation (editorial). December 26, 2006. Conspiracy to Torture. *The Nation* Vol.281(22).

Sothern, Billy. January 2, 2006. Left to Die. How New Orleans Abandoned its Citizens in a Flooded Jail and a Flawed System. *The Nation* Vol. 282(1).

Salah-El, Tiyo Attalah. August 26, 2003. Personal communication.

PART I

Theorizing Prison Experiences, Gender and Resistance

1

POLITICAL PRISONERS IN THE U.S.: NEW PERSPECTIVES IN THE NEW MILLENIUM

J. Soffiyah Elijah

Nearly thirty years ago I began my formal political training about 30 miles down the road at the Africana Studies and Research Center at Cornell University, New York. It was directed at that time, as it is now by Dr. James Turner, my mentor and dear friend. I hold him totally responsible for helping me to keep the right perspective and balance between activism and academia. I wish to applaud the courage of the State University of New York faculty in sponsoring a conference on prisons in the heartland of incarceration for this state. I have mixed emotions about being back in this part of New York State. The "other" education that I received in this part of the state began when I was 17 years old when I made my first of what was to become a long series of prison visits. (Shawanjunk, Wende, Attica, Dannemora, Greenhaven, Coxsackie, Danbury, Leavenworth, Tehachapi, Dublin, Carswell, Allenwood, Lewisburg, etc, etc.) At that time I walked through the frightening walls of Auburn Prison to visit my childhood sweetheart. I remember being struck by the fact that nearly all the prisoners in the visiting room were Black and Latino. Nearly all the guards were white. I even recognized some other former high school classmates who had "disappeared" into that abyss known back home as "upstate". This was also the first time that I saw H. Rap Brown, now known as Jamil Abdullah Al-Amin. He was imprisoned there for Black Panther related activities.

So this is where I cut my teeth and began to understand the interconnections between the State, political repression and the criminal justice system. My remarks in this essay are going to focus on political prisoners and prisoners of war. I have concentrated the last twenty years of my life on efforts to obtain their release. I have represented Marilyn Buck for the past 16 years and Sundiata Acoli for the past 14. Historically, there have been political prisoners and prisoners of war in the United States as we now know it since its inception. As Native Americans fought valiantly to protect their homeland from invasion they were captured, tortured, murdered or imprisoned.

Most of the political prisoners and prisoners of war in the United States today are people of color, primarily men most of whom dedicated their lives to the support of various national liberation struggles and protests against U.S. foreign policy. They come from organizations such as the Black Panther Party, the Black Liberation Army, the Provisional Government of the Republic of New Africa, the Weather Underground and the American Indian Movement, to name a few. I would be remiss if I did not acknowledge the valued support of numerous North American anti-imperialist comrades who also have been incarcerated for their political beliefs and actions. Many of the political prisoners have been incarcerated for over 25 years. They are held in state and federal facilities.

There are nearly 100 political prisoners and prisoners of war incarcerated in the United States. These men and women are incarcerated for their political views and actions. They are understood to be men and women who made and carried out conscious political decisions to fight against social injustice, colonialism, and/or imperialism, and who have been incarcerated as a result of these actions and beliefs. Once in prison, these people continue to adhere to their principles. This definition of political prisoners is the one that has been accepted throughout the international community.

Unlike the concept of political prisoner, the term prisoner of war has been sharply defined in international law. (Relevant citations include the Geneva Conventions and UN Resolutions 2621, 2852 and 3101). The Geneva Convention of 1949 was extended in order to protect combatants who struggle against colonialism and foreign intervention, conferring prisoner of war status on all anti-colonial combatants.

The U.S. does not recognize the category of political prisoner. Therefore, political prisoners are incarcerated on criminal charges. Several of them were framed. Some have been charged and convicted of seditious conspiracy. They have received longer sentences, been isolated in remote prisons, refused parole, subjected to sensory deprivation, denied adequate medical care and demonized by the State.

The fact of the existence of political prisoners is one that has long been denied by the governing officials in federal and state office. In 1978 United States Ambassador to the United Nations, Andrew Young, stated publicly that there were over 100 political prisoners incarcerated in the United States. He was promptly removed from office a few days later by President Carter.

Ironically, the following year, President Carter pardoned several Puerto Rican political prisoners, including Rafael Cancel Miranda and Lolita Lebrón, all of whom had served 25 years for their armed attack on the U.S. Congress in 1954. Their release was the first formal recognition from the White House of the existence of political prisoners within U.S. borders.

In 1988, D.C. District Court Judge Barrington Parker, Sr. acknowledged the existence of political prisoners in this country and ordered the United States and the Bureau of Prisons to shut down a control unit they had built for women at the Lexington, Kentucky penitentiary. The Bureau of Prisons had decided to use the control unit as part of a behavior modification experiment on three political prisoners, Silvia Baraldini, Susan Rosenberg and Alejandrina Torres. The trial court ruled that these women had been sent to the Lexington control unit because of their political beliefs. As a result of Judge Parker's courageous decision in 1986, the women were transferred to other prisons. On appeal, the order to close the control unit at Lexington was reversed and the appellate court held that it was permissible to consider a prisoner's political beliefs and associations when making security determinations not withstanding the First Amendment.

The next decade brought about the release of several political prisoners; some requiring court intervention. For example, Dhoruba bin-Wahad was released from a New York State prison after serving 19 years for attempted murder of a police officer, a crime which he did not commit. Geronimo jiJaga Pratt was released from a California prison after serving 27 years for a murder he did not commit. Both of these men were former leaders of the Black Panther Party who were framed by the FBI's counter-intelligence "COINTELPRO" offensive against political activists during the sixties and seventies.

Despite the release of bin-Wahad, jiJaga and a few others, there are still many political prisoners who remain behind the walls. Almost all of the surviving political prisoners are in their 50's and 60's. Query, why are they still incarcerated? The recidivism rate for prisoners in this age range is approximately 11%. Their health is declining primarily due to medical neglect.

During the past two years Albert Nuh Washington and Teddy Jah Heath died of cancer while serving lengthy sentences in New York State prisons. They had both served over 25 years at the time of their untimely deaths. Requests for compassionate medical releases were ignored or denied. A few years earlier, MOVE member, Merle Africa, died while incarcerated in Pennsylvania as a result of inadequate medical care. Prior to this Ahmed Evans died in the Southern Ohio Correctional Facility of cancer due to medical neglect. In the mid eighties, former BLA member Kuwesi Balagoon died of AIDS in a New York State prison when he received little to no medical treatment despite an obvious rapid decline in his physical condition.

Thirty years passed before any further formal White House recognition of political prisoners and prisoners of war occurred. In a move unanticipated by many, President Clinton released 11 Puerto Rican *independistas* from federal custody in 1999. Their release was the culmination of years of organizing and lobbying by numerous groups and individuals in the Puerto Rican community. Although President Clinton never referred to the *independistas* as political prisoners, his stated reasons for granting their release were a tacit acknowledgment of their status as such. He acknowledged that these prisoners had been incarcerated "between 16 and 19 years as a result of convictions for offenses arising out of their participation in organizations supporting Puerto Rican independence."

As the end of President Clinton's term in office drew near, his office was deluged with petitions for clemency, amnesty, pardon and commutation. The Release 2000 Campaign filed a clemency petition on behalf of all federally convicted political prisoners and prisoners of war. In total, he granted 177 of these petitions; two from political prisoners Susan Rosenberg and Linda Evans. Both of their sentences were commuted to time served without written opinion. This additional recognition of the existence of political prisoners from the White House was a significant step in the campaign to obtain the release of all political prisoners and prisoners of war.

The recent past has seen an increased awareness amongst members of Congress about the existence of political prisoners in the United States. In September, 2000 Congresswoman Cynthia McKinney sponsored a braintrust session during the Congressional Black Caucus' legislative weekend that focused on COINTELPRO and the plight of political prisoners in the U.S. The event was a major success and another significant milestone in furthering the efforts to gain the release of all the political prisoners and prisoners of war. To her credit, Congresswoman Mckinney has continued to lend the full support of her office to this work. Her efforts were pivotal in gaining the support of the CBC to lobby President Clinton shortly before he left office to release the federally convicted political prisoners.

International acknowledgment of the existence of the United States' not so well kept secret is also growing. In November, 2000 nearly 5000 delegates from the international community gathered in Havana, Cuba for the World Meeting of Friendship and Solidarity with Cuba. The final report issued from that body included acknowledgment and support for the release of all political prisoners in the U.S. including Mumia Abu-Jamal.

Over the past 20 years slow, but steady progress has been made in publicizing this issue and gaining the release of some of the political prisoners and prisoners of war. However, a new wave, if you will, of political prisoners is now being seen.

After a politically-charged trial that ended in June 2001, 5 Cuban patriots, (Rene' Gonzalez Sehweret, Ramón Labanino Salazar, Fernando Gonzalez Llort, António Guerro Rodriguez and Gerardo Hernandez Nordelo) were convicted of espionage against U.S. military bases and threatening national security. All of their actions focused on monitoring the actions of and infiltrating Miami-based right-wing groups such as Alpha 66, Brothers to the Rescue, Omega 7 and others that have caused death and injury to hundreds of civilians.

In the wake of the attacks on the World Trade Center and the Pentagon, the use of the nation's jails and prisons for political repression has been renewed. Within hours of the attacks, several of the political prisoners were rounded up and put in administrative segregation, generically known as the hole. NO charges or allegations were levied against them. Some, like Marilyn Buck and Sundiata Acoli (both clients of mine) were held incommunicado for weeks without any access to legal counsel. Social visiting, mail and phone calls are still being denied to Sundiata and his ability to communicate with me was just reinstated last week! My numerous requests to arrange for a legal phone call from Sundiata were flatly refused by the warden at USP Allenwood. Similarly, efforts to have legal communications with Ms. Buck were refused by the Bureau of Prisons. All legal mail was held by the prison and not given to these prisoners. However, it is important to note that the directive to throw these political prisoners in the hole and hold them incommunicado, even from their lawyers, was issued by Attorney General Ashcroft. No doubt, this is an early forecast of things to come.

The most egregious situation is that faced by political prisoner Yu Kiku-mura who has been incarcerated in the super-max federal penitentiary located in Florence, Colorado. Yu has been held there in lock down status for years. Right after September 11th he was moved to a stripped cell, meaning that he has no blanket, sheets, reading material or personal property. The cell is freezing cold all the time and Yu is stripped down to one layer of thin cotton clothing. Again, like the others, NO charges or allegations of any kind have been brought against him.

And there is more. Since September 11th literally hundreds of people of Middle Eastern descent have been rounded up and thrown in jail without being charged with violating ANY laws. Ostensibly, they are being held for questioning. In reality, they are being harassed and politically targeted. Their civil liberties are being violated just like the civil liberties of the political prisoners I mentioned previously. The so-called "shift to the right" feels more like a stampede and recent moves by Congress have demonstrated that there will be no change in this situation for the foreseeable future.

The work to obtain the release of political prisoners and prisoners of war in the United States will have to intensify, move to new levels of sophistication, embrace the international community and exploit all available means of propaganda. I am confident that with a unified effort one day we will welcome all of them back home.

2

WHAT IS IT LIKE IN A FEDERAL MINIMUM SECURITY PRISON?
Notes for Potential Prisoners of Conscience*

Ed Kinane

Under a government which imprisons any unjustly, the true place for a just [person] is also a prison....

If any think that their influence would be lost [in prison], and their voices no longer afflict the ear of the State, that they would not be as an enemy with its walls, they do not know by how much truth is stronger than error, nor how much more eloquently and effectively [they] can combat injustice who [have] experienced a little in [their] own person.

– Henry David Thoreau, "On Civil Disobedience"

These notes are for those engaging in civil disobedience and who therefore may be risking arrest and imprisonment. Doing time probably will be hard on you and your loved ones. It is a major disruption in your lives. But, with preparation and the right mind set, much good can result—both for you personally and for your cause.

You may want to share these notes with your family and your primary support people. *Your incarceration may be harder on those left at home. They have to manage without you and may well get far less solidarity than you are likely to get as a prisoner of conscience.*

My prison experience comes from taking part in several nonviolent protests against the School of the Americas (SOA) at the main gate of Fort Benning in Georgia. The SOA is a U.S. Army school of terrorism and subversion. It trains Latin American soldiers to maintain Latin America as a vast pool of cheap labor for U.S. corporations. It no longer calls itself the SOA: its new name is the Western Hemisphere Institute for Security Cooperation.

In 1996, as one of the "SOA 13," I spent two months in McKean Federal Prison Camp. Then in 1998/99, as one of the "SOA 25," I served 12 months in FPC Allenwood. Conditions and treatment at these two minimum security prisons were rather better than at FPC Danbury -- the women's facility in Connecticut where in 1998 my partner Ann spent six months as one of the "SOA 25." We were sent to federal facilities because our "crimes" occurred on federal land.

***

If sentenced by a federal court to prison for a nonviolent action, whether a misdemeanor or felony, you will probably be sent to a federal minimum security camp. It will probably be in your region of the country. Both my camps were in Pennsylvania, about four hours drive from our home in Syracuse. At your sentencing you may even request that you be sent to a particular camp. The request may or may not be honored.

It is likely you will be given "self-surrender." This means you are not incarcerated immediately upon sentencing; rather, several weeks later you will be notified of the date and camp you must report to on your own. The reporting date may be no more than several days after notification. This interlude between sentencing and incarceration is the time not only to settle your person affairs, but also to do media work. If approached right, media are likely to be interested in your going to prison for a good—or controversial—cause.

Just before going to prison, you might mail yourself there an (unpadded) envelope with items like: address & phone list, press contact list, photos of loved ones, medical needs documentation, a few paperback books, for sharing and for reference include flyers, fact sheets, clippings, etc. on your issue. Most other things you would like to send to yourself would be considered contraband.

I could bring only money and my eyeglasses in with me. A wedding ring would also have been allowed, but no other personal effects. The money was taken and credited to my commissary account (see below). Rules on what you can bring in with you vary; you might phone the camp in advance to check out what its current rule is—which may or may not be respected the day your arrive. Upon entering I was strip-searched ("lift your scrotum, bend over and spread your cheeks"). Then I got a set of army-surplus prison-issue clothes: belt, four undershorts and T-shirts, two or three pairs of pants, two or three shirts, steel-tipped shoes, rain poncho, winter jacket, mittens and cap.

A minimum security camp is not like the prisons you have seen in the movies. It is not "Shawshank." At my camps there were no bars, barbed wire, walls, electric fences, or guard towers. I never saw a firearm. I *could* have walked away, though the penalty would have been severe. Except from 10PM to 6AM, and around count time (see below), I was not confined to the dorm buildings. The mess hall, work site, athletic facilities, etc., were at other sites in the camp.

My two camps looked like suburban community college campuses: one and two story buildings amid lawns and landscaping, with baseball diamonds, basketball courts and other athletic facilities. These included handball and bocci ball courts, horseshoes, ping pong, pool, and weight lifting. I cherished all the green grass and blue skies. Allenwood is on a lovely site surrounded by wooded hills. We had lots of Canadian geese grazing our lawns and pooping all over our sidewalks. Deer often came to our dorm windows looking for a handout. Such critters made the camp seem more humane. Other minimum security facilities, however, are not necessarily so bucolic.

What Is It Like In A Federal Minimum Security Prison?

I was assigned the top bunk of a cramped two-person cubicle in a large room with about 60 other prisoners. If one is over 60, or physically impaired, he or she will probably get the lower bunk. The doorless cubicle provided little privacy. There was a lockable locker for my clothes and personal effects. My bunkie and I shared a small desk and book shelf. We each had a metal folding chair. I used mine to climb up into my ladderless bunk.

In contrast to life "on the street," life in prison is fairly regimented. After a week's orientation, prisoners are assigned a menial job at the lordly sum of 12 cents an hour. At Allenwood even men over 70 were required to work. During orientation you may be able to scout the various departments for a job more to your liking than those "fish" (new first-time prisoners) are typically assigned to.

Once assigned, we could not transfer to a more suitable job for three months. Unicor, a factory system within federal prisons throughout the country, pays prison workers a higher—though still slavishly low—hourly wage. But new or short-term prisoners are not eligible. The handy and huge pool of cheap, nonunionized labor that Unicor exploits is one reason U.S. prisons are proliferating.

If you refuse to work (as some prisoners of conscience do), you go to the "hole." The hole or the "shu"—segregated housing unit—is a medium security punishment cell to which you're confined 23 hours a day, there's little contact with staff or other prisoners—except your bunkmate. I once spent 12 days in the hole—which was in the medium security prison down the road. I was taken there in shackles. Because my bunkie and I found plenty to talk about (Terry was a Viet Nam combat vet and had trained contras in Honduras), the time flew. But if we had been incompatible it might have been rather unpleasant. Some of the "SOA25" spent their first few days in the hole under "observation" because we were sentenced without the customary Pre-Sentencing Report. Our jailors use the PSR to assess whether we are a threat to ourselves or others.

This was my typical weekday schedule: 5:45 AM wake-up; 6-6:30 breakfast; 7:30-10:45 work; 11-noon lunch; noon-3:30PM work; 4:00 standup count in my cubicle; 4:30-5:00 dinner; 10PM count in my cubicle; 10:30 lights off in the dorm. We could use the adjoining game room or TV rooms or phones after lights out. On the weekend, wake-up and breakfast were an hour later. On weekends my time was mostly my own, except I had to be in my cubicle for the 10:30AM standup count. Prisons take these counts very seriously. If you are not where you are supposed to be at count, you can go to the hole. The counts occur several times a day like clockwork. They entail every prisoner in the facility being accounted for. The staff gets into a tizzy if the numbers do not add up, or if a prisoner is not where he is expected to be. The prison goes into lockdown—i.e. enforced suspended animation—until every prisoner is accounted for. Often the problem is that the guards made an error counting.

Given our draconian drug laws, many—maybe most—minimum security prisoners are in for drug "crimes." Most are people of color. None are being incarcerated for violent offenses. Allenwood has a lot of white collar criminals as well. Apart from these, many are probably in prison because they could not afford their own lawyer. Few are a physical threat to society. Many belong in rehab programs or other alternatives to incarceration. Many have families which needlessly suffer by their absence. This is even far more true of women prisoners, most of whom have children.

The dorm often got loud; language was often coarse. Earplugs were contraband, but luckily I was able to get some from guys working heavy equipment. While prisoners and staff were occasionally loutish, I seldom felt menaced. I never felt sexually threatened, although whether younger, more attractive men did, I cannot say. Although several times I heard about fights and, therefore, about those involved going to the hole or being shipped out to medium security facilities, I never witnessed physical violence. Many prisoners had their rough edges, but most seemed decent. Most minded their own business; they just wanted to do their time with as few hassles as possible.

Even some of the guards seemed decent, especially when other staff were not present. Others could be petty or officious or vindictive. Many lacked professionalism and were poorly-trained. Most, but not all, guards were male. Very inappropriately, this was also true at Danbury with its all-woman population.

In Sartre's play *No Exit* hell is other people. For me the worst part about prison was the crowding—crowding in the dorm, in the mess hall, in the visiting room. It can seem like you, your bunkie *and* your neighbors are aware of each others' every move and sound. I did not especially like my first three bunkmates. My fourth was a very likable Colombian soccer player. My fifth and I came from very different worlds; but our time together was stress-free. Along with bunkie can come visits from bunkie's buddies. These can be intrusive. You might seek to transfer to another cubicle. But doing so entails dealing with staff—something I sought to avoid.

One of the nastier realities of prison is snitches. Prisoners can win concessions of various sorts and even get sentences reduced if they inform on others. So, be discreet. Also, do not be nosy, and do not fraternize with staff—other prisoners understandably get suspicious. Snitches can suffer reprisals. It is standard prison etiquette not to ask someone about what got them into prison. The time I went to the hole was because a snitch reported I was talking to an unauthorized visitor—an 83 year-old friend who had no idea he had to go through a screening process before visiting.

At Allenwood, in our residence unit, there were two television (TV) rooms, each with six televisions. Every TV was set on a different channel and, blessedly, was silent. To access audio you had to have earphones, purchasable from the commissary. The TV's were on round the clock. They are a great pacifier.

We were not allowed to possess cash or checks, etc.; our money was held in our commissary account. At a designated hour once a week, we could access the commissary. You wait in a long line to hand your shopping list to a clerk who gathers the items. There is a limited range of junk food, groceries, vitamins, toiletries, clothes, stationary, tobacco products, etc. If you have it, you might want to start your account with about $250. You may immediately want to buy a watch, sneaks, bathrobe, sweat suit, walkman, postage, some food, and a combination lock for your locker.

Although I was *in pauperis*, i.e. the court found me to be without income or assets, while in prison, our local SOA Watch solidarity group mailed me a monthly stipend. The mail room automatically deposited its postal money orders in my commissary account. As I got a hefty fine, very early on my "counselor" asked me to authorize a $25 monthly fine deduction from my account. Many political prisoners refuse to pay their fines. If you refuse, they will find ways to make your prison sojourn more difficult, though not unbearable. This can limit the outreach you are able to do while incarcerated.

If you are not *in pauperis*, you will probably be pressured to pay more than $25. My sense was that my counselor was himself under severe pressure to wring fine money out of prisoners. Apparently the prison gets its cut of fines collected. You will need to go through your "counselor" for most administrative matters. The title is misleading; s/he does not counsel, s/he is a paper pushing cop.

Many staff are resistant to working, much less doing anything for a prisoner, even answering questions. Why such stonewalling? a) It is just another way to put the screws to you; b) the less you know, the more control they have (prison is *all* about control); c) often staff simply do not have the answers and will not admit it; and d) they themselves are oppressed underlings wary of sticking their necks out.

The mess hall served three hasty meals a day, cafeteria style. I was pleasantly surprised: the food was diverse and occasionally tasty. Someone in the kitchen gave a damn. There was enough healthy food for large appetites and there were usually adequate alternatives for non-meat eaters like me. Vegans, or those with kosher or other special diet needs, could arrange a "common fare" diet through their respective chaplain. This may be difficult to do if you have not declared a religious affiliation upon entering prison. At Allenwood, there was a range of religious services and holy days for Christian, Muslim and Jewish prisoners. There was a sweat lodge for Native Americans and the usual legal holidays were observed as well.

Mail call was nightly Monday through Friday. There was no weekend mail call. All incoming mail is opened, inspected for drugs and other contraband, and may be read by staff. Staff usually opened correspondence from my *pro bono* lawyers, unread, in my presence. Receiving a package required prior authorization, but we could receive paperback books if they came in an unpadded envelope. Hard cover books could only be sent by a bookstore or publisher. You had to buy postage in the commissary. I could seal my outgoing mail which normally would not be opened by staff. Each camp may have its own mail regulations. To avoid their mail being returned to them, you might send a copy of the mailing regulations to your frequent correspondents.

As a prisoner of conscience, especially in such a popular campaign as closing the School of the Americas, I received lots of solidarity mail from all over the country. That was heartening, but also awkward, because so many in the dorm got little or no mail. Our prison mailing address appeared repeatedly in the *Nuclear Resister* and in numerous movement newsletters. You may want to answer every note individually; this is time-consuming, but it is a great way to help get others invested in your issue. Alternatively, you might periodically respond with a mass mailing: write a "dear friends" letter and have an outside support person copy and mail it to the list you provide. You can use such a letter to educate and organize.

Smoking was permitted outdoors only. Thanks to the gym and track, etc., many leave prison in much better shape than when they went in. But prison is not a good place to be ill. Sick call is at 6AM. The medical and dental staffs are not necessarily dedicated to your health and well-being; they suspect you are a malingerer. If you have any medical condition, do all you can to deal with it before going to prison. Get your teeth cleaned and repaired beforehand. Prison dentists are notorious for pulling teeth.

We were not allowed to bring in our own medications or have them sent to us. The prison doctor would have to prescribe any meds that we would use, and these usually would be generic and not necessarily those your outside doctor had prescribed. To avoid being assigned a job where I would be on my feet a lot, before I went in I had a podiatrist write a letter documenting my bad feet. When I had to fill out a form regarding my health, I noted my poor hearing. I did this thinking it just might cover me if I was about to be disciplined for not heeding some order over the PA system.

In prison you cannot get phone calls. In a family emergency one might be able to get a call through the counselor or chaplain. At Danbury Ann could make collect calls to anyone—though the phone rates were exorbitant. At Allenwood I could only call numbers I had previously submitted on a list authorized by my counselor. But it was cheaper because I was not calling collect. The charges were deducted from my commissary account. I usually called Ann—we were in prison at different times—in the morning before work to avoid waiting in line to use the phone; in the evening the phone queue could get pretty long. Calls were automatically cut off after 15 minutes. If no one was waiting to use the phone, you could place another call. Calls were subject to undetectable monitoring. Thanks to the monitoring, two of the guys I worked with were punished when one of them got on the line when the other placed a call. Both had commissary and phoning privileges suspended for a few weeks.

Several days a week, for at least several hours, one may be able to receive visits, but usually only if your visitors have returned an application you have sent them and they been approved. Visiting hours and regulations differ from prison to prison. You might get a copy of the visiting regulations during orientation and send them to your potential visitors so they will not run afoul of the rules. Given my entanglements with the law, when Ann was in prison I was not permitted to visit her. When I was in, however, Ann could visit me even though she had done time. For several months at Allenwood, all prisoners were strip-searched after every visit. That seemed to have been a temporary aberration foisted on staff and prisoners alike by a new "get-tough" warden.

Federal prisons have both law libraries and reading libraries. Some reading libraries are wretched, for instance, at Danbury; some are quite good such as the one at Allenwood. I was able to use interlibrary loan to borrow books from the county library system as well. At Allenwood, the law library had a ten-cent-a-copy photocopy machine accessed with a photo identification/commissary card. Furthermore, if one does not have a high school diploma, one will be required to take the GED course. Other optional skills and academic courses may be available, although not for credit. At Allenwood, these courses were mostly taught by prisoners. You may find yourself offering to teach one.

Each point in your penal journey—arrest, trial, sentencing, self-surrendering, going to the hole, release—is an opportunity for doing press work in your home town, with your alumni and professional organizations, or faith community, etc. After my sentencing, our local daily ran an editorial, "Going to Prison for a Good Cause." To get effective press out of your civil disobedience action, read Jason Salzman's excellent *Making the News: A guide for non-profits and activists*, Westview Press, 1998, paperback, $19.95, 289pp. It is not egocentrism to use the personal hook to publicize your cause, or the injustice of your prosecution, or the abuses of your incarceration, or of the penal system as a whole (see attached bibliography).

**

The late Phil Berrigan used to say, "Use their time against them." I thought of my time as a federally-subsidized sabbatical or retreat. Many prisoners of conscience use their time "accompanying" fellow prisoners: being a tutor, a resource, a friend. In prison I read scores of good books. Through correspondence I "met" or deepened my relationship with good people. I took satisfaction in the simple low-consumption lifestyle—low by U.S. standards, not by *campesino* standards. Whatever deprivation I might have suffered was a passing inconvenience compared to what Latin Americans suffer at the hands of School of the Americas grads. Given what was at stake, I felt my prison time was a pittance. Knowing that our prison witnessing was helping to build the campaign against the SOA was a sustaining joy. By 2003, the SOA campaign has yielded over 150 prisoners of conscience for a total of over 60 years in prison. As I update these notes, 30 more SOA Watch activists face prosecution for crossing the line at Benning, Georgia in November 2003.

Being in prison is consciousness raising—like going on one of those movement delegations to Chiapas or Colombia. There is much to be learned—especially by those of us with middle class origins—from the stark experience of those who have led much harder lives, or those who have gotten a much rawer deal.

The U.S. prison system is burgeoning. It can only do so through an enormous amount of injustice. Its essential that activists gain firsthand experience in this Gulag in order to help retard its proliferation. Being a deliberate prisoner of conscience is qualitatively different from serving time either as a victim of the system or as a victimizer of others. It is as different as honor and stigma.

Frequently people wrote expressing sympathy for my "lack of freedom." This led me to reflect on the constraints and opportunities that go with (intentionally) being in prison vis á vis being out on the street. Each side of the gate had a different configuration of constraints and opportunities. But I am not sure whether as a prisoner of conscience I had more constraints or fewer opportunities than when I was on the street. I do know that prison was where I needed to be.

When I got out, I became a more sought after speaker and had more credibility as an activist. I came out more empowered than when I went in. I am a freer person now precisely because I followed my conscience, committed civil disobedience, and experienced incarceration.

Note

* Originally published in Ed Kinane and Ann Tiffany's "The Gandhian Wave: A Civil Disobedience Handbook." "The Ganhian Wave" was compiled in 2000-2001 in binder-form and is no longer being assembled and distributed.

COMPELLING READING ON U.S. PRISON ISSUES

Being in prison is the ideal time to bone up on prison issues. To frame your experience and round out your picture of the entire Gulag, here's a brief bibliography. I read all of these either in, or before I went to, prison.

— *The Nuclear Resister*, a wonderful tabloid focusing on civil disobedience, trials and incarcerations of antinuclear, anti-imperial and disarmament activists. Excellent coverage of anti-SOA CD actions. Address: c/o Jack & Felice Cohen-Joppa, POB 43383, Tucson, AZ, 85733.

— *Prison Legal News*, a highly respected 40-page monthly, edited by prisoners. Address: 2400 NW 80th Street, #148, Seattle, WA 98117-4449; one year $18 prisoners, $25 individuals, $60 law firms & institutions.

— Amnesty International, *United States of America Rights for All*, NY, October, 1998. See especially the chapter on prison conditions.

— Daniel Burton-Rose, Dan Pens and Paul Wright (eds.), *The Celling of America: An inside look at the U.S. prison industry*, Common Courage, 1998. Excellent analysis of the U.S.' fastest growing industry.

— Samuel H. Day, Jr., *Crossing the Line: From editor to activist to inmate*, Fortkamp, 1991. A lively autobiography.

— John Dear, S.J., *The Sacrament of Civil Disobedience*, Fortkamp, 1994. Of particular interest to devout Catholic activists.

— H. Bruce Franklin, *Prison Writing in 20th-century America*, Penguin, 1998. A rich anthology of fiction and nonfiction, poetry and prose, about prison.

— Jennifer Haines, *Bread & Water: A spiritual journey*, Orbis, 1997. Intense, meticulous exploration of doing uncompromising resistance *within* prison.

— Mumia Abu-Jamal, *Live From Death Row*, Addison-Wesley, 1995. Tells his own story. Timely. Infuriating.

— Sister Helen Prejean, *Dead Man Walking: An eyewitness account of the death penalty in the United States*, Vintage, 1993. As gripping as the film. Useful appendices on the death penalty issue.

— Elihu Rosenblatt (ed.), *Criminal Injustice: Confronting the prison crisis*, South End Press, 1996. Excellent companion volume to *The Celling of America*.

The following are several useful books I've come across since my release:

— Samuel H. Day, Jr. 05121-045 (ed.), *Prisoners on Purpose: A peacemaker's guide to jails and prisons*, The Progressive Foundation, Madison, WI, 1989. Includes first-hand reports from various prisons and jails, not only federal institutions.

— Clare Hanarahan, *Jailed for Justice: A Woman's Guide to Federal Prison Camp*, Asheville, NC, 2002 [order from chanrahan@ncpress.net]. Useful advice not only for women. Clare did six months as an SOA Watch prisoner.

— Howard Levy, M.D. and David Miller, *Going to Jail: The Political Prisoner*, Grove Press, 1971. Practical guidance from the anti-Viet Nam War era.

— Clive Sharp, *How to Survive Federal Prison Camp: A Guidebook For Those Caught Up in The System*, Loompanics Unlimited, 1997. *Not* geared to political prisoners.

— Committee to End the Marion Lockdown, *Can't Jail the Spirit: Political Prisoners in the U.S.: A Collection of Biographies*, Fifth Edition, 2002, Chicago, [order from ceml@aol.com]. *Not* focused on minimum security prisoners.

3

SOME FACTS AND ANECDOTES OF WOMEN ARRESTED AND IMPRISONED IN THE UNITED STATES

Mary Barr

ARREST

National Numbers

In 1998 women comprised 22% (3.2 million) of annual arrests (Chesney-Lind, 2000). Black women are eight times more likely to be arrested and Hispanics five times more likely to be arrested than whites (The Sentencing Project, 2003). Most women who use illegal drugs while pregnant are white, yet in several studies, the vast majority of women reported or arrested for drug use while pregnant are women of color (The Guttmacher Report, 1998).

Issues

The majority of women are arrested for non-violent drug related offenses (Women's Economic Agenda Project, 1994) Women who were abused or neglected have a 77% higher chance of being arrested than those who did not experience abuse or neglect (Greenfield and Snell, 2000). Most of these women are mothers who do not report having children for fear of them being taken into the foster care system (Ibid.).

Police abuse remains one of the most serious and divisive human rights violations in the United States. The excessive use of force by police officers, including unjustified shootings, severe beatings, fatal chokings, and rough treatment persists because overwhelming barriers to accountability make it possible for officers who commit human rights violations to escape due punishment and often to repeat their offenses. Also are many reported and unreported sexual assaults and torture by police officers which are not, strictly speaking "excessive" use of force but are unjustified and criminal assaults (Human Rights Watch, 1998). A common enforcement tactic is offering money to an obvious or known drug user to procure drugs for an undercover officer. The person buys from the closest dealer, takes the drugs back to the officer and promptly gets charged as if they were the actual drug dealer. Any sale of a hard drug, even a $3.00 vial of crack, is a felony. Sometimes the undercover agent offers a fee and asks where they can procure drugs. Merely pointing them in the right direction is a felony considered, "Acting in Concert."

Illustrative Anecdotes: New York City

Two police cars screech to a halt in front of me nearly giving me a heart attack. My breath is coming hard and I tell the police I feel faint. They tell me to shut up and hand cuff me roughly behind my back. An officer shoves me into the police van, purposely bouncing my head off the frame, the pain forming tears in my eyes. Gypsy, who was standing with me, says f—- you to the officers and three of them throw her down and start kicking her. I look on in horror, crying for them to stop. They throw Gypsy into the van with me and fourteen other women. All of them are familiar to me. While I am the only white woman along with 12 black women and 3 Hispanics, we all look similar. Tired, scared, skinny and beaten. Most of us have bruises and facial scars. Some are missing teeth. I am missing a finger from an assault. All of us have been attacked by men, arrested by men, and condemned by men. Few of us have ever lifted a hand to harm another. Some of us are crying, not only because we know the ordeal to come, but for our children.

There is Angel (trespassing) whose three children stay with her mother. She used to see them often but it has become too hard to hear them cry at her departure. There is Tameka (acting in concert), whose twin boys are the only children I know of whose father is caring for them. There is Gypsy (loitering for the purpose of prostitution, but now the officers claim she was resisting arrest), who refuses to talk about her children. There is Ada, (conspiracy), who says she has no children but we all know better by the look in her eyes. And me (sale). When I had gone to a social worker seeking a program for myself and my children two men from Child Services came to my home and took them from me. My heart was broken and I have given up all hope of life.

There are those that lead by fear and those that lead by respect. I have little respect for the police. I was physically abused by white middle and upper class male customers at least 500 times in three years and the police knew this was routine treatment of prostitutes. In three years there was only one 'sting' operation to arrest Johns and it made the front page of the paper so the community would think they were being fair. I was arrested 45 times in three years even though at least six officers were regular, paying customers of mine. I know the prostitution area I have been arrested in is directly in front of an illegal sweatshop. I have seen an officer visit and chat amiably with the manager there. I have also seen him accept a bribe from a pimp and watched him let six women go free and later arrest me. I have also seen two officers rough up a young black male drug dealer and take his money and drugs. The young man and I were happy not to report it because we were spared arrest. The police did and said anything in front of me because they thought I would die in the streets. I am afraid of the police with good reason. I was raped, on separate occasions, by an off duty detective and a uniformed officer. I was lucky to have been physically abused only once in my 45 arrests. I was arrested falsely numerous times. And now some police that arrested me a half dozen times are claiming that I sold them $10 worth of crack.

Booking

The officer will take you to a police station. You will be advised generally as to the charges against you. However, these charges may be changed later and stated in more detail by the office of the prosecuting attorney or in some instances by the grand jury. You may be required to participate in a lineup, to prepare a sample of your penmanship, or to speak phrases associated with the crime with which you are charged, to put on certain wearing apparel or to give a sample of your hair. You should ask to have your attorney present during any of these procedures. You have an absolute right to counsel, if you are asked to participate in a lineup after you have been formally charged by the prosecuting attorney or indicted by a grand jury. You also may be required to be fingerprinted and photographed. You will be arraigned at a court session or your attorney will file a written plea on your behalf. An arraignment is no more than a plea of guilty, not guilty, or no contest to the charge. If you plead not guilty, a trial date will be set. If you plead guilty or no contest, a sentencing date will be set, generally after the court has received a pre-sentence investigation report from probation and parole (Russel Mace, Esq.).

You have a right to know the crime or crimes with which you have been charged. You have a right to know the identity of the police officers who are dealing with you. This is your right to statute and by custom. You have the right to communicate by telephone with your attorney, family, friends, or bondsperson as soon after you are brought into the police station as practicable. The police have a right to complete their booking procedures before you are allowed to use the telephone. You have the right to be represented by counsel at all critical stages of your case. If you cannot afford an attorney, the court will appoint an attorney to represent you free of charge, if you qualify under existing criteria as an insolvent person. This right pertains to any offense, however, trivial, for which any imprisonment whatsoever might result. Constitutional rights may be waived or given up voluntarily. Before you say or sign anything that might result in waiver of a constitutional right, weigh your decision carefully (Russel Mace, Esq.).

Illustrative Anecdotes: New York City

None of us are read our rights. When one lady asks why, an officer replies, "Because we ain't askin' you any questions. There ain't no question about it, you are under arrest." The three other officers in the van join him in laughing. As soon as we get to the station we are all begging to be uncuffed; some of us have been cuffed for five hours and all of us are hurting. When the officers are in a good mood they cuff one hand to the chairs we are placed in. Gypsy is dragged up a ramp by her hair crying all the way. This is another way to convince the others she resisted arrest. An officer asks my name and I spell it out for him, B-A-R-R-A-C-L-I-F-F. As usual, the officers make a joke out of my name. I pick out the officer with the longest name, purposely mispronounce it, and ask loudly how to spell that one. The officers tell me to shut up and ask me if I'd like them to 'lose' my paperwork. When the officers are angry with us they can pretend to 'lose' our file which would result in an extra day of confinement in a freezing cold, filthy holding cell.

None of us are placed in a lineup or asked for any information other than our fingerprints. We have all been arrested for crimes that the police said they saw us do. There is no physical evidence; no money, and no victim. After finishing our paperwork the women are placed in a small cell and the males are left outside cuffed to the chairs. If we are very lucky we are allowed to smoke, and luckier still if we have cigarettes. We start to beg the smoking officers for cigarettes and they blow smoke in our direction and laugh. We also ask to use the phone and are ignored. Soon 30 other women are brought in and placed in the cell until there is not an inch of space. Those that don't fit are handcuffed outside with the men.

After six to eight hours on the floor we are transported to cells in central booking where we will await trial. They are known as the tombs because they are dark and freezing cold. We huddle on the concrete floor trying to stay warm as the cold seeps into our bones. Women with asthma are sharing their inhalers. One lady has a seizure and is carried out by two officers. Women who are addicted to heroin or methadone are beginning to be ill and many of them are vomiting or having diarrhea in the one urinal. It is not shielded from the outside and the male guard just reads his magazine while we try to pee without sitting in the mess. After many hours we are given a bologna sandwich and some juice. A male prisoner comes down to clean out the cell. We are placed in single file in the hallway while he sloshes buckets of water over the floor. Once that goes down the drain we are put back inside and the floor is even colder. I doze off and on, huddling with the others on the floor to try and keep warm. I wake up starving and I look around for uneaten sandwiches. We are all filthy from the floor and our hair looks like rat nests. None of us smell too good. After two and half days we are finally, looking like this, taken to see the judge.

SENTENCING

National Numbers

In 2000, 68% of all felons convicted in State courts were sentenced to a period of confinement, 40% to State prisons and 28% to local jails. Jail sentences are for short-term confinement (usually for a year or less) in a county or city facility, while prison sentences are for long-term confinement (usually for over a year) in a State facility (US. Dept. of Justice, 2000). Year 2000 FBI and National Criminal Justice Statistics report the average sentence for rape is 20 months; for breaking and entering it is 14 months, for drug possession 88 months, which is 7 years. The majority of women are convicted for non-violent drug related offences and, of women convicted of violent crimes, the majority are convicted for defending themselves or their children from abuse. Average prison terms for killing husbands are twice as long as for killing wives (Turning the Tide, 1998). Some women with comparatively minor infractions are sent to super–maximum security prisons (Amnesty International, 1999). Many women are caught up in long mandatory minimum sentences, the majority of which are because drug kingpins are rarely foolish enough to be caught carrying narcotics. They hire other people to transport drugs for them. These couriers are often caught with drugs in their possession, charged with serious felonies and given long mandatory prison sentences (Correctional Association, 2001). Since most of the arrestees are low income they are assigned a public defender. According to a 2001 Legal Aid Society Newsletter, the budget cuts imposed on them left 370 defenders for a client list that numbers over 200,000 per year; this is in NY but is indicative of national policies.

Illustrative Anecdotes: New York City

Most of my 45 arrests were for loitering for the purpose of prostitution. The first time I was arrested I pled not guilty. Five minutes before I was up before the judge I met my public defender. He asked me if I had bail money. I didn't. The prosecutor told him, as if I were not there, that if I pled not guilty I would stay on Rikers Island for 90 days before my trial, but that if I pled guilty I could go home. I pled guilty. This time I am charged with my first and only felony for supposedly selling $10 worth of crack. I tell the public defender that all he has to do is check the records to see that the officers were very well known to me. How stupid would I be to sell them drugs? He asks that if he were to defend a 'crackhead' against the New York City Police Department, which he won't, what would I do if we won? I would have to go right back where I was and things would be made even harder for me. Plus if we lost at trial I could get 3 years but the prosecutor is offering a city year, which is 8 months. I plead guilty. When I am brought to yet another holding cell I see none of us from my vanload have escaped sentencing.

Ada is nearly hysterical because she was arrested as an accomplice to her husband's drug dealing, even though she never saw him sell and he didn't keep drugs in the house. She had suspected he was doing something illegal but her strict Catholic/Latin upbringing made her feel she had no right to question him. She is scared she will be sent away for 25 to life even though she has never committed a crime.

None of us have a quarter to use the pay phone hanging just out of reach of the cell. We ask the guards for a twenty-five cent loan and the standard answer is, "If I gave everybody a quarter that asked for it, I'd be broke by now." We all try to get some sleep on the floor. We still have to go through processing on Rikers Island and it will be almost six days from the beginning of our ordeal before we get a bed and a threadbare blanket.

IMPRISONED

National Numbers

There are over 150,000 women imprisoned in the United States, more than any other country (Sokoloff, 2001). Women represent the fastest growing population in prison. Between 1980 and 1993, the female prison population increased about 313%, for men the same period the prison population increased 182% (National Women's Law Center, 1995). Between 1990-1998 the number of women in prison increased by 88%, on probation by 40% and on parole by 80% (Chesney-Lind, 2000). Women comprise 11% of the U.S. jail population. There are fewer prison facilities for women and prison services of all types were created for men. 25% of women are political prisoners (Women's Economic Agenda Project, 1994). Black women are incarcerated at a rate eight times that of white women. 5.1 % of black and Hispanic women are likely to go to jail at least one time during their lifetime as compared to .5% of white females (The Sentencing Project, 2003). On December 31 2001 State prisons were operating at 16% above capacity and Federal prisons at 31% above capacity (Bureau of Justice Statistics, 2001).

Issues

16% of women prisoners surveyed in 277 prisons had less than an eighth grade education, 45.8% had some high school and only 22.7% were high school graduates. 53.3% of women held no job prior to incarceration (Snell, 1991). Education is provided to minors only and some facilities have been sued for not providing that. Of those prisoners who had jobs, two thirds reported never receiving more than $6.50 per hour (Welsh, Anglin and Pendergrast, 1993). More than half the women in prison have been physically abused and 39% sexually abused, with many being survivors of both types of abuse (The Sentencing Project, 2003).

In 1999 State and Federal prisons held an estimated 721,500 parents of minor children. Of State women prisoners, 64.3% reported living with their children 28% reported the caregiver as the other parent 52.9% reported a grandparent, 25.7% reported other relative, 9.6% reported foster care and 10.4% reported friend or other. Of female Federal prisoners 73.4% reported living with their children (Mumola, 2000). Because there are fewer facilities for women an incarcerated woman is usually much further from her home and family than the average male prisoner. These distances cause transportation problems and deprives women of contact with their children (National Women's Law Center, 1995). More than 100,000 minors have a mother in jail (Bloom and Owen, 2002). Along with use of restraints on pregnant and sick female prisoners, reports of rapes and other sexual abuses—including male officers touching women's breasts and genitals during searches or watching them when they are naked or showering—are widespread in US jails and prisons. Some women with comparatively minor infractions are sent to super–maximum security prisons, where conditions are particularly harsh requiring prisoners to be in full view at all times, violating the woman's privacy and dignity (Amnesty International, 1999).

Health Issues

Women are substantially more likely to be serving time for a non-violent drug offense than men. More than half the women in prison reported committing their offense under the influence of alcohol/drugs. More than half the women had used alcohol/drugs in the week before committing their current offense (Snell, 1991). Substance abuse treatment availability is only available for 5-15% of populations incarcerated and illegal drugs are easier to get in facilities than counseling (Barr, 2000). A quarter of all women incarcerated are mentally ill (The Sentencing Project, 2003). 12.2% are diagnosed with serious mental illnesses, more than double that of men (Teplin, 2001).

Health care for all prisoners is substandard but women face a double stigma of being ignored and considered complainers. Facilities in many states have been accused in class action lawsuits of denying essential medical care to women with cancer, lupus, sickle cell anemia, AIDS and other life threatening conditions (Merrimen, 1998). 3.6% of women incarcerated in state and federal prison were HIV positive in 2000. The HIV rate of prisoners is about 4 times the rate of the US general population (Bureau of Justice Statistics, 2000). Hepatitis C is now the number one communicable disease in state prisons. They estimate as many as 40 percent of all women prisoners as compared to 30 percent of all male prisoners have been infected with the virus (DeGroot, 2002). Injection drug use is a major factor in the spread of AIDS and Hepatitis C in prison with one-quarter of prisoners having injected drugs in prison. Nearly half of prisoners have shared needles. 9 to 20 percent of federal inmates are victims of rape. The main argument against distribution of condoms in correctional facilities is that it might appear to condone sexual activity (American Foundation for AIDS Research, 1999). Needle exchange outside of prisons is difficult to put into legislation, the chances of implementation inside prison are minimal (Id.).

Six per cent of women are pregnant when they enter prison. In almost all cases the woman is abruptly separated from her child after giving birth (National Women's Law Center, 1995). 25% of all adult women in prison have either given birth in the year prior to their incarceration or are pregnant at the time of their arrest. A survey of state prisons reveals that less than 50% have written medical policies regarding pregnant women and only 48% offer prenatal services. Of these 48%, 21% offered prenatal counseling only, 15% offered counseling to help the mother find suitable placement for her after birth and only 15% had lighter or no work policies for pregnant women (U.S. Dept. of Justice, 2001). Women are forced to give birth with their legs shackled. One woman was forced to give birth to twins with her legs shackled. The children died (Amnesty International, 2000).

Illustrative Anecdotes: Florida and New York City

The first time I was in jail, and the only time I was incarcerated in Florida, was in a trailer deep in the Florida swamps. There were 50 women in the small trailer I was in. We were lined up next to each other in bunks. We gave each other privacy by not looking at each other. I covered my head with my sheet. The guard always made sure we had tobacco and books so that we wouldn't get in fights from 'nerves' as she called it. We knew we were lucky not to have been transferred from Dade County lock-up where there was worse overcrowding, no books or free tobacco, and tempers ran high. We were also lucky that we didn't have to work the swamps.

There was no television but we got plenty of news from the prison grapevine. One day a 64 year-old man had a stroke working the swamps in the 100 degree Florida humidity and the weed-whacker he was using cut off his leg. They didn't spare us from working the swamps because we were women, but because this little trailer housed the pregnant women and women with serious health issues. In the 45 days of my incarceration for possession of paraphernalia, two women died; one from cancer and one from AIDS. I was two months pregnant and me and the other 'preggies' never got any pre-natal care or vitamins. We were simply housed in this space that was considered less stressful and safer than regular facilities.

I believed it was safer since my short time in Dade County lock up provided some hard lessons. I had been offered a job with one of the male officers. Each officer is assigned a section of the prison to maintain and cull from the population for workers. I was happy to mop floors for $3.50 a week. When I reported for work the officer called me into his broom closet/office and asked me to 'do my job' while unzipping his pants. He said he would be my good friend and also make sure I had cigarettes. I wanted to cry and scream but I started thinking that the opposite of 'friend' was enemy, and I was scared to death. He said he didn't like using condoms and picked me since I was already pregnant and HIV negative. I was so relieved when a few days later I was transferred to this safer facility. In Florida we heard horrific stories of worse prisons like Rikers Island where I was now heading. I was eventually incarcerated there 41 times in the space of three years and eight months.

On Rikers Island there is a special cellblock for pregnant women. I was pregnant during at least five of my incarcerations since my arrests were so close together, but was never housed in the 'preggie' dorm because my stays were only 10 days. This cellblock had the same conditions as all others but the women received vitamins and fruit twice a day. Also, when they complained they may have been given a pass to the clinic more easily if it wasn't head count time or during a security search or drill. This didn't preclude pregnant women from being raped, as I well knew, or from getting drugs or hurt in fights. One innovation on Rikers is that women could keep their babies in the nursery for up to a year and a half after giving birth. Many did not want to because their sentences were longer than that and they were afraid the baby would be traumatized at separation. Many chose to give them up for adoption. It was sad to see a woman carted out shackled to a stretcher, but sadder still when they came back to the cellblock for regular prisoners. We gave these women space and shoulders to cry on.

One day I was walking up the hall and passed two pregnant women, two paralyzed women in wheel chairs, two deaf women and one woman with dwarfism! America's most UNwanted. There is also one crowded cellblock for mentally ill women. I was in there once to deliver the newspaper. It was the filthiest cellblock imaginable. Women were barely supervised and I watched as a man I presumed was a doctor handed out their medication. As soon as he was done he scooted out of there.

I lived in the street but was lucky to never get ill or be infested with lice. On Rikers Island there was such a bad outbreak of lice you could see their eggs in our eyelashes. When the facility finally got enough lotion for us to use, our clothes were not replaced. We were re-infested because hand-washing is not enough to rid the clothes of lice. I was so mad that I placed my mattress, uniform, sneakers, socks and underwear in the middle of the dormitory floor as a protest. I was lucky that the guards were afraid of catching lice so instead of placing me in solitary confinement for my actions they got us all new mattresses and clothes.

On another incarceration I caught chicken pox. I was released into the community still incubating the disease. While I was given the obligatory pap smear, when my results were positive they never mailed them to me. It wasn't in their job description. As a result I was living with ovarian cysts and Hepatitis C that may have been easier to treat earlier.

There were women sharing needles because while drugs were easy to sneak inside, syringes weren't. Also women performed oral sex on each other without dental dams. These behaviors helped propagate the rate of HIV, Hepatitis C and other communicable diseases. I heard stories of beatings and rapes by male guards. I also heard of women being told by guards that they would be placed in solitary on family/children visitation day if guards did not like them or for favors and silence.

During one of my early incarcerations I borrowed three cigarettes from a woman who wanted six in return. When I brought cigarettes from the commissary I looked for her but could not find her. I was released in my usual ten days and arrested two weeks later. Upon my return to Rikers Island the woman asked me where her cigarettes were. I had no money this time and I begged the guards, most of whom smoked, to please give her the cigarettes. They did not. She and two other women beat me before some officers came to stop them.

Another common misconception is that personal grooming items are supplied to prisoners. Due to overcrowding many prisoners don't have a job and if they have no one to send them money they can't buy supplies in the commissary. I was one of many of those in this position. Only half a bar of soap and sanitary napkins are given for free, but often are unavailable. Shampoo, toothpaste and deodorant are costly. Because of the lack of toothpaste I developed cavities. Since I was housed in a city facility the only option I had was to get them pulled.

At that time (1993-1996) there were around 300 beds on Rikers in drug treatment for the 2,000 women housed there. In 2003 there are only 100. To get into treatment you had to have no record of violence for the past ten years. This could be difficult among women who often fought in self-defense against their mates, or were raised in a hostile environment. I had no history of violence but couldn't get in the programs until my 41st incarceration landed me a city year, which is eight months. The worst thing for me was the boredom. No books, no school, no phones (unless you have money) and the food really is substandard. This is fertile ground for trouble and more reasons to do drugs and have unprotected sex.

When I finally entered one of the programs they had representatives from drug rehabilitation centers and other social programs come in to do client intake. I took one residential treatment program up on the offer. I didn't have any identification or money to send for my birth certificate so the representative was kind enough to send for it out-of-pocket. I also had been homeless and could not prove my residency. I will not describe how I got around that. The program also arranged to pick me up at the gate upon my release. Imagine the women who did not get this lucky. Finally, after 45 arrests, 41 incarcerations and many times begging social workers and judges for help, I was discharged into somewhere other than the street.

RELEASE FROM IMPRISONMENT

Drug treatment is only available to 15% that need it (SAMSHA, 1999). While there is a general shortage of treatment centers for drug users, facilities that cater for women's needs are even scarcer. Many in-patient treatment centers do not accept pregnant women and may drop women from treatment if they become pregnant. The reasons for this can range from a lack of sex-segregated accommodation to a lack of facilities to deal with pregnancy. Most treatment programs are unable to provide the prenatal medical services or the extensive support these women need. On the other end, prenatal care programs often do not have the resources to cope with the personal, social, medical, and other problems of drug-dependent pregnant women. A fact little thought of is that abortions are offered to these women.

The 2000 National Household Survey on Drug Abuse found that 3.9 million people who needed treatment did not get it and treatment professionals estimate that only 1 in 10 people receive the treatment they need. Increasingly, the only way for people who do not have the financial means but need drug treatment to access it is through the criminal justice system. After being arrested for drug related crimes, some states and jurisdictions divert offenders into treatment as a cost-effective and humane alternative to incarceration, yet drug courts and other diversion programs are available only to minute percentage of eligible and needy individuals and these models problematically rely heavily on non-therapeutic drug testing and coercion (Drug Policy Alliance, 2003).

The average cost to incarcerate one person in jail is $64,000 per year and $32-42,000 in prison. The average cost is $26,000 a year to send a parent and two children to a residential treatment center, which includes adult and child psychologists, education, anger management, parenting and job skills/placement. For a single person in a similar facility it only costs $17,000-21,000 per year and for outpatient facilities the cost can be as little as $2,500-5,000. Treatment has been proven 15 times more effective than imprisonment for reducing crime, and the two biggest deterrents to crime are education and employment (The Rand Corporation, 1996).

Many people were homeless, jobless and uneducated upon their arrest (See Section I). Many may have lost their homes and jobs because of their incarceration. Many states have implemented laws that exclude anyone with a drug charge from living in sponsored housing and will even evict their family members if they allow them to spend the night. Many states do not allow people convicted of a drug charge to receive student loans. Health concerns may have worsened or developed while imprisoned (See Health Issues).

During incarceration, women usually experience situations that can have an impact on their self-esteem. Such experiences may cause mothers to change so that they may no longer be the warm, caring parents they once were. Additionally some mothers may be angry with themselves, and with society for their situation. Children may have developed new friends, interests and activities. To abandon these and invest time in building a relationship with a mother that has been absent may not be so important to children. Another concern for them is that their mother may leave again. The mother may take these as a sign of rejection (Henriques, 1999).

Illustrative Anecdote: New York City

The program I entered did not take pregnant women or children, and the programs that did had a waiting list of over two years. I was happy to be there even though it was not really geared for women and their needs. As in jail, around 10.3% of the folks there tested positive for drugs. They were usually given a second chance. I was serious about building a life. I was lonely but went about the stages of the program and found it to be helpful. I became accustomed to the 9-5 structure again. I got my paperwork in order and I received medical checkups from head to toe. I also received one-on-one psychological counseling twice a week. Many people attended the on premises GED classes but since I already had mine I was placed in a job training program. I learned to use a computer and other office equipment.

There was a family court advocate on staff who helped me get in touch with my children. My son was two-and-a half and my daughter one when they were taken. I was lucky the children's father had a reliable family who enabled him to get the children out of the system. In Narcotics Anonymous meetings I heard many women share that after ten years of sobriety they were still fighting for custody. My children not only remembered me, they had missed me, and were happy to begin visitation.

I was also lucky that, unlike many others, my reading and presentation skills allowed me to interview well for jobs. When you speak with confidence sometimes they don't ask the dreaded question, "Have you ever been convicted of a felony?" I started as a receptionist in a software development company and moved into a studio apartment. One of the barriers to getting children out of the system is that boys and girls are required to have separate rooms. If you can't afford a two bedroom, you're out of luck. I was worried about taking my kids out of their familiar environment so I was okay with having them only on weekends.

I signed up for the ex-offender college grant that New York City used to provide. One problem with that is I had to attend fulltime and after one semester of working fulltime and going to college I was exhausted. I gave up college. I can't say enough how good it made me feel to have gone. I learned, I networked with like-minded people, and I contributed to my classes and classmates. I began studying on my own at home—everything from public policy to treatment methodologies.

A mentor of mine asked me to speak at a conference in Florida and soon I was speaking regularly in universities and for awhile even co-hosted a NYC talk show! I learned that the public had little understanding of addiction or incarceration. I also learned that, nationally, only 15% of prisoners receive any counseling so I founded Conextions Inc, a non profit organization, to educate the public and prisoners on addictions and related health and justice system issues. I came full circle when I was asked to work as a consultant on Rikers Island in the same program I had graduated from. I worked there from November of 2000 to January of 2003. I brought what light I could into an environment that had gotten even worse since my release.

Currently I am taking time off for health needs and to write my memoir. I have been married to a great man for five years. My children still spend the weekends. While we have problems from the separation, I can deal with them because I started with fifteen months of rehabilitative treatment and grew from there. Two things drive me to continue my advocacy. When I remember that none of this would have happened to me if there was treatment on demand, and over 150,000 other women that are incarcerated should be living a happy life too. And they could if only everyone knew what I know. They are worth it.

RECOMMENDATIONS

1. Changing legislation so that substance use and abuse is placed in the hands of health care professionals and out of the hands of law enforcement would greatly:

    a. reduce police racial, sexual and economic profiling, violence and corruption.

b. reduce violence against police and violence over territory.

c. reduce spread of diseases.

d. reduce the amount of addicts.

e. reduce the harm, driving under the influence, overdoses etc. from drug use.

f. reduce the amount of street prostitution by half or more.

g. reduce funds for ineffective incarceration and re-direct them to education, job skills, mental health, prevention, treatment and harm reduction programs.

h. reduce the break up of families and the cycle of crime and addiction.

i. reduce the black market so that it is more manageable for the police.

2. In place of that we should:

a. re-direct funds for police to learn investigation and detection and encourage police departments to reward the quality of arrests not the quantity.

b. re-direct funds for prisons into education, job skills, mental health, prevention, treatment and harm reduction programs.

References

American Foundation for AIDS Research. 2003. http://www.amfar.org

Amnesty International. 1999. http://web.amnesty.org/library/index/ENGA MR510011999

Barr, Mary. 2000. Drugs in Prison. http://conextions.org/html/drugs.html

Bureau of Justice Statistics: HIV in Prisons. 2001 http://www.ojp.usdoj.gov/bjs/pub/pdf/hivp01.pdf

Incarcerated Parents and Their Children. 2000. http://www.ojp.usdoj.gov/bjs/pub/pdf/iptc.pdf

Prisoners in 2001. http://www.ojp.usdoj.gov/bjs/pub/pdf/p01.pdf

Correctional Association. 2002. http://correctionalassociation.org/women_proj.html

Drug Policy Alliance. http://www.drugpolicy.org/drugwar/access/index.cfm

Henriques, Zelma Weston. 1982. *Imprisoned Mothers and their Children: A Descriptive and Analytical Study.* Washington, D.C.: University Press of America.

Human Rights Watch. 1998. Report "Shielded from Justice: Police Brutality and Accountability in the United States." www.hrw.org/reports98/police/

JusticeWorks Community. 2001. Mothers In Prison Fact Sheets. http://www.justiceworks.org/factsheets.htm

Mace, Russel, Esq. "What to expect when you are arrested. Your rights when you are arrested." http://www.macelaws.com/Criminal_Defense/information_about_arrests.htm

National Women's Law Center. 1995. http://www.nwlc.org

Rand Corporation. 1997. http://www.rand.org/publications/RB/RB6003/index.html

The Sentencing Project. 2003. Women in Prison Fact Sheet. http://www.sentencing-project.org/pdfs/1032.pdf

Sokoloff, Natalie. 2001. Violent Female Offenders in New York City: Myths and Facts, *Crime and Justice in New York City*, Vol. 1. A. Karmen, (Ed.). Thompson.

Substance Abuse and Mental Health Administration. 1999. http://www.samsha.gov/statistics/statistics.html

4

GENDER, INCARCERATION AND PEACEMAKING: LESSONS FROM GERMANY AND MALI*

Mechthild Nagel

In September 2003, a woman prisoner was denied access to abortion in the state of Indiana. She did not want to carry the fetus to term while incarcerated. In 1999, the Michigan state legislature considered adopting a bill that confirmed what prison critics have known all along: prisoners do not have any civil rights. Thanks to the 13th Amendment to the US constitution, slavery is codified in prisons. The occasion for that legislative discussion was a visit scheduled by an international human rights delegation of a women's prison where prisoners' rights were systematically violated. Needless to say, Human Rights Watch was denied entry since US officials do not consent to international monitoring of its prisons, let alone detention centers where immigrants are being held. The precarious status of prisoners is also internationally codified, as the USA signed on to the international covenant against slavery—with reservations—in 1929: Slavery is illegal, except in prisons. On the basis of this statute, the US courts have argued that prisoners are prohibited from entering into collective bargaining agreements and from voting. But prisoners are counted in the census and for purposes of political apportionment. Many states have extended voting rights prohibition to ex-felons, an issue that certainly was highlighted in the 2000 presidential election in Florida, a state that has barred hundreds of thousands of Black men and women from voting.

I wish to focus on women's experiences in the criminal justice system, in part, because they face a different set of challenges than men do and because women's experiences tend to be ignored in general studies on the prison system. This is not meant as a comprehensive study but rather to highlight a few persisting patterns faced by imprisoned women which have a certain cross-cultural relevance: a) The failure to recognize women's rights as human rights; b) women's victimization prior to arrest; c) demonization of "fallen" women; d) the dilemma of turning prison into home. I will look at two countries' model prisons to illustrate these prevailing patterns. Wardens of women's prisons in Germany, the USA, and Mali have told me that women do not belong in prison (The German warden was quite frank in noting that she'd be happy to find a different job for herself, if today, all women's prisons were to be closed.). Yet, we still arrest and incarcerate women at alarming rates, especially in the USA where

Black women have become the targets of the War on Drugs, both at the federal and state levels (cf. Frazer and Barr's articles). What tools and analysis should abolitionists use when contesting gender-specific incarceration and proposing genuine paths of reform? I will draw cross-cultural and transnational parallels of imprisonment, e.g. vis-à-vis conditions of women's prisons, and I will suggest peacemaking practice as viable alternative to prisons.

In the 1990s a global political consensus emerged that 'women's rights' are also 'human rights' (Bunch, 1995). In particular, the Beijing Women's Conference set forth an ambitious agenda and in many countries in the global South, its recommendations were implemented by returning delegates who acted as pressure groups on local and national politicians and policy makers. In an era where many of us in the global North found ourselves battling post-feminist ideologies and policies, particularly, in the US, activist-scholars in the global South began circulating ideas and papers on "putting women at the center of analysis." I believe this focus is necessary, especially when it comes to critiquing the current prison system. Specifically, a gender focus on human rights' issues needs to integrate racial-sexual political economy. Such an analytical framework is very important in analyses of welfare reform and other structural adjustment measures and in studying the trends in criminalizing women of color around the world.

In a recent paper, Julia Sudbury (2002), who works with the abolitionist group Critical Resistance, argued that women of color and Black women in particular are faced increasingly with the threat of mass arrest and incarceration, not only in the United States but globally. Angela Y. Davis (2000) has also noted that it is quite startling to visit such white, homogenous countries, e.g. the Netherlands, and find a large number of Black women in its prisons. Indeed, there is a disproportionate incarceration of Black women and indigenous women in such countries as Australia, Canada, and Great Britain (Sudbury, 2002, pp. 59-60). What I wish to introduce here is the concern that the *criminalization of women of color is a human rights issue*. This was highlighted in the recent UN Conference on racism, xenophobia, and religious intolerance held in Durban, South Africa in September 2001 (Davis et al, 2001). Unfortunately, the political progress made in Durban was eclipsed by the events of September 11, 2001. I believe it is important to give a brief sketch of the mis-recognition of women's rights as human rights occurs, especially as at it affects poor women of color.

Sudbury (2002) chronicles the Americanization of the Drug War in Great Britain and highlights in what ways immigrant women are being targeted by immigration officials in the global North. Women prisoners in the UK report that they are being used as "mules" or "decoy" for major drug transports and they blame were poverty and coercive tactics (Sudbury, pp. 65-67). Within the US, the entrapment strategy developed against women is that they are accused of selling drugs, when in reality they often "hold" (sometimes without their knowledge) drugs for a boyfriend who is a drug dealer. Often, he pleads to a lesser charge and the girlfriend is sentenced to twice as many years of hard time, because she does not testify against him—out of loyalty, fear, or both (Johnson,

2003). The harsh penalties faced by women need further explanation. Crime statistics indicate that women's imprisonment, especially African American women, has increased at a much higher rate than imprisonment rates of men since the inception of the War on Drugs.

The justice system is fraught with patriarchal attitudes as 'deviant' women do not fit the ideal of a lady. Judges can be contemptuous of women who fail to conform to domestic ideals and engage in conventionally "immoral" strategies to obtain a better future for themselves and their children. Such judges (mostly men) like to invoke the idea that "an example has to be made" and they follow the script of a racialized patriarchal logic. A sentenced prisoner in Great Britain says that the judge "used me as an example because he knew I was pregnant" (Sudbury, p. 66). In Paula Johnson's anthology, *Inner Lives*, incarcerated African American women discuss racial discriminatory practices: white women with the same offense get a lesser sentence or probation/counseling, whereas Black women do hard time. A paternalistic script is invoked to assist a white working class woman with her 'drug problem', whereas a punitive script is employed to mark the Black working class woman as a "drug dealer;" instead of receiving drug treatment African American women are disproportionately sentenced to 15 years to life and lose child custody as a result of lengthy sentences and federal child custody laws (Johnson, p. 48).

If women who are criminalized as drug dealers face judicial retribution, demonization of sex workers is even more prevalent in the judicial system the world over. A warden in Germany, whom I interviewed, told me about a 22-year-old sex worker who was sentenced to seven years for pouring sleeping pills into her client's drink in order to rob him. The warden said that the male judge's own fear must have played a role in this excessive sentence. She also noted that the language of the verdict was bizarre. The judge justified the harsh sentence this way: the offender "can't play doctor; she could have killed the client." Sex workers have long been stereotyped as 'fallen women,' and Nawal el Sa'adawi's novel, *Woman at Point Zero* (1983) dramatizes this patriarchal logic and critiques it. The protagonist, Firdaus, narrates her journey of becoming a sex worker. She is in prison awaiting execution for killing her pimp (in self-defense). Firdaus is executed, and yet her voice lives on in this fictionalized account written by Sa'adawi who interviewed a sex worker while Sa'adawi herself was imprisoned for her political views. The groundbreaking anthology *Global Sex Workers* (Kempadoo and Doezema, 1998) also serves as an important corrective to the prevailing societal attitudes of sex workers as fallen women and/or of being hapless victims, deprived of any agency. This study of sex workers and their organizations opens up a discourse for resistance and redefinitions of voluntary versus involuntary prostitution. Similarly to the targeted prosecution of (transnational) poor women of color in the global War on Drugs, racism, too, plays an important role in the selective prosecution of criminalized sex workers and of those who appear to be sex workers solely on the basis of their continent of origin, e.g. African women living in Italy (Angel-Ajani, 2005).

The third area of demonization of women offenders concerns 'domestic' offenses: when battered women kill their abusive spouses or boyfriends. In the US, psychologists have done decade-long research into what has come to be known as "Battered Women's Syndrome." Pioneered by Lenore E. Walker in the 1970s, studies were done on the cycles of violence and on how women felt entrapped in abusive relationships. Killing the abuser became the only option they felt they had to end the cycle of violence (cf. Dittmann 2003, p. 60). Despite expert testimony to the jury about this cycle of violence in which abused women find themselves entrapped, more often than not these women have been demonized and sentenced to disproportionately long sentences or even death sentences, as in the case of Carla Faye Tucker. Her case sparked international solidarity, and even the Pope intervened to plead for commutation of the death sentence. Perhaps, Tucker won great acclaim because she was a model prisoner and became a born-again Christian. But to no avail. Tucker was executed under the reign of Governor George Bush of Texas.

While death row and capital punishment represent the bleakest side of the carceral complex, I like to turn to the peculiar case of prisons becoming homes for women. I shall describe two prisons: one in Germany, a first world country, and one in Mali, a third world nation. Both prisons are administered by female wardens at the time of the interviews.

The women's prison in Hamburg, Germany, tries to care for women with compassion. Hilde van den Boogart, the warden, highlights the need for sensitivity training for male guards who, unlike in the United States, are not permitted to go into personal care areas! She advises them to watch out for their own paternalistic attitudes. The prison offers the following programs to help in rehabilitation: job placements for released women in the area (which requires networking with area placement centers); a project with prisoners and high school girls (youth assistance program); and educational programs, such as German for Foreigners and basic literacy programs (Boogart, 2001).

It is interesting to note that immigrant female prisoners often encourage and help German illiterate women. Long-term educational programs are difficult to schedule due to the average stay of 10.5 months. Shorter programs are preferred. They have developed partnerships with Hamburg to place ex-convicts in schools or jobs. Women are required to work in prison but they have to choose from three different job placements. If prisoners refuse work, they face disciplinary arrest (23 hrs/day). Boogart also commented that they should have a chance to change jobs once. She cited lack of concentration due to noise as a key problem. The prisoners should have a probation period for a job for six weeks. In 2001, they were paid 17 DM/day (ca. $9.00/day). The warden explained that if they got paid more, they would have to pay rent...

When asked about the security level of the prison, she scoffed at the idea of having a maximum secure facility for women. Boogart also focused on the importance of having women live with their children, even when these attended regular schools (women don't run away when they have children to take care of). She also discussed issues arising from weekend furloughs (women feeling a sense of guilt, not pleasing guards when they stay longer than the allocated "vacation"), but she expressed her concerns about guards abusing their authority. On the other hand, she felt that racism was not an issue among the staff, even though a sizeable number of women of color are imprisoned—immigrants make up 20% of prisoners. She noted that these women do not group together, unlike Turkish male prisoners in men's prison, partly because they are a very heterogeneous a group. Besides sensitivity training, the warden wants to work with women who are actually afraid of other women (especially their own mothers); she noticed that some women lose all self-esteem when their mother comes to visit, trying to please her and behaving in rather infantile ways.

The prison was enlarged from 45 to 95 beds in 2001. Fifty per cent of the prisoners are mothers, most with young children. The fathers rarely take care of children, so that most of them end up in foster homes. When convicts are pregnant, the warden tries to negotiate with the judge to release them early or keep the children with them up to the age of schooling. The warden has built up good contacts with the clemency board (*Gnadenbehörde*). Another women's prison in northern Germany actually has a separate mother-child area with kindergarten and school. Older women, above 60 years, serve as "grandmothers." The facility is an apartment complex; there is little danger of escapes because their children live there, too.

Finally, when I asked the warden about alternatives to incarceration (ATI), she responded that these ATIs occur mostly in juvenile justice and are offered under the label "projects instead of prison." She advocated that these projects ought to be carried over to adult court. (Note however, that in Germany, 80% of felons receive fines, not a prison sentence.) For women felons, the warden advocates no prison, or early release. She says that it is not acceptable for prisons to become home. Yet, Boogart emphasized that "prisons cannot be expensive enough," i.e., there should be many more rehabilitative programs subsidized by taxpayers.

An illustration of the problems of the prison system in the USA was revealed at a church based conference in upstate New York (2000) entitled, "What good can come out of prisons?" One of the speakers was Elaine Lord who was at the time the warden for the women's maximum security prison in Bedford Hills, NY, which is hailed as a model prison in the United States. She told the sad story of a woman who was desperate to get re-admitted to prison because she had no community on the outside, no job, and no family to take her back. She was re-arrested on "parole violation," sitting in a Donut Shop all night across from the prison. Prison had indeed become her home. The warden concluded that most of the women in her facility do not belong there. They have had harrowing histories of violence in their childhood, and since the New York state mental health hospitals were closed in the 1990s, many mentally ill patients become homeless and end up in to jail or prison. They end up forming emotional relationships if not intentional communities with other prisoners and even sympathetic guards.

The warden of the main women's prison in Bollé, Mali told me that they do not have problems with recidivism, with the exception of one woman who stole upon her release—in order to be readmitted to the women's prison! So here, too, at least in this instance, the prison turns into a home. For many women, the prison actually becomes a sanctuary where genuine love for one another is developed; a feeling that some of the women may experience for the first time in their lives! They tell the warden: "'Madame, at home I will not have food, a bed, a place to shower.' There are people who told me that their whole life until they came to prison they had not slept in a [Western] bed.'"(Kouyate, 2002)

Kouyate, the warden, emphasized that she runs the prison so that the women's stay is "comfortable and to assure their reintegration into society as well as their post-carceral life. It does not matter what you do [but] if you do not provide them with a life project they risk coming back. We are a reintegration center. . . . We must help these people to find jobs. These hopes cannot be realized without means. We need the financial means to start co-ops in which these people can continue to make use of the skills they have learned in prison."

The majority of women incarcerated in Mali were previously domestic workers of upper caste Malian families. They are accused or convicted of infanticide; and as prison officials readily admitted the father of the infant in all of these cases are male members of the family the young, unmarried woman worked for, or the *patron* himself. This is particularly dire for these women since women are associated with life and incapable of committing "war", i.e. killing somebody. In fact, if a woman dies in child birth, this is akin in this culture to having died in war! But it may also be the case that women are compelled to kill the child if the father is of lower caste origin (Koné, 2003).

In Mali, the women's prison does not have a mess hall. The planners rejected a Western panopticon architecture in favor of a more African house/compound structure. Young children stay with their mothers, and there is a separate play area. The prison administration emphasized that it wants to help women who killed their babies resocialize with the help of prisoners who are mothers and who keep their babies while in prison. Each dorm room houses about 5-8 women and the eldest is declared the mother who keeps order and makes important decisions. Women are also trained to make garments, soap, and are provided with a rudimentary school room with a few books to read. Most women are illiterate.

Even though this prison looked like a sanctuary as opposed to the men's prison downtown and American prisons I have visited, most women would still prefer freedom of movement. One young woman was beaming and told me that she was to be released the next day. Some women are offered continuation of training in the prison after their release, but most do not want to return because society will view it as if they were re-incarcerated (Togola, 2002).

Conflicts that arise between women prisoners get resolved the "African way." There are overseers (*surveillantes*) who intervene before quarrels degenerate into fights. We watched a conflict resolution scene, where, as Togola, the public relation officer of the prison, explained, "both parties mutually apologize to each other. They do this by holding their arms behind their backs" and kneeling. This practice is quite different from women prisoners being written up for provocation (including touching or embracing each other) in American prisons.

Kouyate had visited US prisons in 1997 and was struck by the predominance of African American women prisoners. Questioning the warden of the Boston women's prison, she was given a "superficial" answer: "Blacks do not want to work. They do not do anything. They sell drugs. They dance." Bollé prison in Mali, on the other hand, exudes a spirit of humanity and compassion; it has been ranked a model prison and reintegration center and the warden made a point of creating a "communal prison system" which is quite different from the French cell system (Kouyate, 2002).

What strategies can we learn for the abolition of prisons?

In Africa, every administrator I spoke with announced that prisons are a colonial invention, but unfortunately, given the predominance of the laws of the former empires, attempts at change are futile. Yet, Kouyate, like Boogart, the German warden, tries to negotiate early release, often with good success: "There are a lot of poor people here, but there are various degrees of poverty. For those people without family or any kind of support, we try to 'sensibilize' judges to expedite the process of trials or release" (Togola, 2002). In Mali, imprisonment is frowned upon by society and judges who give out harsh prison sentences may face harsh criticism. Prison is a last resort of punishment for people, usually reserved for those who are socially displaced, i.e. people who have migrated from another African country or who have left their rural ancestral home for the city where they are without their kin, imam and other social networks.

Mali has a caste system and one of these groups is the *jeliws* (griots), both men and women, whose main job is to keep peace in the community. They intervene on any level, from spousal disputes to those between heads of state, to solve disputes and issue solutions for redress, if an offense is committed. The main objective is to find a solution quickly, to minimize the damage, and to assure that future generations of the feuding parties and families may continue to intermarry. *Jeliws* enjoy great authority and power in Mali society.

Polygamy seems to be a great source of tension in Mali culture. I heard the story of a woman who killed her husband because he had married a second wife. The offender was banished from the village and had to seek exile at her paternal home. Nobody proposed turning her in to the police and ultimately prison, despite the severity of the crime. An extreme example of the influence of custom on Malian views of criminal behavior is if a marital dispute arises in the kitchen area of the house, and the husband is killed. No action is taken, because Malians would ask 'What is his business in the kitchen?' The kitchen is off limits to adult men.

There are obvious complications that arise from comparing differences in peacemaking strategies between cultures: to what extent are we encouraged to support traditional practices? A Western woman might frown on the Malian practice of banishing men from the kitchen. Whose human rights are we supporting? When can appeals to universality be made which do not smack of patriarchal, paternalistic or other practices of subordination? As we wish to pay attention to cultural specificity, it is helpful to ask, what works? Can we map out an alternative vision for peacemaking, putting women at the center of such praxis analysis? I take my cues from a South African women's rights activist, Mmatshilo Motsei, who developed a women- and community-based model of empowerment and violence prevention for a very successful women's shelter in Soweto, South Africa. Her model, which addresses domestic violence among other issues, encompasses a collective and spiritual strategy. It provides an alternative way of thinking about domestic violence, which has been guided by expert-driven psychological, individually focused assessment—the *modus operandi* of the battered women's movement in the USA (Nagel, 2001).

In North America, Native American and Canadian women, too, have been traditionally in the center of peacemaking and are reemerging as forceful voices in these neo-colonial times. Their criminalization as a result of white supremacy has focused on forced education, forced sterilizations, and in general a forced adaptation of the white man's way of life. Nevertheless, as countless native women tell, "we don't go away." In Black and Latino communities, high school students have been agitating against imprisonment with slogans, such as "Education, not Incarceration" (in particular, in Brooklyn, NY and Oakland, CA). The late 1990s have seen an upsurge in reformist and abolitionist demands, and it is time that we conceive of visions of an egalitarian society that relies neither on prisons nor on other conventional penal systems, which only further systemic inequality, rather than eliminate it. Even criminology, which has aided the ideological justifications of Western penality with its emphasis on incarceration, has changed its way, led by pioneers, such as Harold Pepinsky who coined the sub-discipline of criminology of peacemaking (Pepinsky et al, 1992) to counteract a criminal justice system founded on violence. As prison critics and activists discuss what novel perspectives work to undo the centuries old naïve faith in a broken system, I encourage us to look for inspiration and models outside Western paradigms, such as indigenous practices from Native America to the Mande world of West Africa. It does not suffice to acknowledge the human rights of an incarcerated woman if one does not seek tools for dismantling the chains that bind her. Reforming prisons as an end in itself will not accomplish the disappearance of prisons, but reforming prisons with the goal of abolishing them, might just bring about genuine peace.

Note

* This research was supported in part by a Faculty Research grant provided by the research council of SUNY Cortland. Many thanks to Kassim Koné who was a research partner and assisted in transcription and translation of the interviews conducted in Mali during August 2002.

References

Angel-Ajani. 2005. Domestic Enemies and Carceral Circles: African Women and Criminalization in Italy. *Global Lockdown* Julia Sudbury, (Ed.). New York: Routledge.

Blackwell, Maylei and Nadine Naber. 2002. Intersectionality in an Era of Globalization. The Implications of the UN World Conference against Racism for Transnational Feminist Practices—A Conference Report. *Meridians* 2(2): 237-248.

Bunch, Charlotte. 1995. Transforming Human Rights from a Feminist Perspective. In Peters et al.

Davis, Angela Y. 2000. Critique of the Prison Industrial Complex. Paper presented at the International Conference on Penal Abolition (ICOPA IX), Toronto, May.

Davis, Angela Y. and Cassandra Shaylor. 2001. Race, Gender and the Prison Industrial Complex. California and Beyond. *Meridians* 3(1): 1-25.

Dittmann, Melissa. (July/August) 2003. A Voice for Women in Prison. *Monitor on Psychology* 34(7): 60-61.

El Sa'adawi, Nawal. 1983. *Woman at Point Zero*. London: Zed Press.

Johnson, Paula C. (Ed.). 2003. *Inner Lives. Voices of African American Women in Prison*. New York: NYU Press.

Kempadoo and Doezema. 1998. *Global Sex Workers: Rights, Resistance, and Redefinition*. New York: Routledge.

Koné, Kassim. 2003. Personal communication, September.

Nagel, Mechthild. 2001. On the Limits of Feminist Cross-Cultural Analysis: African Women and Human Rights Discourses. *Issues in Africa and the African Diaspora in the 21ˢᵗ Century*. Seth N. Asumah and Ibipo Johnston-Anumonwo (Eds.). Binghamton: Global Publications.

Pepinsky, Harold E. and Richard Quinney. 1991. *Criminology as Peacemaking*. Bloomington: Indiana University Press.

Peters, Julie and Andrea Wolper (Eds.). 1995. *Women's Rights are Human Rights. International Feminist Perspectives*. New York: Routledge.

Shakur, Assata. 1987. *Assata. An Autobiography*. Chicago: Lawrence Hill Books.

Sudbury, Julia. 2002. Celling Black Bodies: Black Women in the Global Prison Industrial Complex. *Feminist Review* 70:57-74.

Interviews with:

Mme Koyate, warden, Bollé women's prison, Bamako, Mali, August 2002.

Mr. Togola, PR person, Bollé women's prison, Bamako, Mali, August 2002.

Hilde van den Boogaart, warden, Hamburg, Germany, June 2001.

PART II

Theories of Punishment and State Violence

5

IMPRISONED BODIES: THE LIFE-WORLD OF THE INCARCERATED*

Drew Leder

Why pay attention to the experience of the imprisoned? There are several important reasons, some sociological in nature, some phenomenological. I begin with the former. One reason, in twenty-first century America, to focus on inmates is simply because there are so many. The United States now incarcerates over two million men and women (www.ojp.usdoj.gov/bjs/prisons.htm). In 1972, the United States held a little over three hundred thousand inmates (Ibid.). That this has increased six-fold in the last three decades is a result of a myriad of factors including the war on drugs with its focus on criminalization and punishment, and an overall trend toward longer sentences and reduced use of parole. The incarceration binge has continued largely independent of criminal activity. Crime has decreased for the last nine years (www.cjcj.org/index.html, 2000), during which time the prison population has risen precipitously.

Our incarceration rates are six to ten times as great as similar Western industrialized countries. For example, we hold more prisoners in one *state* (California) than do the nations of France, Germany, Great Britain, Japan, Singapore, and the Netherlands *combined* (www.fbi.gov/ucr/ucr.htm). The United States, though it has but 5% of the world's population, holds fully one-quarter of the world's prison population (Schlosser, 1998, pp. 51-77).

We might say the U.S. has embarked on a unique social experiment. In response to a complex variety of social ills, we respond with one "simple solution": place an ever-increasing proportion of our citizens in cages. Needless to say, this strategy has impacted disproportionately minority populations whose social position is already disadvantaged. Though African-Americans compose 13% of Americans, they represent 46% of all inmates in U.S. prisons. Fully 63% of inmates are either Hispanic or black (www.hrw.org/reports/usa/2000).

For sociological reasons alone it is thus important to pay careful attention to the experience of these two million. Their presence has been erased from the common society, but must not be from our scholarly and public discourse. Otherwise, the wisdom of our prison "solution" will continue to go unchallenged.

In addition to the sociological import, the experience of inmates has phenomenological meaning. Phenomenology developed as a branch of philosophy dedicated to investigating and describing the structures of human experience:

time and space *as lived*, movement and perception, the embodied self in its encounter with objects and others. But what happens to all these when a human being is confined for decades on end often in cells the size of a normal bathroom? What then becomes of lived temporality and spatiality? What then the relation to one's own embodiment, or that of other people? To investigate these is to understand better the human capacity to construct a life-world even in the most constrained of circumstances.

From both a sociological and phenomenological standpoint, issues of power are key within this world. The severe constraints mentioned above are imposed by state power in response to individual behaviors judged intolerable. We might say the prison exists to disempower the individual, and re-empower the threatened state. Yet the prisoner is not passive in this equation. His or her construction of a life-world is not only provoked by mechanisms of power, but constitutes a strategic response to them, sometimes carefully reasoned through, sometimes pre-thematic. I will thus examine the inmate's life-world as an active constitution. We will find that the inmate's experience of space, time, and body are interwoven with strategies of resistance, reclamation, and escape vis-a-vis a hostile environment.

Philosophically, I will draw on the work of a variety of Continental philosophers, including Heidegger's phenomenology of the life-world, Merleau-Ponty's focus on the lived body, and Foucault's attention to the body in the field of power relations. I will also draw heavily on work I did with inmates, mostly serving life sentences, in the maximum-security Maryland Penitentiary. As a volunteer, I taught some 10-13 men (it was an all-male prison) in a not-for-credit philosophy seminar that continued over two years. We studied a broad range of texts, including several in Continental thought by authors such as Nietzsche, Heidegger, and Foucault. The inmates used concepts from such works to analyze their experiences of life on the street, and in maximum-security prison. The conversations were so powerful and illuminating that I began taping them. From transcripts I produced edited dialogues which are published, with my own comments, in a recent book, *The Soul Knows No Bars: Inmates Reflect on Life, Death, and Hope* (Leder, et al., 2000).

This paper relies heavily on these dialogues, cited here by page numbers in parentheses. My goal is to allow the inmates to articulate their own life experience, though I gather their insights into an overarching framework. The voices we hear are mostly those of African-American men from an inner-city environment, unusual for their level of educational achievement (largely secured through prison college-extension programs which have subsequently closed down as a result of the 1993 Omnibus Crime Bill). I make no pretense that this is a representative cross-section of all inmates. If anything, categorical thinking about all 'prisoners' and 'criminals' has tended to feed the incarceration binge. Yet I believe the individual voices here represented do shed light on the range of human responses possible in conditions of incarceration. We may also find aspects of the analysis applicable to other institutions. Foucault argues that in the modern regime of 'discipline,' similar mechanisms of power are at play not only in prisons, but in the military, schools, workplaces, hospitals (Foucault, 1979, pp. 135-28). The work of reclamation, escape, and integration I discuss may be employed by individuals within those institutional settings.

Ultimately, we may learn from inmates something even more general about human strategies for coping with adversity and restraint. "I could be bounded in a nutshell and count myself a king of infinite space, were it not that I have bad dreams" (Hamlet II, pp. 263). So says Hamlet, struggling with an inward dilemma—or so might say someone suffering from a debilitating disease, or the constraints of poverty, or other existential limitations. And so say the inmates. Bounded by the nutshell of a prison cell, the inmate can strive to be king of infinite space and time—but contends with a world of bad dreams.

LIVED TIME

Husserl (1964), Heidegger (1962), and many other Continental philosophers have distinguished between lived time and clock-and-calendar time. The latter is grounded metaphysically by Newton's vision of an absolute time that flowed forth equably, independent of observers. It is susceptible to mathematical measurement, can be divided into standardized increments, even plotted geometrically as on a timeline. By way of contrast, lived-time, time-*as-experienced* is a complex and vari-able phenomenon. Past, present, and future do not simply unfold consecutively as on a time-line. Heidegger suggests that, in a sense, the future comes first (ibid., p. 378). Our future goals and anticipations organize our present activities, and even our interpretations of the past. Nor does experiential time unfold in equable increments. Time may slow down, as when we check the clock repeatedly during a tedious lecture, and are stunned to find the minute-hand all but paralyzed. At other times we wonder "Where did the time fly?" A day of delightful play may seem gone almost before begun. Yet, after the fact, it might expand in pleasant memory, while the tedious lecture contracts to insignificance.

Ultimately, our experience of time has much to do with the rhythms of our daily life and our extended projects. Waking and sleeping, washing and eating, works begun and accomplished, friends and family encountered, special events, and the change of seasons, all combine to create a textured temporal field. Often, this field can be altered, even shredded by "life on the street." The problems of the inner city – drug addiction, chronic poverty and unemployment, disrupted family-life, community fragmentation, loss of hope concerning the future, all have the power to distort lived temporality. Yet life on the street is nonetheless a life, with its own goals, rhythms, activities, and interactions.

All this is radically disrupted by a prison sentence. Lived-time is supplanted by an abstract Newtonian framework of mathematically-measured calendar time (Prison Conference, SUNY Cortland, 2001). "Twenty years" says the judge. This is time turned into alien beast – or *automaton* we should say, given its blind and abstract nature. Twenty years are to be taken from a person's life. They belong not to him or her but the state. Time itself has become something that *must be served,* an instrument of disempowerment. This is true not only on the macroscopic scale but in the intricate management of daily time to which an inmate is subjected. When you sleep, hours in and out of the cell, limited opportunities for action, will be largely pre-determined by prison authorities—not natural inclination.

A massive disordering of temporality can ensue. The past may be brooded over as a scene for repetitive regret, if only at having gotten caught. The experienced present may be slowed almost to a halt by the lack of things to do, the boredom, the paucity of meaningful projects offered to inmates as they are "warehoused" for their duration. Experience of the future may be transformed, to use Minkowski's terms, from one of "activity" to one of "expectation." He writes, "Through its activity the living being carries itself forward, tends toward the future, creates it in front of itself." (Minkowski, 1970, p. 83). However, "expectation" involves an inversion of lived-time. While awaiting an event which we do not control, instead of moving toward the future, "we see the future come toward us and wait for that (expected) future to become present" (ibid., p. 87). We are paralyzed in anticipation. The expected future "absorbs, so to speak all becoming," allowing the present "only a shadowy existence" (ibid., p. 89), shriveled up and constricted. This is the predicament of many prisoners counting off the years on the way to an expected release date. Instead of living richly and purposively, they are trapped in a desiccated present, watching the future march oh-so-slowly closer (ibid., p. 87).

This constitutes a brief description of the altered time that threatens to overcome the incarcerated. But the individual remains capable of responding to and resisting such vectors. I will now turn to a variety of strategies whereby inmates re-work temporality. This theme will be introduced by an excerpt from our prison class discussion on phenomenological notions of lived-time.

> **Donald Thompson:** I think the problem is that guys in here spend most of the time just discussing the good ole days, the glory days, "When I had my car, these two jobs, or those five girls." Or "When prison was better" or "Instead of knives and machine guns we had forty-five magnums." If you try to talk about the future it's just not acceptable.

> **Selvyn Tillett:** I've seen guys with a couple life sentences plus some numbers behind it, saying "Yeah, my wife will be waiting for me like the old days." I be thinking, "Are you out of your mind?" I wouldn't say it is because they'd be ready to fight, but they're trapped in *that past.*

> **John Woodland:** Quite a few guys try to live in the past. I like living in the future, thinking about what my life is going to be. But I think one thing most of us try to avoid is the *present.* Because the present here is the most painful (Leder, et al., p. 86).

Articulated here is a strategy of resistance I will call "escape." Trapped in a painful present, the men seek ways to escape into the past or future. In its most deficient form, this can devolve into a sterile, even self-destructive escapism. The discussants are aware that dwelling in an idealized past can be a waste of time, perhaps even a set-up for a repetition of bygone failures. Rather than actively advancing in life one retreats to a static past.

But the strategy of escape need not always be escapist in the pejorative sense. Happy memories can be a source of strength and comfort. "Thinking about what my life is going to be," as John does, introduces hope and ambition. Heidegger's writes of lived-time as involving a series of *ecstases*, etymologically from the Greek for "standing outside" (Heidegger, p.377). To live in and for the future, like John's, allows a door to swing open so one stands outside the prison cell. Freedom is not then something just to be "expected" at a future date, as in Minkowski's sense of debilitating expectation. Rather, imagining the future introduces an element of freedom into the prisoner's current life-world.

Resuming the inmate discussion:

> **Q (an alias):** I see it a little differently. To me, time is like a dragon I have to slay. If I can master the present, I will have used my time to *redeem* time. Then I can go back and offer something to people who never had to be in that situation...I get up in the morning at 8:30 and I don't get back to my cell until about 10 p.m. Between those times I'm constantly involved in activities that are beneficial and what I want to do. I'm reading materials I intend to use in the future for political work, and philosophical literature, concentrating heavily. The time flies for me, you know? Sometimes I can't even find enough hours to complete what I wanted.

> **Wayne:** I call this *"doing time"*--when you use every available moment for your benefit. When you have time to sit back and mope and worry, is when *time begins to do you* (Leder, et al., p. 86).

In contrast to the strategy of escape, I will call this the strategy of "reclamation." The living present is reclaimed as a scene for fulfilling and purposive action. One is back to "doing time" instead of having time do you. Q cites satisfying activities that give meaning and richness to his day, even one spent in prison. The temporal alienation introduced by the imposition of sentence is successfully overcome.

The strategy of "escape" emphasizes flight from an oppressive reality. The strategy of "reclamation" emphasizes redeeming that reality: the life-world is re-humanized. However, this polarity I sketch is far from absolute. Like the yin-yang symbol, such opposites bear within themselves seeds of one another, and can flow together and harmonize. This harmonizing of opposites is an ideal in Taoism, and has its merits in a prison setting.

For example, we see this harmonizing in Q's description of being "constantly involved in activities that are beneficial....reading materials I intend to use in the future." Perhaps Q started by reclaiming the present, discovering the joys of reading possible even in prison. This reading may then have stimulated new visions of a life post-release. Reclamation leads to escape. The progression can also be reversed. Perhaps Q liked to escape to an imagined future. Envisioning what he wants to do post-release (and Q is the only living participant in my class who has been released) may have then helped Q find meaning in his prison days. Escape leads to reclamation.

Which ever movement came first, I will call this blending of escape and reclamation "integration." From the Latin *integratus*, meaning "renewal," or "made whole," we see the power of integration in Q's ability to both affirm his incarcerated present, and to see it as a route to a different and better future. The "*ecstasies*" of time are effectively integrated, making whole again lived temporality. This can lead to an enhanced sense of the self's integrity, as it dwells in a re-integrated world.

This analysis would be overly sunny if it didn't mention a series of obstacles to this integrative work which can make it almost impossible for many. Take the example of Q's intellectual labors. He is unusual in having been highly educated before being imprisoned for drug dealing. Some 70% of inmates have a degree of functional illiteracy, and prison schools are ill-equipped for the massive remedial effort needed. Even for strong readers prospects can be discouraging. Prison libraries are woefully underfunded, and have restricted rules on utilization. Inmates and their families often have few financial resources to purchase books. Prisoners may only be allowed a small number of books in their cells, because it constitutes a "fire hazard." Those attempting to send books in from the outside world (as I have done) often find it is treated as a security hazard, rejected because it does not come directly from the publisher, or that it mysteriously disappears in the prison mailroom. Certain types of literature – including, for example, religious materials—may have to be approved by a censoring authority. On and on it goes, as barriers within and without make it difficult to accomplish the integrative work mentioned above.

LIVED SPACE

Phenomenologists, Heidegger a prominent example, have distinguished between geometric space and the lived-spatiality of human experience. The former, like the Newtonian conception of time, is an abstract, calculable entity. It can be plotted using Cartesian axes, as can any particular spatial point (this itself a theoretical concept, since points have no dimensionality). Space thus conceived is a contentless void, stretching uniformly and infinitely in all directions.

Spatiality-as-lived is something wholly other. It is oriented by our embodiment, which vectors space into what lies ahead and behind, right and left, up and down, accessible or withdrawn from our sensorimotor powers. Moreover, our lived-space is filled with meaningful "places" that orient our life (Casey, 1993). There is the home in which we dwell, places of work and recreation, social gathering and solitude. We experientially dwell not only in a house, but in nested environs—a neighborhood, city, natural landscape—that can become a wider home shared by other "homies."

Yet all this is vulnerable to displacement. Just as the pronouncing of sentence rips the convicted out of the temporal life-world, so, too, out of a previous fabric of lived spatiality. "Twenty years" spoken means twenty years during which the sentenced cannot return to his or her home. He or she cannot wander, cannot even see, the familiar neighborhood, nor—except for dislocated visits—friends and family who dwell there. Even the world of nature is largely ripped away, but for a patch of dirt or sky.

What does the prison put in place of these places? First, we might say it offers *constricted* space. The inmate's ability to roam freely has been forfeited. Hereafter, he or she will dwell in zones of brutal restriction—the narrow cell, the tiered building, the hemmed-in yard, the prison compound.

This is also a *ruptured* space. Contrast the experience of walking across an open field toward the distant horizon with space experienced by an inmate. Everywhere bars, fences, barbed wire, tall walls, cut through space separating limited *heres* from unreachable *theres*. The outside world, hitherto the place of all places, is severed off from access.

We might also call this space as *disoriented*. The spatiality of home and neighborhood is oriented by vectors of meaning, possibility and preference. Far less so is the spatiality of prisons. They are often laid out in geometric grids, substituting an abstract Cartesian space for the more humane contours of ordinary habitations. Architecture here is dictated by issues of security and surveillance, not oriented by the desires of the home-dweller. Moreover, the prison usually stands in no meaningful relation to the natural landscape into which it is thrown, or the life of surrounding communities. A life-world of nested places gives way to space structured as an instrument of control.

This can even give rise to a *reversed* spatiality. German phenomenologist Bollnow writes about the primacy of the "home," broadly understood, in centering one's life-world (Bollnow, 1961, pp. 31-39). But prison tends to reverse all the meanings of home—security, privacy, comfort, freedom of choice. The guards are there to keep you in against your will, not protect you from intruders. Whereas the boundaries of home establish a zone of privacy, prison walls do the opposite; they compress you together, often in overcrowded conditions with hundreds of other criminals. This is "maximum security" for the outside world, not those dwelling within the prison. There's a door to your "home" cell, but you don't have the key. You're not free to go in and out as you please, but your enemies, the guards, can. You have a big picture window, but it faces inward where there's no view. In contrast to home as a place of settled dwelling, you can be transferred at a moment's notice by administrative fiat. This, then, is home in reversed caricature. Instead of establishing a positive center to lived spatiality, the prison "home" is like the epicenter of a flushing toilet, centripetally sucking away the world.

The newly-incarcerated must contend with this disordered spatiality as he or she did the disordering of time. Again, with reference to inmate dialogues, we will see a variety of strategies to re-humanize the world.

John Woodland: We always had a concept around here about keeping yourself distant from prison activities and the prison mentality. Don't participate in a whole bunch of prison groups, don't get caught up in playing football, basketball, don't think about fixing no cell up to make it comfortable. Let it stay raggedy. You want to keep a mindset that this is not some place for me to get comfortable.

Michael Green: I agree. I got a friend that every cell he moves in he paints to the max. I *refuse* to paint one of these cells or lay it out like it was home. To me it's just a place where you exist.

Charles Baxter: [*laughing*] I understand what Mike's saying because I'm one of those dudes—I call my cell my *palace*. As a matter of fact I just got it painted last week and paid the dude four packs to do it. He painted the floors, my ceiling, the whole thing. I got my Oriental rugs laid down. I don't care where I'm at, I'm going to make it heaven while I'm there. Even in this hellhole, I'm going to find some heaven.

Wayne Brown: It's different being in a double cell. I could feel at home laying on my bunk. But when I got up and took one step to the wall, I felt like I'm in a danger zone 'cause I had somebody else on the top bunk. I was under their scrutiny. There's somebody watching....

Tray Jones: Yeah, when I used to sleep in a double cell, if I was in there with a person I didn't like, I felt like Wayne. But when I was in the cell with T—the only cell buddy that I really got along with—a bond developed, and in our closeness we were so brotherly....It seemed like had *more* room in the cell with him than I do now when I'm alone. We'd play cards and talk, and it felt like there was a lot of room! (Leder, et al. pp. 57-8)

In this discussion, John and Michael emphasize a strategy of escape. That is, they cope with the disordered world of prison by refusing to become complicitous with it. Instead they imaginatively escape beyond its barriers, not allowing themselves to feel at home in a cell. Rather, they orient to the outside world, considering *that* their true home, albeit one from which they are temporarily exiled.

Charles adopts an opposite strategy, one that I have termed reclamation. He is determined to make himself as at home in prison as possible. If spatiality has become constricted, ruptured, disoriented, even reversed, Charles will do what is possible to reverse the reversals. He will make of his cell a palace. With paint and oriental rugs (and Charles is a Muslim Imam) he will fight to humanize, even divinize his surroundings into an earthly/heavenly home.

Wayne and Tray remind us that such strategies are never affected alone. A human being is always a social being, inhabiting a world with others. As such, lived space is not constituted by the solipsistic individual, but is a shared construction, deeply influenced by those around us. Wayne's life-world is constricted by the alienating "scrutiny" of a cell mate. However, Tray shows how the sympathetic Other assists the process of reclamation. An experience of communion and community has the capacity to radically expand lived-space.

To further the analysis, I introduce two more comments:

> **Charles Baxter:** And the cell's where you actually get your schoolwork done, or work for organizations you're in, or work to get out of prison. Man is created from one cell, right, and as man grows he adapts into another cell, and that cell's also a place for growth and development. When you read the Koran and the Bible you'll see that different prophets went to the *cave* for comfort and isolation. And the cell's like that cave (ibid., p. 56).

> **Tray Jones:** My space ain't too restricted because I think of myself as on an *odyssey*. Even in here. I don't look at this as my home; it's just an experience that's necessary in order for me to get where I'm going. I believe I'm here because I lost my road. That's what I'm searching around for, the road to the larger society. In the meanwhile I'm supposed to be restricted in space. I take the stoic outlook--my space is supposed to be restricted but my ideas don't have to be, and that's where I find all my freedom....When I was on the street, I had *less* space than I do in prison. I would only associate with the criminal elements....Since I've been in prison, I've met people with sophistication, people from different races....We meet here, and get a chance to rest and get out of our immediate world, and we can think about things we couldn't on the street (ibid., pp. 75-76).

In these comments we hear eloquent statements of what I have termed the strategy of integration, combining elements of reclamation and escape. Both men positively affirm—and thereby reclaim—aspects of prison life that might otherwise seem alien. For Charles, the limitations of the prison cell reminds him of the Prophet's cave, a place for growth and development. Tray, torn out of his driven world of drug dealing, uses prison as a haven for thoughtful exploration. Again, this process is assisted by others, whose diverse perspectives broaden his own.

Reclaiming the possibilities immanent within the prison world is the very tool that allows these men transcendence. That Tray is pinned in place (serving a sentence of life plus twenty years) has launched him on an odyssey. So, too, Charles, on a spiritual journey which unfolds in his Prophet's cave. Here are examples of the strengths of the integrative strategy. The limits of prison space and time are used to trigger a life-world expansion.

EMBODIMENT

I now turn to what has been implicit in my previous analysis; the place of the body in the inmate's life-world. The notion of embodiment I use is not to be equated with the body in its sheer physicality—a piece of Cartesian *res extensa*, or the anatomico-physiological entity described by medical science. In such frameworks, the human body is thematized as a thing in the world, like a desk, tree, or automobile. The properties of the human body can then be characterized—as can those of other material entities—using the language of mathematical description and mechanical analysis. Yet, as Merleau-Ponty explores in *Phenomenology of Perception,* the body is not just a thing in the world: "The body is our general medium for having a world" (Merleau-Ponty, 1962, p. 146).

It is through our embodied perception and motility, reflection and expression—not just a purified rationality—that we experience a world of objects, people, and meanings. That which grounds my experience has been called the lived body *(Leib* in Husserl's German) imbued with subjectivity, as distinguished from the object body *(Körper),* viewed as thing in the world.

Earlier I said that prison tends to replace the richness of lived temporality and spatiality with a kind of geometrical and dehumanized time and space. We now see this is in every way correlative with a shift in embodiment. The body is *ec-static*—it naturally stands outside itself through its ability to perceive across a distance and move toward its goals. It is engaged with a world beyond its limits. But these projective capacities can also be blocked. A tall wall brings the body to a halt. We cannot see over or move through the wall. The imprisoned body is not primarily active subject, advancing through space as it chooses, but a thing that is held, observed, and controlled. The prisoner is reduced to the status of contained object within a confining world. Prison thus reminds us that the body is inherently ambiguous. To use Merleau-Ponty's language the lived body contains an *écart*—a fissure, or divergence (ibid., pp. 123-124, 130-155).

The living body is always both perceiver and perceived, a constituting subject and a worldly object. The restrictions of prison have the capacity to turn this two-sided nature into an outright opposition experienced between self and embodiment.

Other situations provoke this sense of opposition. When one falls ill, or is hampered by physical incapacity, one's own body may emerge as an alien thing. In health, the body was an unproblematic and largely unthematized seat of self. Now it surfaces as Other. The sick body blocks one's will, undermines one's projects, may threaten one's very life (Leder, 1990, 70-83).

This is not quite the existential situation of the body incarcerated. Unlike illness, where an alien power arises *within* the body, the prisoner is more like to experience hostile forces located *outside,* in the incarcerating system, guards, and bars. It is social constraints that immobilize the body, not its own disabilities. Nevertheless, the body can seem as a co-conspirator. If one did not have a body, one could not be observed, punished, and restrained in this way.

Another imperfect analogy to the situation of the prisoner may be found in the experience of female embodiment within a patriarchal culture. As de Beauvoir discusses, women are often identified particularly with the body, and taken as object for the male gaze and use. (de Beauvoir, 1974). Insofar as women internalize this gaze they come to regard their own body as the thing in the mirror which must be rendered properly attractive, fit, and constrained in order to be socially acceptable. Whereas Merleau-Ponty writes about the body's "I can" structures of ability, (Ponty, p. 137). Iris Young writes that women often internalize an "I cannot." They learn an objectified style of embodiment that limits their capacities—for example, how to "throw like a girl" (Young, 1980, pp. 130-176).

Similarities abound to the position of the inmate. He or she is also made into an Other, an object under an omnipresent gaze. The inmate's body is everywhere constrained. The institution reinforces the experience of the "I cannot"— I cannot move freely, leave the prison, secure privacy, pursue my preferences. The prisoner's bodily location, dress, and actions are largely dictated by the state. A woman in a patriarchal society may be reigned in by subtle reinforcers (for example, "My, you look pretty today in your dress"). In a prison situation, the forces of confinement are much more blatant, fashioned of bars and barbed wire, threats of longer sentences and solitary confinement. Nevertheless, both cases provoke alienation from one's body. The body renders the self vulnerable to outside powers.

An alienated embodiment can also result from living as a "minority" member in a racist society. This is relevant to the 63% of inmates in the U.S. who are African-American or Hispanic. In *Black Skin, White Masks,* Frantz Fanon writes about a formative encounter with a young boy who becomes frightened at seeing a "Negro." Confronted with his blackness, culturally associated with primitiveness and defect, Fanon feels "imprisoned." "My body was given back to me sprawled out, distorted, clad in mourning" (Fanon, 1967, pp. 111-113). The experience of being literally imprisoned may compound this distortion. The imprisoned body, like the black body in Fanon's description, is associated with violence and deficit, objectified by a fearful gaze, appropriated by hostile others. Exploration of the complex interplay between race, gender, ethnicity, and incarceration is an important topic for future work.

Given the prisoner's alienation from the body, it is not unusual for him or her to wish to cast it off, or transmute it into a non-human form—say that of a bird seen flying over the wall. The human body keeps one chained to earth. Yet this embodiment can also be reclaimed or escaped in a variety of ways which I will now explore. I begin with an inmate's remark (part of a discussion which was excerpted earlier) on the prison as "home."

> **Tray Jones:** But you can never really have a home in here. Because the officers could come with the key anytime they want and uproot you. Like right now, everything that I own I brought out with me (my toothbrush and all) because *I'm the cell*, my own body, rather than some hole cut out of space (Leder, et al., p. 56)

This comment reminds us that as much as prison renders the body "Other," possession of the state, it can also reaffirm the body as the self's one true possession and locus of power. We see a similar paradox in the case of illness. The sick person may feel both alienated from the body, which surfaces as a hostile Other, and more closely tied to the body, hyperaware of its functions and solicitous of its well-being in a way that was unnecessary in health. So, too, may the inmate become solicitous of the body. With so much else of the world ripped away, the body remains to be reclaimed—guarded and cultivated with care.

This strategy of reclamation takes many forms. Tray Jones affirms the body as a zone of privacy and security. Often the inmate's first task is to bolster the lived body against possible assaults from guards or other inmates. Many prisoners develop the body's energy and skills, through weightlifting, sports, yoga, and various forms of work, insofar as these are available. Inmates also develop the body as a locus of self-expression. Prisoners have produced amazing artistic creations with the most limited resources. A certain style of walk, dress, or mode of speech may help assert one's power and individuality. Then, too, the body can be a source of pleasure. Even within a depriving environment, gratifications of music, movement, sexuality, and drug use often remain obtainable.

The presence of others can assist in bodily reclamation. In Merleau-Ponty's words, we inhabit "intercorporeal being" (Merleau-Ponty, p. 143), our experience of self and world intertwines with that of those around us. Tray mentions the threat posed by invasive guards. Yet, earlier he spoke of a brotherly cell-mate whose presence expanded lived-space when "we'd play cards and talk." The communion of prisoners with one another, sympathetic employees, and outside visitors, can help the inmate reclaim embodied wholeness. This is a challenge in the face of the disciplinary gaze. Foucault discusses how the architecture of the "panopticon" serves to keep potentially rebellious bodies under surveillance (Foucault, pp. 195-228).

The inmates respond:

> **Mark Medley**: When you're virtually under twenty-four hour surveillance--like the new prison in Jessup--there's also a way you can *resist* or *escape*. Autistic thinking. Total absorption in fantasy. "I'm building an island and this is what my water source will be, and the kind of plants I'll have . . ." You can absorb yourself in this for hours and hours and resist being conditioned by the discipline.

> **Charles Baxter**: I was in Supermax, and a lot of the brothers in there, they escape by a lot of reading and studying--African history, the Bible, the Koran. They realize they're being watched, but they escape to something that gives them, you know, hope and inspiration.

> **Donald Thompson**: But there's another side. Before I came here I was very violent. It didn't take much for me to strike out at another person--different ways--a baseball bat, a brick, a gun. But since I came in here I've had one fight. Knowing that I'm being watched has made me control this violence. And as time went on it helped me discipline myself, 'cause my intellect eventually kicked in (Leder, et al. pp. 44-45).

Donald's comment is an example of the strategy of reclamation. He has found a way to turn even the disciplinary gaze—potentially alienating and disempowering—into a source of personal power. He cannot escape being watched, yet he uses this to help him overcome his own violent impulsivity. The result is a greater sense of self-mastery.

Comments by Mark and Charles remind us that the imprisoned body can not only be reclaimed but strategically escaped. Mark Medley, rather than affirming discipline, as does Donald, chooses to escape it via fantasy. Through "autistic thinking" he all but vacates the body, giving it over to the authorities but as a lifeless thing. Charles Baxter makes reference to the escapist power of reading available even when confined in Supermax (imum security)—a place where the "worst" inmates are isolated in their cells twenty-three hours a day.

Is the body genuinely escaped through such activities? Not exactly. The very means by which the inmates "transcend" the body are rooted in the body's own capacities. Mark distracts himself with visual imagery, constructing a perceptual scene which calls upon body-memories. Charles holds a book in his hands and scans it with his eyes, using his brain to process symbols and formulate thoughts. The body is as involved in activities of the "higher intellect" as it is in weightlifting or sex.

Yet, as I discuss in *The Absent Body*, certain activities, because they put out of play or background large regions of the body, and involve modes of projection and self-transcendence, can seem *as if disembodied* (Leder, 1990, pp. 180-185). In reading, for example, we often sit still. The body's movements are reduced to subtle eye-scans and sub-vocalizations. The physical words on the page become as if transparent to the meanings they signify, which are processed by brain activity unavailable to our senses. Imaginatively, we feel transported out of our immediate locale to other times and places, or a world of non-physical ideas. Such factors combine to create an experiential sense of escaping the body, of being pure mind or spirit. We have seen how such experiences help many an inmate cope with confinement.

Strategies of integration combine elements of escape and reclamation. We see this implicit in Charles' comments. Even in the extremes of Supermax body-confinement, he and his "brothers" can reclaim their situation and use it as a launching pad for transcendent escape.

THE PENITENTIARY

In doing this integrative work, inmates, often unknowingly, operate according to the original meaning and intent of the penitentiary. "Penitentiary" is a term coined in the 1770's to define what was then a new vision of penal correction. (The Maryland Penitentiary, where I taught, is the oldest continuously operating penitentiary in the Western world, having first opened—or closed?— its doors in 1811.) Rather than endorsing harsh corporeal punishment, the penitentiary movement, led by Quakers, sought to humanize, even spiritualize criminal justice. The prison cell was modeled on the monastic cell.

Just as monks retreated in confinement and isolation to repent their sins, so might criminals, emerging reformed by the experience.

We have seen that certain prisoners do accomplish something like this in prison. In integrative work, the very conditions of confinement are used to enlarge the self and its life-world. There is a genuine, and positive, existential re-formation.

The irony is that the contemporary penitentiary does so much to undermine this process. Conditions are harsh and overcrowded. Treatment by prison authorities is often dehumanizing, demeaning, and radically disempowering. Opportunities for educational, therapeutic, and occupational advancement are sadly deficient. The prisoner seeking to positively transform the self battles hostile forces at every turn.

I will give a few examples from personal experience. Due to a change in the status of the prison to medium security, most of the men I worked with were abruptly transferred en masse to other prisons. The sense of community we had painstakingly built was shattered. (This is not unusual in a prison culture where close relationships and inmate-communities are often seen as a security threat to be countered by transfers.) Further teaching there on my part was discouraged. Around this time, the 1993 Omnibus Crime Bill also cut off Pell Grants, which fund higher-education for low-income Americans, to all prisoners. The result was a whole-scale closing down of prison college extension programs. Soon thereafter, the governor of Maryland (a moderate Democrat) announced he would not approve the parole of any inmate serving a life-sentence, despite any positive recommendations from the parole board. The message is that any process of self-reformation the "lifer" engages in will neither be recognized nor rewarded by the state. This serves to undercut just the sorts of motivated prisoners with whom I was working. Most recently, my own attempt to volunteer as a philosophy teacher in a women's prison was rejected by the warden. The stated reason had to do with issues of "space and security."

Whereas Charles' envisions the cell as a Prophet's cave, all too often it is more like Plato's cave in the *Republic*. To illustrate the state of the unenlightened he used the metaphor of prisoners chained within a cave. Their necks are fastened so they cannot turn to see the light at the cave mouth. All that is visible to them are dark shadows cast on the wall. These they take to be reality, having no object of comparison.

Though metaphorical, it seems an apt image of many a prison. Educators, counselors, and others who might bring "light" from the outside world are often woefully absent. The inmates are left primarily amongst "shadows"—the society of frequently contemptuous authorities, other criminals, and the memories of their previous misspent life. For most, there is little of a positive nature to pursue. Not surprisingly, upon release from this cave, the inmate is often poorly equipped to re-enter the broader society. Incarceration has torn them from the fabric of their previous life-world. It has infantilized and disempowered them. The prisoner who emerges is often angrier as a result, and more dysfunctional.

He or she is out of touch with new cultural developments and technologies which others take for granted. Then there is the permanent label of ex-con, making it harder to find a job and forge a new identity. Is it any wonder that the rate of recidivism is so high for released inmates? This, then, reinforces a stereotype that rehabilitation does not work, justifying harsher prison conditions.

I have heard it said that if a mad scientist wished to create a system designed to *increase* criminality, he or she would come up with something like our modern prison system, now caging more than two million Americans and peripherally effecting tens of millions more of their dependents, family members, associates, and friends.

Yet to see only this bleak picture is to miss the power of the person to escape, to reclaim, to integrate, even the harshest of worlds. The inmate is not only the passive recipient of punishment. He or she is also an active constitutor of the world, capable of creating freedoms.

Note
*   A previous version of this paper was published in *Social Justice*, 31, 2004, pp. 51-66. It was also published under the title "Imprisoned Bodies: The Life-world of the Incarcerated" in *The Phenomenology of the Body: The 20ᵗʰ Annual Symposium of The Simon Silverman Phenomenology Center* (ed., Daniel J. Martino, 2003, pp. 1-18).

References

Bollnow, O. F. 1961. Lived-Space, *Philosophy Today* 5.

Bureau of Justice Statistics, "Prisoners in 2000."

Casey, Edward S. 1993. *Getting Back Into Place; Toward a Renewed Understanding of the Place-World*. Bloomington: Indiana University Press.

de Beauvoir, Simone. 1974. *The Second Sex,* trans. H. M. Parshley. New York: Vintage Books.

Fanon, Frantz. 1967. *Black Skin, White Masks*. New York: Grove Press.

F.B.I.'s Uniform Crime Report, www.fbi.gov/ucr/ucr.htm.

Foucault, Michel. 1979. *Discipline and Punish: The Birth of the Prison,* trans. Alan Sheridan. New York: Vintage Books.

Gordon, Lewis, ed. 1997. *Existence in Black: An Anthology of Black Existential Philosophy*, New York: Routledge.

Heidegger, Martin. 1962. *Being and Time*, trans. John Macquarrie and Edward Robinson. New York: Harper and Row.

Human Rights Watch, May, 2000. Punishment and Prejudice: Racial Disparities in the War on Drugs www.hrw.org/reports/usa/.

Husserl, Edmund. 1964. *The Phenomenology of Internal Time-Consciousness*, ed. Martin Heidegger, trans. James S. Churchill. Bloomington: Indiana University Press.

Justice Policy Institute. May 2000. The Punishing Decade: Prison and Jail Estimates at the Millenium. www.cjcj.org/index.html.

Leder, Drew, et al. 2000. *The Soul Knows No Bars: Inmates Reflect on Life, Death, and Hope* Lanham, MD: Rowman and Littlefield.

Leder, Drew. 1990. *The Absent Body.* Chicago: University of Chicago Press.

Merleau-Ponty, Maurice. 1962. *Phenomenology of Perception*, trans. Colin Smith. London: Routledge and Kegan Paul.

Merleau-Ponty, Maurice. 1968. *The Visible and the Invisible,* ed. Claude Lefort, trans. Alphonso Lingis. Evanston, IL: Northwestern University Press.

Minkowski, Eugene. 1970. *Lived Time: Phenomenological Psychopathological Studies,* trans. N. Metzel. Evanston, IL: Northwestern University Press.

U.S. Department of Justice. 2000. Prisoners in 2000. www.ojp.usdoj.gov/bjs/prisons. htm.

Schlosser, Eric. December 1998. "The Prison-Industrial Complex," *The Atlantic Monthly,*

"Thinking About Prisons: Theory and Practice," October 2001. State University of New York at Cortland.

Young, Iris. 1980. Throwing Like a Girl: A Phenomenology of Feminine Bodily Comportment, Motility and Spatiality, *Human Studies* 3.

6

TIME AND PUNISHMENT IN AN ANESTHETIC WORLD ORDER

Greg Moses

In the visceral imagination of collective opinion prison is a place where you do time. "Do the crime, do the time." Through this equivalence between crime and time, prison is prescribed as the site where time shall be stripped down to barest needs: "bread and water," perhaps, but no more. Such is the popular formula. The prisoner who has caused pain and suffering shall be made to feel pain and suffering through a particular regimentation of time. By the way, if acts of brutality and humiliation are smuggled with appropriate discretion into the process of imprisonment, so much the better from the popular view. Prison life is therefore demanded as a life of essential deprivation, punctuated by accidental terrors that few would call for out loud, but which fewer would be diligent to scandalize.

This popular, visceral imagination of prison life is, in many ways, the very monster of prison itself. But who has the strength to grab this Grendel's claw and rip it from the shoulder of the popular beast? It would seem easier by comparison to pulverize a prison wall. The imaginative appetite for punishment may be more easily appeased whenever crimes are not directly brutal, as in cases of financial embezzlement; or where injuries are self-inflicted, as with addiction; or when perpetrators are perceived as truly tragic cases themselves, as with the recent case of the mother who drowned all five of her children. But for the rapist, murderer, and child molester, there is a particular chill and revulsion that attends the image of the perpetrator, where it is felt that time for such prisoners should be stripped away like a waking death.

If we agree that a kind of calculus is created through public imagination that in turn becomes a palpable force in the politics of prison policy, I want to select for consideration today the side of the equation that deals with time. I want to explore the deprivation that is imagined in order to reveal how its terror works. When doing time is imagined as time stripped away, I want to linger over the studied cruelty that lurks. Leaving unexplored for the moment the emotional heft that pulls the imagination down when contemplating our most disparaged crimes, I want to attend to the side of the scale where we place the imagined counterbalance of maximum-security time. I am aware that this emphasis on the imaginative calculus does not address the crucial issue of structural deployments in punishment. Maximum-security convictions are more likely imposed upon poor and nonwhite suspects. But if this is the case, then it is perhaps one reason why the popular imagination of time deserves consideration, since it attends so little to the grating effects of prison time. It is possible to dismiss the pain of such time partly because the popular imagination can dismiss the populations who feel it, not necessarily because those populations are in fact the only offenders, but because their time as poor and nonwhite already counts for less.

The following inquiry looks at the meaning of time to see what happens when we demand a certain form of time as punishment.

I.

"You can't see or do time," writes Evan Pritchard in his book, *No Word for Time*. Pritchard's point is that time itself cannot be experienced in isolation, apart from events through which duration is manifest. There is no such thing as pure time, stripped away from all events. When time does impose itself upon experience as a pure thing, argues Pritchard, we should look not further into the nature of time itself, but into the nature of activity that isolates our sense of time as something divorced from events. Prison, for Pritchard, is the perfect example of activity that peels time away from the world. "You can't do time unless you are in prison" (p.18).

No Word for Time is Pritchard's exploration of cultural valuations that emerge as he recovers his American Indian heritage through a series of conversations, rituals, and revelations. Here he finds that the Algonquin people have no word for time apart from the befores and afters that relate events to one another. The river flooded yesterday. The sun will come out tomorrow. Such expressions presume temporal relations, but time itself goes unremarked.

When Pritchard argues for the value of understanding time in the context of events, I am reminded of the esthetic philosophy of John Dewey. Like Pritchard, Dewey resists the temptation to isolate time. Dewey is more interested in the way we ordinarily experience time in the rhythm of events. For Dewey, rhythm is a pre-condition of experience. Whenever we complain that there is no rhythm, we confirm Dewey's claim that we expect some rhythm to be found. From this perspective, our experience of a lack of rhythm would prompt us to inquire into the context of activity that would give rise to the complaint.

Where we find no rhythm in Dewey's sense, I think we find pure time in Pritchard's. Where rhythm absorbs us, we don't speak of time itself. Both Pritchard and Dewey seem to know what they warn against. "Time is not real," warns Pritchard, "unless you are in prison" (p.18). Among the Algonquin, there are no prisons. By exploring the esthetic potential of experience itself, where rhythm and beauty are fruits of nature, Dewey is also encouraging vigilance against anesthetic structures of activity.

Dewey introduces the concept of rhythm as fundamental to his esthetic conception of form. His approach to esthetic philosophy naturalizes the potent effects of art by showing how our experience of beauty reveals something about the structure of reality. Artistic form is possible because experience itself is formed. According to this view of things, form is defined generally as the, "operation of forces that carry the experience of an event, object, scene, and situation to its own integral fulfillment" (p.137). Esthetic form is rhythmic, because beauty as we know it participates in the surges, pauses, harmonies, and conflicts of energy that contribute toward a completed experience. "The first characteristic of the environing world that makes possible the existence of artistic form is rhythm" (p.147).

In his essay on, "The Natural History of Form," which comprises the seventh chapter of *Art as Experience*, Dewey writes lyrically about rhythm. "The larger rhythms of nature are so bound up with the conditions of even elementary human subsistence, that they cannot have escaped the notice of [humans] as soon as [they] became conscious of [their] occupations and the conditions that rendered them effective" (p.147). The rhythm of day and night, summer and winter, new moon through full moon, life, death, decay, and rebirth—these are the larger operations of forces that structure our experience. Where the rhythms of nature are inescapable, human rhythms dance in step. Planting takes place in the Spring, harvesting in the Summer and Fall. Where human rhythms intercede, nature is transformed. Edison's electric light, Ford's car, Gould's railroad, Carnegie's steel—each invention transforms the rhythm of nature. The rhythms of so-called fine art intercede as experiments in the form of experience. We come away from art refreshed through its revelations and transformations of rhythm.

Pritchard, in his treatment of singing and dancing, writes about an ancient connection between song and prayer. "Each of the hymns of the early Vedas were sung, with specific rhythms and pitches, much as they are today" (p. 90). Likewise, in the varied drum patterns that accompany American Indian song, deep meanings of the cosmos are ordered into traditional form. During the ceremony that takes place in the Native American sweat lodge, each initiate hears her own song with her own beat. Meaning, argues Pritchard, is born not of language, but of gesture. "Among Western metaphors, dancing is perhaps the closest we can come to describing the essence of the Algonquin way" (p.55).

So far, the treatment of rhythm as the fullness of time has been loose and lyrical. We have conjured an image more than an argument, a picture of nature and humanity moving in rhythmic form. And yet our vision of movement and energy has not yet exhausted what Dewey would claim. "The very concepts of molecule, atom, and electron arise out of the need of formulating lesser and subtler rhythms that are discovered," writes Dewey (p.149). Mathematics and number reveal and impose rhythm, sometimes expressing those rhythms that are the most universal of all.

A generous review of the concept of rhythm, found in the work of Pritchard and Dewey, refreshes Plato's admonition, that rhythmic education is at the core of the human curriculum, "for rhythm and harmonious adjustment are essential to the whole of human life" (Protag. 326b). Success, achievement, flourishing, growth, progress, fulfillment—these are the terms that are associated with human experience in the work of Pritchard, Dewey, and Plato. To closely paraphrase Dewey in nonsexist language: since humans succeed only as they adapt their behavior to the rhythms of nature, their achievements and victories, which ensue upon resistance and struggle, become the matrix of all esthetic subject matter, the common pattern of art, and the ultimate condition of form (p.150). In the experience of our daily triumphs we find the conditions for beauty of any sort. It is not just the pulse or pace of activity that interests us. Rhythm fascinates us because it suggests conditions that can be ordered to fulfillment.

In art, Dewey is partisan to a critical preference that he calls naturalism. Of course, nature provides objective conditions and materials that the artist must use:

> But naturalism in art means something more than the necessity all arts are under of employing natural and sensuous media. It means that all which can be expressed is some aspect of the relation between [humans] and [their] environment, and that this subject-matter attains its most perfect wedding with form when the basic rhythms that characterize the interaction of the two are depended upon and trusted with abandon. (p.151)

Not only the materials, but the rhythms of artistic form are to be conceived as natural gifts. Dewey's lyrical celebration of natural rhythm entices us toward a profound and joyful trust in the structure of experience and nature. For Dewey, a "genuine naturalism" in art would disclose "deeper and wider sensitivity" to "rhythms of existence" (p.152). Beautiful rhythms are always rhythms of experience in nature.

In sum, for Dewey, rhythm is an "ordered variation in changes." Therefore, rhythm is not, "a uniformly even flow, with no variation of intensity or speed" (p.154). For instance, rhythm is not the tick, tick, tick of clock time, nor the dull marking of years, months, weeks, or days. Such are the features of the anesthetic, the unbeautiful, the lack of experience in nature. Note how we often portray prison time as the time that is simply x'd out.

Turning to further consideration of prison time, there are three obvious areas that deserve to be explored, if we want to undertake a thorough investigation of the implications of what Dewey, Pritchard, and Plato say about rhythm and time. First, we may understand how the popular, punitive appeal of prison lies in its reputation for denying time and rhythm. Second, we may explore how time and rhythm are nevertheless smuggled into the system as irrepressible human demands. Third, we may explore the general effect that prison has as an institution, when viewed chiefly through our focus on rhythm and time. As a result of this investigation, we might provide critical considerations that might, in turn, help to slow the social reactions that now fuel the heated prison boom in America. Today, I will only begin to explore consequences of the popular concept of prison as a site of pure time, without rhythm, anesthetic in its void.

As a guiding principle for this investigation, I am working against the assumption that prison only has effects on prisoners. As much as possible, I would like to keep a close watch on the ways that prison is a forceful tool of social and political values for various classes of non-prisoners, whether they be prison workers, their families and communities; victims of crimes, their families and communities; the relatively removed citizens whose public opinions fuel the political climate that favors prisons; or finally, very close to the prisoners themselves, their families and communities, too.

The concept of prison time, therefore, is not a concept confined to prison life, but a concept of growing importance in the life of the larger society in which prisons participate. Prisoners did not invent prisons, nor do prisoners serve as the most effective proponents for the increasing demand for prison time. Therefore the presence of prison time, although crucial to the lives of prisoners, is also in important ways somehow essential to the arrangement of American popular philosophy. When Americans demand more prison time, they are making assertions about the meaning of that time for their own lives. The citizen who never expects to enter prison nevertheless demands more of a specific form of prison time. The call for prison time expresses a philosophy in which the presence of prison time becomes more and more important to the stabilization of a worldview for those who always imagine prison time as necessary for someone else.

To begin the application to prison, I want to suggest that the popular conception of prison time derives its visceral appeal from an implicit model of time that is roughly similar to the concepts and critiques suggested by Pritchard, Dewey, and Plato. When we desire prison time, we desire a time that is stripped of life's events and rhythms. In fact the prison policies of the past five years may be viewed as an attempt to further purify the concept of prison time. Education shrinks, programs disappear, and parole is denied. The ability to do "good time" is systematically erased, the better to enforce a singular regime of time that is strictly barren and absolutely useless. The ultimate logic of this policy leads toward solitary confinement, otherwise known as "the box" where 4.4 percent of the New York Prison population accounts for 31.6 percent of the suicides.

References

Dewey, John. 1980. *Art as Experience*. New York: Perigree.

Pfeffer, Mary Beth. Dec. 16, 2001. "Suicides High in 'Prison Box,'" *Poughkeepsie Journal*.

Plato. 1961. *Collected Dialogues of Plato*. Edited by Edith Hamilton and Huntington Cairns. Bollingen Series LXXI. New York: Pantheon.

Pritchard, Evan. 2001. *No Word for Time*. San Francisco: Council Oak.

7

BEYOND THE WALLS: DISPERSING THE RESPONSIBILITY FOR CRIME*

Clayton Morgareidge

PRISON AS AN IDEOLOGICAL STATE APPARATUS

Prison is an instance of what Louis Althusser calls a "Repressive State Apparatus." As Christian Parenti points out, "Repression manages poverty," and poverty plays a central role in the exploitation of labor that makes capital profitable (2001, p. 20). "Criminal justice regulates, absorbs, terrorizes and disorganizes the poor" (ibid., p. 27).

Louis Althusser contrasts the Repressive State Apparatus (or RSA) with the Ideological State Apparatus (or ISA). His favored example of the ISA is the school, because it trains citizens in the virtues of work and patriotism as well as inculcating, by precept and discipline, the necessary attitudes and skills for fulfilling the roles assigned to them by their social class in the capitalist mode of production (Althusser, 1971, pp. 155-56).

There are, however, no *purely* repressive, or *purely* ideological, state apparati. The school has its repressive side. The police functions ideologically, teaching us that the law has its eye on us. An RSA is one that "functions massively and predominantly *by repression*..., while functioning secondarily by ideology," while an ISA "functions massively and predominantly *by ideology*, but it also functions secondarily by repression...." (ibid., p. 145). It seems to me that prison functions as "massively" by ideology as it does by repression. This essay will consider prison as an ISA and will try to articulate and criticize *just one* of the ideological claims it makes.[1]

WHAT PRISON TEACHES: SOLE RESPONSIBILITY

Every state apparatus invites us to read off from its existence the principles that make sense of it, that make it just. Prison locks up *individuals*, specifically those individuals who are found at the scene of a crime. If this is just, it must be that individuals *deserve* to be in prison, and that they deserve to be there because they, and they alone, are *responsible* for the crimes they committed. It is this idea, that the people in prison are solely responsible for their crimes, that this essay is intended to subvert.

The message of prison is a corollary of a broader principle of capitalist ideology: that individuals are solely responsible for, and therefore deserve, whatever the system hands them. As long as due process is observed, people deserve whatever trouble they get into, as well as the wealth and power they accumulate. This idea both guides and justifies the job market, the welfare system, and the criminal justice system. It explains and legitimizes the spectacle of ostentatious wealth side by side with degrading poverty. Individuals, not social structures, are responsible for teen pregnancy, drug addiction, unemployment, poverty, and crime.

ACCEPTING INDIVIDUAL RESPONSIBILITY

One liberal-progressive response to prison's assignment of blame to its inmates is to *deny* that prisoners are responsible, and to put the blame *instead* on such factors as racism, poverty, and the structural inequalities of capitalism. This view, which is regarded by many as "the bleeding-heart" approach, argues that these social (or structural) conditions give rise to unmanageable rage, mental illness, or even brain damage, which in turn drive individuals into crime.

Certainly there are individuals who have no moral responsibility for crimes they have committed—people who live in a state of paranoid delusion (Hodgins, 1993, p. ix), or who are unable to control their violent impulses because of neurological damage suffered at the hands of brutal parents (Mansnerus, 2001). But it does no favor to most prisoners who have committed murder or rape or who have terrorized people in armed robberies to deny that they are responsible for what they have done. To attribute their actions entirely to forces outside their control deprives them of the agency they need to alter their lives for the better. It reduces them to objects to be theorized and manipulated by officials of the state. Finally, we cannot have compassion for prison inmates unless we see them as responsible agents who choose their actions on the basis of motives we can, at least vicariously, share with them. But you cannot put yourself in the place of another person unless it *is* a person and not just a bundle of impulses and neurological damage (Frederick, 2001, pp. 84-85). Frederick asserts:

> It's true that slavery was wrong. It's true that racism and classism and economic oppression have warped the dreams and ideal that empower people enough to believe in themselves. It's true that the justice system and the political system and the economic system all seem aligned against certain segments of the society. There is a very great deal of evidence to support these charges. It doesn't matter. To allow these factors to direct one's course of action in life is to give up the opportunity to stand as a human being with will and potential and value. To allow oneself to be buffeted about through life by the storms of existing in a black skin or a female skin or a poor skin is to concede the very inferiority that we rage against. Every prisoner who would strive to understand and truly regret the lifestyle that brought him to this point must be able to see these societal failings as only minimally relevant. In the daily battle for the rest of his or her life, each prisoner must look for ways to see past his or her own existence.... It's difficult but necessary that each man here learns the concept of being responsible for his actions (ibid.).

So let us say that most crimes of the kind we would regard as heinous are committed as a matter of conscious and deliberate choice and that their perpetrators are responsible for them. Nevertheless I hope to show that they are not *solely* responsible for them and that therefore prisons as they exist must be abolished or radically reformed.

I must explain, first, that I am not concerned in this chapter with "nominal" crime—actions defined as crimes by the law but which do no injury to persons. Also, I will focus primarily on violent, one-on-one crimes, as distinct from corporate crimes, even though the latter do more harm. The reason for my focus is simple: those who rape, murder, beat, and rob people in person are the ones found in prison, and my project here is a critique of the principle that those in prison deserve what prison does to them.

NOT WITHOUT REASON

Lonnie Athens conducted extensive interviews with 58 prison inmates about the violent crimes they had committed, including many for which they had never been arrested. He concluded that the men and women he talked with acted consciously and deliberately. They interpreted the likely intentions and attitudes of their victims and other features of the situation, and they decided "that they *ought* to take violent action" (Athens, 1997, p. 33).

Athens's account is consistent with Kant's theory of motivation. For Kant, an "incentive," such as anger or lust, "can determine the will to an action only so far as the individual has incorporated it into his maxim ([in other words,] has made it the *general rule* in accordance with which he will conduct himself)..." (Kant, p.32). One is not a violent criminal or an outlaw by natural instinct, and one does not become one through non-conscious processes. Rather, one has chosen to live that way. One adopts the maxim, or general rule, to live violently or non-violently, within the law or against the law, cooperatively or antagonistically (Athens, p. 61).

However, the fact that we make this choice does not mean that we *alone* are responsible for it. The best way to make this clear is by giving a Kantian twist to Marx:

> Men and women make their own lives by the maxims they choose, but they do not choose them just as they please; they do not choose them under circumstances selected by themselves, but under circumstances directly encountered, given, and transmitted from the past (McLellan, ed., 1977, p. 300).

Let me pause to make the philosophical issue clear. Our question is this: What is the most illuminating form of explanation for understanding the actions of human beings? One view is that each of us alone chooses what we shall do and that choice arises out of the very core of ourselves for which we and we alone are responsible. If our souls are corrupt, it is because we have freely chosen to forsake the better path. This conception of absolute free will goes back to the early Christian theology of St. Augustine, and it continues to serve the interests of those who see no moral objection to prisons as they exist. A second view is that individuals and their actions are simply the *products* of past and present conditions, and it is on these that all the responsibility for crime should be placed. This view eliminates the agency of the offender and thereby his or her power to live differently. The position I am arguing for is that individuals *do* choose their actions and the principles of their lives, but that they do so in circumstances in which brutal and hateful choices can appear entirely necessary and even justified. This means that *both* the individual *and* the circumstances must be held responsible. The responsibility must be *dispersed*.

To see how the decision to follow the path of violence may seem reasonable, let's look at Lonnie Athens's account of how violent criminals are made (Athens, 1992). (I will save for another time the important task of providing a parallel account of other kinds of criminal lives.)

On the basis of his case studies, Athens concludes that violent criminals go through a four-stage process he calls "violentization." The stages are brutalization, belligerency, violent performance, and virulency. Each stage prepares the way for the next without making it necessary. Schematically:

Condition: Brutalization

Many children find themselves in a set of circumstances, inflicted by a parent or older sibling, which Athens calls *brutalization*. It has three elements:

Violent subjugation—the use of violence to subjugate the child to the will of another.

Coercion—violence and invective to *compel subordination*

Retaliation—violence and invective to *retaliate* for disobedience and insubordination.

Personal horrification—experiencing the violent subjugation of someone you care about (e.g. a child hearing his mother being beaten up in the parents' bedroom).

Violent coaching—being trained and encouraged in violence by someone with a credible record of violence. Brutalization provokes a reaction.

Reaction: Rage and shame

The brutalized person typically feels extreme anger at the tormentor and fantasizes violent revenge. He also feels shame at being too weak to defend himself and the other victims he cares about. (Does he chose whether to have these feelings? Is he responsible for having them?)

Rage and shame are *problem-posing* emotions. They call for deliberation about what action to take. The outcome of the deliberation, will be a decision, the formation of an intention. If attractive and realistic alternatives are not offered, this intention is likely to be *belligerency*, the second stage of violentization.

Response to problem: Belligerency

The individual decides to respond violently the next time she is seriously provoked and if she judges there is a good chance of success.

This resolution results, when the time comes, in *action*, Athens's third stage.

Violent Performance

The performance may not succeed, or may have mixed results. If so, the individual may either try again, making use of what was learned the first time. Or he may give up the resolution of violence and deal with the provocations of his rage and shame in some other way. On the other hand, if the experiment succeeds and the person who challenged him is seriously injured or killed, this produces a strong social and emotional *reaction*. Reaction (to success): Pride, empowerment, respect. The individual receives respect and fear from those who know what he did. He gains a new and gratifying sense of empowerment and pride. His rage is slaked and his shame vanquished.

He must now decide whether to adopt a policy of violence. In light of his dramatically improved self-esteem and reputation, he is almost certain to do so, thereby moving to the fourth and final stage:

Response: Virulency

At this point, our "hero" has adopted the maxim that he or she is willing to use extreme violence in response to the slightest provocation or to achieve any goal. Such a person is dangerously violent.

So Who's Responsible?

There are two moments of choice in this story: the question of belligerency and the question of virulency. In the first case, one is trying to decide whether to attempt a violent performance. In the second, the violent performance having been successful, our protagonist is deciding whether to embrace violence in a big way. In both cases, she is aware that there are alternatives. Especially at the point before belligerency, she may want to follow the example and the precepts of her teachers or religious counselors. But given the real conditions of her life, the strength of her feelings, and the advice from coaches in violence, she finds the path of peace unrealistic. She makes what is arguably, under the circumstances, a rational decision to act violently.

As I mentioned earlier, violentization is not inevitable once it begins. Early intervention by a teacher or counselor may prevent someone who is beginning to experiment with violence from continuing to perform violent acts. Athens emphasizes that the process proceeds at the will of the individual; one *decides* to use violence to deal with provocations. Yet one does not choose the provocations, or the range of resources and options one has for dealing with them. Moreover, although one is not *driven* into violence by blind passions and uncontrollable urges, strong passions (fear, humiliation, rage, shame, and pride) play a major part in the provocations to which one must respond.

I present Athens's account of how "dangerous violent criminals" are made not because I think it explains every instance of violent crime, but because the *kind* of explanation it offers seems right. People do choose the lives they lead; they are responsible agents. But they make their choices under circumstances they did not choose, and for which they are not responsible, circumstances which provoke and limit their choices.

They do not deliberate and choose in circumstances in which most of *us* had to decide how to live—those of us who write and legislate about these issues. They are, to put it mildly, in very stressful conditions in which it is difficult, even impossible, to give all the possible choices a fair hearing. The lived experience of someone undergoing brutalization limits his or her horizon of choice; options that look real and preferable to us, either do not exist for this person or seem unrealistic or foolish. What has gone wrong is not that the will of the violent person is defective or dysfunctional, as theories of crime as mental illness would have us believe. Nor is the problem that the will is depraved or corrupt, as Augustinian Christianity claims. Rather, the will of the violent individual has *a restricted range of imagination*; it can imagine only violence because it came to maturity under conditions where violence was the only, or the best, imaginable response.

So although violent people (and other criminals) are responsible for what they do and who they are, many *other* things—persons and institutions and conditions—are responsible as well. Responsibility must be *dispersed*.

The point of assigning responsibility for something that has gone wrong is to identify a point of intervention: who or what do we try to change in order to prevent something from happening again and to repair the damage that has occurred. In this sense, someone who has voluntarily done violence or any other kind of harm to us is responsible: we need to intervene in whatever way is appropriate to get them to accept the responsibility, to make amends, and to change their ways. But dispersing the responsibility for crime means locating and intervening in the conditions under which people are provoked to make bad choices. What are these? Where does responsibility go when it is dispersed?

Athens work focuses on families with one or more violent parents and on "turbulent" and "malignant" communities where children are likely to be brutalized by gangs (Athens, 1997, 148-151). Violence is not, on this account, a direct response to oppression and inequality. What provokes a boy, for example, to choose violence as a way of life is not an indifferent teacher or a racist landlord or the inability to buy food; it is the pressures of brutalization by people he is living with, his family or older boys on the street.

But of course economic and social structures have an impact on violent crime in a number of indirect but important ways. For example, not all violence is committed by the extremely violent types whose development we have just surveyed. People who are marginally violent are more likely to act violently when frustrated by unemployment and poverty. Marginally violent parents and older siblings will be less prone to brutalizing children when they have jobs and housing they can take pride in.

CONCLUSION

Prisons say to us: "We hold within our walls those who are to blame for the crime you fear, and whatever we do not contain is without blame. Do not question what goes on behind these walls, for our inmates deserve whatever happens to them here. *They* did the crime, and so must do the time." We need to learn how to reply to this endlessly repeated message. Overlooking or denying the responsibility of criminal offenders for their actions does not help them and only discredits reformers in the mind of the public. Let's insist that those who are guilty of harmful crimes are responsible for them, that they really did choose to act badly, with the exception of those who are evidently mentally or neurologically ill or damaged.

The claim that criminals choose their lives is often used to justify their condemnation. But if we take a good look inside the world in which these men and women were forced to make their choices, we may well doubt that *we* would have chosen any differently. None of us create the circumstances, fortunate or unfortunate, in which we learn how to live. We have no grounds in the differences between criminals and ourselves to refuse them their dignity. We do have reason to confront them with expressions of both outrage and sympathy. We do need to forcibly restrain them from doing more harm, and we need to do what we can, while respecting their dignity, to bring them to a cooperative point of view. New institutions, bearing no resemblance to prisons, will have to be invented for these purposes. At the same time, we need to think more deeply into the complex social mix that includes the disastrous circumstances in which many children must figure out how to live. We need to learn how to claim *our* share of responsibility for crime.

Notes

* Many thanks to Sevin Koont for her careful reading of an earlier draft, as well as to Jan Haaken, George Bradley and Marc Marenco.

1. My topic here is prisons as ideology represents them, not prisons as they are. The latter, but not the former, contain only those who are guilty of crimes. Real prisons, of course, contain many other people as well: political prisoners, the wrongly convicted, and those guilty only of nominal crimes.

References

Althusser, Louis. 1971. Ideology and Ideological State Apparatuses. *Lenin and Philosophy*. New York: Monthly Review Press.

Athens, Lonnie H. 1992. *The Creation of Dangerous Violent Criminals*. Urbana and Chicago: University of Illinois Press.

Athens, Lonnie. 1997. *Violent Criminal Acts and Actors Revisited*. Urbana: University of Illinois Press.

Frederick, Gregory. July-August 2001. Prisoners are Citizens. *Monthly Review*. Press.

Hodgins, Sheilagh, ed. 1993. *Mental Disorder and Crime*. London: Sage Publications.

Kant, Immanuel. 1998. *Religion Within the Boundaries of Mere Reasons and Other Writings*. Cambridge: Cambridge University Press.

Mansnerus, Laura. July 21, 2001. "Damaged Brains and the Death Penalty." *New York Times*.

McLellan, David, editor. 1977. *Karl Marx: Selected Writings*. Oxford: Oxford University Press.

Parenti, Chrisitan. July/August 2001. "The 'New' Criminal Justice System: State Repression from 1968-2001." *Monthly Review*.

8

HATH WE NOT EYES?: THE CASE FOR JUST MERCY DENIED IN PREJEAN

Diane Antonio

"Just mercy" is the balm after the storm. It cares for those who do or suffer wrong. This paper theorizes "just mercy" as an act of care, informed by justice, that entails a positive openness and responsiveness to the moral and legal claims of the embodied wrongdoing or wronged other. First, this essay examines the impetus for a theory of just mercy in Derrida's discourse on justice. It then explores the practical application of just mercy in context of a care and embodiment ethic. Finally, I discuss how just mercy is denied in the film and Prejean's book of *Dead Man Walking* (Prejean, 1933, p. 5). From the state of Louisiana's failing to heed the humanity in the murderer's face back to Salem's unholy somataphobia that justified violence against the body of the feminine (Nussbaum, 1999, p. 158)—the moral blindness of these communities indicts our own refusal to sanctify the other.

THE IMPERATIVE OF JUSTICE VS THE SPIRIT OF JUSTICE

In Derrida's view, the state's merely following the cold letter of the law does not fulfill the promise of the coming of justice. "Law is pusillanimous... blind...and legalistic" (Caputo, 1997, p. 150). Derrida problematizes justice by dividing it into two moments or impulses. The "imperative of justice" or "justice as law" is general. It corresponds to "objective law" or application of just rule. In contrast, the "act" or "spirit" of justice demands the "equitable honoring of faces" (Derrida, 1969, p. 54). Derrida writes:

> How are we to reconcile the act of justice which must always concern singularity, individuals, irreplaceable groups and lives, the Other, or myself as Other, in a unique situation, with rule, norm, value or the imperative of justice which necessarily have a general form...? If I were content to apply a just rule without a spirit of justice...I might be protected by law (*droit*), my action corresponding to objective law, but I would not be just (Derrida, 1990, p. 949).

These two conflicting forces—the imperative and the spirit of justice—threaten to split the justice-seeking community apart. But it is also at the site of juridical/moral tension generated by these two impulses (i.e., applying just rule vs honoring the singularity of the other; that visionary justice is "yet to come" (a-venir).

In considering the uniqueness of the other, the becoming of justice necessarily implies the very law that it must exceed. Only when it goes beyond rule, lives out the "honoring of faces," can justice, perhaps, become that which "refounds" law and politics (ibid., p. 971). Derrida suggests further that there are "unsatisfied appeals" for visionary justice that give rise to a transformative "increase in or supplement to justice" as merely law (Derrida, p. 957). In my view, this is where "just mercy" takes fire. Derrida's elusive justice is an "experience of the impossible," a kind of madness. But over time, a morally maturing community's dissatisfaction with the effects of purely *law-referencing* justice (objective, circumscribed legal response to claims of wrongdoing or wronged other, respectively and typically accompanied by emotions of outrage, contempt, vengefulness, desire for prudence, fairness, rightness or rectification of wrong done) drive it toward just acts. These would be acts of *life-reverencing* justice. One such paradigmatic act would be to invoke the openness, the potentially healing force of mercy (an attitude of care that is taken by a collective power toward the transgressing or transgressed upon other (Kittay, 1999, p. 108)). This merciful and pragmatic attitude of care is typically accompanied by common emotions of compassion, desire for stabilization of family or community in the face of violence, including need for liberation from the past, pursuit of emotional or spiritual healing, or construction of ideal version of self or society. "Just mercy" would then emerge as something more than the just application of law or even visionary justice in the abstract sense of judicial "fresh judgment." ("No exercise of justice as law can be just unless there is a 'fresh judgment'" (Derrida, p. 961)).

With all its honoring of faces, Derridean justice worships from afar. It focuses attention more on the concept of the other's singularity, than on the brute facts of relationship with the other. Insofar as just mercy freely enacts "fresh judgments" within a context of flesh-and-blood care, just mercy exceeds justice (ibid.), is a ministry beyond the mystery of justice. That is, "just mercy" would be a profound expression by the community of the ever-becoming of justice, refreshed by and in dialogue with mercy. Why not call this phenomenon "merciful justice" instead of "just mercy"? There are three reasons why "just mercy" is the more just denomination, two semantic and one substantive. First, "merciful justice" does not capture the nature of ongoing, post-juridical, post-sentencing justly merciful acts, e.g., in the daily treatment of prisoners. Derrida identifies "justice" with "fresh judgment" in court. Secondly, "merciful justice" does not connote the ability to function in the private sphere as well as does "just mercy." And thirdly, and most substantively, the term, "merciful justice," puts the emphasis on the wrong ethical "family tree." The ethical relation that drives what I call "just mercy" is not primarily predicated upon Derrida's ontology of justice or on justice ethics, but upon the care ethic of a memory-based obligation to attend to the needs of the embodied other. "Mercy" is the child of care (ibid.).

TOWARD AN ETHICS OF EMBODIMENT

Acting on the "spirit of justice" is a responsiveness that is "owed to the Other, before any contact, because it has come, the Other's coming as the singularity that is always Other" (Chanter, 1995, p. 234). In a fundamental way, one "equitably" responds to the unique other, not because of a social or even a divine contract. One opens oneself to the call of the other just because one is there in the world—a world full of others, that is, a plenum, intertwined with one's own flesh. On this account, being in the world obliges, or at least, compels one to respond to the demands of human relationship. But what about an explicitly ethical relation to others? Derrida decries the limitations of traditional ethics. Even so, finding "fault" with those who do not responsibly heed the other, he passionately indulges in a discourse of moral relations. He has a "hyperbolic ethical vision of pure forgiveness" (Derrida, 1991, p. 51) and "mad" justice. He approves of Levinas' "ethics beyond ontology" (Derrida, 2001, p. 202). He exhorts one not to "escape the complex polemics of contemporary legal, political, and ethical disputes" (Caputo, p. 140). And he does so by calling one to a shockingly generous relationship to the Other.

Ultimately, this compelling call to heed the other encourages an ethical project that is founded, not on the sovereign power of the state, but on the primal bond and shared idiom of bodily subjectivity. After all, the primal relationship Derrida describes is none other than a relationship of lived body-to-lived body. One is conjoined with embodied human others by the shared phenomena of sense perception, passion, desire, and most importantly, by one's personal set of emotion-charged memories about what it is to be human, to be loved, to be cared for.

Moreover, since the other is always an incarnate subject, with concrete, corporeal-based emotions, perspectives, and intentions, fulfilling any ontology-grounded imperative to heed the other requires a practically applicable ethics of embodiment and care. Such an ethics asks the basic question: what are the moral implications of embodiment?

In the more narrow context of penal reform, an ethics of embodiment would focus on the following sorts of questions. What do the dominant cultural imaginaries ("the register, the dimension of all images, conscious or unconscious, perceived or imagined") (Gallop, 1985, p. 61), popular philosophical, theological, and so on, dictate about the transgressing body subject?[1] How do they direct that certain gender, class and racially coded wrongdoing (and wronged) others be treated in court and in prison? When they commit crimes, are these groups of racially, class and gender-coded lived bodies imaginatively and valuationally constructed as subjects or objects, potentially good or inalterably evil? Who in the society is empowered to interpret the culturally inscribed bodies of transgressing others? What responsibility does the collective have for creating a culture in which all lived bodies can flourish, even transgressing ones? And, most relevant to our discussion, how can a care ethic of just mercy be applied to the lived bodies of others as part of a project of social justice?

"JUST MERCY" AS AN ETHIC OF CARE

Crafting a viable concept of just mercy toward embodied subjects is dependent upon the acknowledgment that there is an ethical obligation to give appropriate care to otherbodies in the first place. Building on Derrida's insights, this obligation to heed the call of the other is grounded in body-to-body sensual and perceptual relationship, mutual experience of passion, and bodily and emotional memory. In my view, it is the latter—emotional memory—that most strongly encourages and embodiment ethics of just mercy to flourish in the polis.

But, as Nel Noddings has suggested in the context of care ethics, it's not just any memory (1995, p. 16). Noddings describes two moments in this ethical process. First, "the memory of our own best moments of caring and being cared for sweeps over us as a feeling—as an 'I must'...in response to the other" (ibid., p. 10). Secondly, the "I ought," a genuine moral sentiment and impulse emerges upon deliberative evaluation of the caring relation as "good" (ibid., p. 13). "Just mercy" is a moral impulse derived from individual memory of having been recognized and cared for as a dignified embodied other (all adult human beings who have survived infancy must have received at least minimal care. Also, there is considerable evidence that one has access to memories of care, from as early as the first year (Meyers, et al., 1994). In my view, collective recognition of the moral mandate to offer "just mercy" to the lived bodies of others would be analogous to personal recognition of the obligation to enact an "ethic of care" (Nussbaum, 1990, p. 98). In the 1920's, the jurisprude Williston affirmed this kind of "external manifestation of mutual assent," and the possibility of individuals' enacting corporate moral values through law, institutions and practice (Gilmore, 1974, p. 43).

Erupting out of the dialogue between justice and mercy, just mercy resonates with justice's abstract law, rule or right-referencing impulse, along with the desire for fairness or rectification of wrong done to embodied subjects, as opposed to a desire for revenge. Because of the reverence for life that invokes just mercy in the first place, it would be likely to give more weight to the considerations of practical care than to rule in judicial or societal decision making. So what is the relationship between "care" and "just mercy"? When applied to the public sphere, "just mercy" relies upon a communal sense of obligation to attend to the specific moral (e.g., to be treated with human dignity by one's particular prison guards) and legal claims (e.g., to have one's penalty reduced upon evidence of authentic rehabilitation) of the otherbody. As such, just mercy shares the emotion-charged focus of an ethics of care upon the more concrete and/or day-to-day needs of the embodied human other. "Care" is, more primally, an individual, positively active response to the physical and emotional needs of the otherbody that is based on the private memory of having been cared for (Noddings, 1995, p. 16). In turn, "mercy," in the context of "just mercy" in the civic domain, is a caring perspective based on historical memory, experience, or witness of a public-sphere forgiveness of debt. Without their individual memories of care, it is probable that the exigencies of "just mercy" would not even be recognized by a people. As such, "just mercy" is not only engendered by the body politic's memory of or experience of forgiveness in the public realm. It takes root, initially, in individual, embodied memories and experience of private care and forgiveness. Just about all human beings have had some early-life experience of forgiveness, however minor, temporary, or incomplete, and whether directed toward self or others. These can range from parental forgiveness for children's household infractions like not finishing one's spinach, to mom's letting dad "out of the doghouse," to reconciliation with a best school friend after some serious betrayal of trust. The most benevolent personal and cultural narratives of care, born within a unique history of political interactions, come to merge in just mercy.

Here are some case-by-case applications of just mercy (a law, rule or right-referencing, memory-based attitude of care that inspires openness and respon-siveness to the call of the embodied wrongdoing or wronged other). The dis-position to just mercy can sensitize those rationally pursuing justice in court (police, judges, juries, attorneys, plaintiffs, spectators, the public-at-large) to the values of context, discretion, equity, uniqueness of individual situation. Judge, jury and other citizens following the trial pursue an honest understanding of what, in victim's and perpetrator's physical, economic, or political lives needs to and can be mourned (for instance, a good life lost to murder), supported (dignity of rape victim or prisoners' privacy rights) or, eventually, reformed by the common body (for example, harms such as racial discrimination (Walker, 1998, p. 65)). A disposition to just mercy might determine an individual judge's decision to include in court defendants' histories (Nussbaum, 1995, p. 94) of abuse, racism, oppression or poverty. This can lead to more "sympathetic assess-ment of the defendant's background and character" and positively influence not only sentencing but reforms in the subsequent treatment of prisoners in every-day life (such as in matters of diet and hygiene, racial discrimination, sexual abuse, inhumane conditions of execution, etc. (ibid., p. 55)).

Recognition of what Nussbaum calls "social deformation of character and desire" (ibid., p.96) can encourage a sense of collective responsibility in citizens' following the case, for some conditions of violence (Sarat, p. 161). As Dworkin says, the individual citizen participates in a political and social process "whose success and value are communal in the strong sense that he or she shares fully in the pride or shame of the collective decision" (i.e., legislation, adjudication, enforcement, institutions and practices (Dworkin, 2000, p. 187)). In regard to just mercy toward the wronged, Helen Prejean urges the busy law enforcement and legal community to display more patience and compassion with the emo-tional phone calls of victims' families, and to make assistance programs more accessible to crime survivors (Prejean, 1993, p. 225). Ideally, in connection with some court cases, the communal disposition to just mercy can accelerate a puri-fying end of resentment within that legal/social collective, Nussbaum's "refusal to hate" (Nussbaum, 1990, p. 210). This would not be a premature amnesia, but a foregoing of bringing up fiery emotions surrounding the crime. Or it may even invoke the mystery of forgiveness. Justice-seekers' respectful, timely and sympathetic hearing of the voices of crime victims may empower the relevant community to integrate shared traumatic experience more successfully than any one individual member of family (Arendt, 1964, p. 261). The moral society begins to pay attention to care issues in a legal setting, including self-care in the sense of releasing itself from the cycle of blood debt.

INSIDE AN ETHICS OF EMBODIMENT; JUST MERCY DENIED IN COURTS AND PRISONS

Before turning to *Dead Man Walking*, let's examine in the abstract what it means for a community to deny just mercy to embodied subjects. Wherein is the collective moral failure? First, from the perspective of embodiment ethics, the "just mercy"-denying polity does not take up a common disposition of mercy toward other body subjects under law. That is, a life-reverencing, memory-based attitude of care that entails l. an active moral, imaginative, and emotional *openness* to the uniquely situated other body (Sarat, 2001, pp. 91, 245); 2. a positive, compassionate responsiveness to the bodily/emotional/cultural situation of the transgressing or wronged embodied other.

Secondly, consistent denial of just mercy reveals a morally immature community's inability to recognize or act upon its dissatisfaction with purely rectifying law, a dissatisfaction that invokes just mercy in its legal dimension (just mercy can also exist in the private sphere). Sadly, the denial of just mercy does not allow the creative dimension of moral valuation to come to full flower in the public realm.

DEAD MAN WALKING

The film, *Dead Man Walking*, depicts a law-abiding *polis* that refuses the gift of just mercy to a transgressor. While he is on death row, the convicted murderer, "Matthew Poncelet," (a composite of actual death-row prisoners in Prejean's book) does receive situationally-sensitive bodily, emotional and spiritual care from "Sister Helen." (This character is based on Sister Helen Prejean, the real-life Roman Catholic nun and author of the non-fiction book from which the screenplay was derived.) Interestingly, there is a strong suggestion throughout the screenplay that Helen's ability to care for others emerged from personal, experiential memory of maternal caregiving. For example, the quietly powerful influence of her mother's style of caring becomes evident on the eve of Poncelet's execution. When Sister, who has sought the haven of her mother's house, confides that Poncelet doesn't offer much to love, Helen's compassionate mother reminds the nun of her own dark side. For, as it turns out, in the throes of a childhood fever, young Helen had lashed out, and given her mom a black eye. Her mother says pointedly "But I held you...tight."

Helen's mimesis of this maternal ethos is introduced by the first shot of the screenplay. It is (fictive) color film footage from the sixties, crudely entitled

"Helen's Big Day." Sr. Helen is decked in bridal white and becoming a nun. After the ceremony, she stands, smiling, shoulder-to-shoulder with her mother. In the climactic execution scene, she will re-enact this very stance of maternal care to stand shoulder-to-shoulder with Poncelet. Seeing the condemned man's shivering with fear, she will call out: "Can somebody get him a shirt. He's cold." As he begins his death march, she will gently re-focus his vision: "I want the last thing you see in this world to be the face of love. Look at me." It will be she who gives the animal warmth of a touch on the arm, as Poncelet goes to his violent death.

Even so, Austin Sarat, author of *When the State Kills*, is critical of Prejean's confessor relationship to the prisoner in the film (ibid., p. 225). He says Poncelet's confession of guilt infantilizes, shames and demeans the wrongdoer. This criticism rests on the mistaken premise that Sister Helen is herself an arm of the violent and secret state apparatus and Western imaginary of guilt and punishment. I would argue, rather, that in the personal sphere, and as a member of the smaller civil rights community, Sister Helen acts with a just mercy that is subversive to and goes beyond the harsh patriarchal imaginary regarding sin and retribution. She loves Poncelet and evokes love from him. She insists on his humanity. She fights institutional cruelties inflicted upon him, with her own body and breath. When the prison Chaplain Farley will not allow music that "stirs up emotion" to be played for Poncelet as he walks to execution, she sings the hymn *a capella* instead. In her book, she condemns bodily injustice toward prisoners—tiny cells, inadequate lighting, heating and ventilation, limited telephone calls on Death Row. She wants prisoners to be able to do meaningful labor, and to compensate victims of criminal cases, as in civil cases. She even subverts harsh theological views of the sinful body that appear themselves at odds with Christ's beatitudes (Prejean, p. 196). For example, right before the execution, she prays for the granting of the killer's own wish that he "not fall apart" and lose bodily dignity. She puts the state's attitude toward Poncelet into corporeal (and Derridean) terms: "So cold, so calculated this death."

As a woman, Sister Helen's own feminine-gendered body is yet another site of both church-and-state institutional power struggles that distracts from the rendering of just mercy. Sister Helen resists this gender oppression. She disobeys Chaplain Farley's contemptuous directive that she "not flout authority," that is, she should don her habit and not expose her woman's form and "bleeding heart" when visiting the prison. When Matthew chooses Sr. Helen over Farley as his spiritual advisor (a Constitutional right), the prison opposes her nomination, ostensibly because of her participation in an anti-death-penalty demonstration. But Sister Helen discerns that "the prison wants to block women as spiritual advisors to inmates on death row" (ibid., p. 41).

As to the question of collective responsibility for, at least, creating some conditions of violence, Sister Helen does mention that Poncelet grew up in poverty and neglect. However, I agree with Sarat that the film does not adequately explore this controversy, or flesh out the "flattened" narrative of Poncelet's crime to a "whole life" in social context (Sarat, p. 171).

The film, and book that inspired it, raise other important questions in regard to a communal ethic of just mercy. In the film, the young killer was eventually executed by the state of Louisiana in a sadistically specular punishment. He was displayed behind a glass window to the hostile witnesses of his execution. He was strapped to a table, given a lethal injection, and then held up for viewing, arms out-stretched, crucifixion-style. He died under the understandably vengeful gaze of his enemies (the grieving families of the young couple who were brutally raped and murdered by him and his companions). Perhaps we do not want to know whether the chemically-induced paralysis of his lungs resulted in a horrible sense of strangulation before he died, since the condemned was rendered immobile by the drug. ("His face just goes to sleep while his insides are going through Armaggeddon," says Hilton the lawyer.)

What, if any, debt of just mercy (a caring response to his personal and cultural situation of embodiment, including classist injustices, drawn from our own resources of care and forgiveness or from witnessing public clemency toward others) did the American collective owe this true-life criminal other? Do we, in whose name the state kills, bear some common burden for turning a blind eye to his bodily terror and passional pain (Deigh, 1996, pp. 236, 243)? Is it true for cultures that, as Sister Helen says, there is "some peace" at the end of hatred? If one "forgives" the fullest extraction of blood debt, "do our memories...become more pure?" (Robbins, 142) Does our communal ethic, our best version of ourselves, include compassion toward the bodies, if not the souls of cold-blooded killers? If not, should it? The human "to-come" (*l'avenir*), fresher judgment, the "going where we cannot go" of just mercy are at stake. Hath we not eyes?

Notes

1. By "body subject" I mean an incarnate human consciousness whose unique perspective on the world, intellect, desires, emotions, will, and most significantly, moral agency are inseparable from her bodily existence. As moral agent, the "body subject" projects her intentions onto the world and interacts with other body subjects/moral agents (intersubjectivity) through the physical media of her corporeal gestures, movements and language.

References

Arendt, Hannah. 1964. *Eichmann in Jerusalem: A Report on the Banality of Evil.* New York: Penguin.

Caputo, John, 1997. Justice, If Such a Thing Exists. *Deconstruction in a Nutshell, A Conversation with Jacques Derrida.* New York: Fordham University Press.

Chanter, Tina. 1995. *Ethics of Eros, Irigaray's Rewriting of the Philosophers.* New York: Routledge.

Code, Lorraine, Mullett, Sheila and Christine Overall. 1992. *Feminist Perspectives, Philosophical Essays on Method and Morals.* University of Toronto Press.

Deigh, John. 1996. *The Sources of Moral Agency.* Boston: Cambridge University Press.

Derrida, Jacques. 1990. "Force of Law, 'The Mystical Foundation of Authority." *Cardozo Law Review*, 11 (5-6).

_____. 1991. At This Very Moment in this Work Here I Am. *Rereading Levinas*. Bernasconi and Critchley (Eds.). Bloomington: Indiana University Press.

Caputo, John D. (ed. & commentary). 1997. *Deconstruction in a Nutshell, A Conversation with Jacques Derrida*. New York: Fordham University Press.

_____. 1997. *On Cosmopolitanism and Forgiveness*. New York: Routledge.

Dworkin, Ronald. 2000. *Sovereign Virtue, The Theory and Practice of Equality*. Cambridge: Harvard University Press.

Gallop, Jane. 1985. *Reading Lacan*. Ithaca: Cornell University Press.

Gilmore, Grant. 1974. *The Death of Contract*. Columbus: Ohio State University Press.

Kittay, Eva. 1999. *Love's Labor, Essays on Women, Equality and Dependency*. New York: Routledge.

Levinas, Emmanuel. 1969. Lingis, Alphonso (trans.). *Totality and Infinity, An Essay on Exteriority*. Pittsburgh: Duquesne University Press.

Myers, N. et al. 1994. Fifty Months of Memory: A Longitudinal Study in Early Childhood. *Memory* 2(4): 383-415.

Noddings, Nel. 1995. Caring. *Justice and Care, Essential Readings in Feminist Ethics*. Virginia Held, (Ed.). Boulder, CO. Westview.

Nussbaum, Martha C. 1990. *Love's Knowledge, Essays on Philosophy and Literature*. New York: Oxford University Press.

_____. 1995. *Poetic Justice. The Literary Imagination and Public Life*. Boston: Beacon Press.

_____. 1999. *Sex and Social Justice*. Oxford: Oxford University Press.

Prejean, Helen. 1993. *Dead Man Walking*. New York: Vintage Books.

Robbins, Tim. 1997. *Dead Man Walking, The Shooting Script*. New York: Newmarket Press.

Sarat, Austin. 2001. *When the State Kills, Capital Punishment and the American Condition*. Princeton: Princeton University Press.

Walker, Margaret Urban. 1998. *Moral Understanding; A Feminist Study in Ethics*. New York: Routledge.

9

MORAL PANIC IN THE DRUG WARS: THE CONSTRUCTION OF EXCLUSION ERA CHINESE AMERICAN AND CONTEMPORARY AFRICAN AMERICAN DRUG USERS

Somjen Frazer

> *The control that drugs wield over users is seen as insidious, one that creeps into the user's mind and body and "takes over"; the drugs is attributed a kind of diabolical or "black magic" power that overwhelms and dominates the user. It exerts a power that manifest parallels with other dreadful agents that embody "stealth and treachery," that "invade" the user, that "contaminate, pollute, corrupt, taint and befoul," that "penetrate human tissue" and "never end," never quite seem to go away. The public finds widespread drug abuse riveting and terrifying in part because of these genuine primal fears.*
> —Erich Goode and Nachmen Ben-Yehuda
> "Moral Panics: Culture, Politics and Social Construction"
> (1994, p. 161)

Since Nixon's successful 1968 presidential campaign, the United States has seen a seemingly unprecedented attack on drug use in America. As I write, New York State policymakers are debating the efficacy of the Rockefeller Drug laws, notoriously harsh legislation which proscribe mandatory sentencing of drug users to long prison terms for small amounts of narcotics, especially crack cocaine (Tonry, 1995, p. 120). Elementary school children are being taught to "Just Say No." Somewhere in Latin America, United States helicopters are burning coca plants. These variations on drug use prevention demonstrate that current fears of drug use have occupied so much policy and media attention that they warrant the label "moral panic."

This moral panic, like all such panics, does not emerge out of nowhere. This paper attempts to provide a sort of "history of the present," an answer to questions about the genealogy of the current panic in a specific period, the Chinese Exclusion Era (1882-1943). The power of drug use to inspire moral panic is evident in Goode and Ben-Yehuda's metaphors: disease, invasion, pollution, magic, and penetration. These elements are present in both Chinese Exclusion literature concerned with the perceived opium habit of Chinese people and in current fears about African American drug use. In both moral panics, disease literature contests moral explanations of drug use, "otherizing" language is used to identify the groups targeted as drug users, and fears about the possibility of the spread of drug use to those who are not the "other" (white elite and middle class people) affect the ways the "other" is treated by the mainstream.

These patterns compose a "moral panic." Paraphrasing Cohen, I apply the term "moral panic" to a

> condition [in which] a group of persons emerges to become defined as a threat to societal values and interests. . . [is] presented in a stylized and stereotypical fashion by the mass media . . socially accredited experts pronounce their diagnoses and solutions. . . it has . . . serious and long-lasting repercussions and might produce such changes as those in legal and social policy or even in the way society conceives itself," (Goode and Yehuda, 1994, p. 155).

This chapter will compare the ways in which moral panic is represented in media and expert discourse, while questioning the ways in which the production of such discourse contributes to the "moral panic" explosion of the problem of drug use.[1]

Contemporary popular images and discourse around drug use, as well as some contemporary expert scholarship, have constructed an image of a drug user who is black, urban, and poor.[2] As Marc Mauer has argued in his book *Race to Incarcerate: the Sentencing Project*, this image has led to policy which unfairly targets minorities and does not reduce drug use. The African American drug user trope has become normalized because it fits other discursive patterns in the American polity which reify nationalism and exclude those who do not fit national identity. These discursive patterns have a specific history, which includes slavery, Chinese Exclusion, American Indian genocide, and many other practices which upheld the power of white, wealthy, Protestant, heterosexual men. Rogers Smith refers to this history as "the ascriptive tradition," which he argues exists simultaneously in America with a more liberal, egalitarian tradition a well as multiple other traditions (Smith, 1997, p. 6). The contest between these traditions has been fought in the media, the electorate, and in the minds of Americans throughout history.

Given the high stakes in drug policymaking, it seems strange that Americans have not looked to our prior collective experience to inform current concerns. It is as though we have forgotten the moral panics which led to prosecutions of other minorities accused of disproportionate drug use. The similarities between the images and rhetoric of the contemporary drug wars (defined here as the Nixon Era to the present) and those of the Chinese Exclusion Era remind us of the centrality of moral panic to our vocabulary of "otherness" and exclusion. In addition to rhetorics of morality and public health, images of street gangs, often called "highbinders" or "tongs" in the Exclusion Era, symbolize the kind of person who uses drugs in both time periods considered. The images of violence surrounding the tongs and the contemporary African American gangs are another mechanism (along with drug imagery) that an oppressed minority is constructed and conflated with violence, primitivism and difference, thus perpetuating justifications for their oppression.

In considering the discourse in these two eras, which helped define how the white majorities in America understood, legislated against and treated (in both senses) two disenfranchised minorities, I will be looking at both "expert" and popular images of drug culture. "Experts" on the Chinese and opium smoking during the Exclusion Era included missionaries and settlement workers who proselytized in Chinatowns, public health and government workers who studied Chinatowns as centers of disease and vice, and the sociologists who emerged in the early twentieth century as new "experts" on social problems. Popular discourse included journalists' books and articles as well as material culture. Current work on the "drug wars" comes from many disciplines and ideologies; I will chiefly be concerned with the shifts in scholarship and the contesting accounts of and solutions to the "drug problem" in America. Because there is such a rich body of scholarship concerned with images of black drug culture and urban ghettos, and because these images are so pervasive, I will not be considering these images extensively but rather will rely on the work which inspired and precedes this paper.

It is easier to compare the construction of racist images when they can be relegated to the foibles of a former era. By choosing to compare recent historical trends with those of the Exclusion Era, I simultaneously treat each "expert" source concerned with the "drug wars" as both a source of information and as a reflection of the racialization of drug offenses which I am critiquing and interrogating. Rather than allowing this slippage to compromise my analysis, I propose to question the category of "expert" not just for the Exclusion Era, but throughout history, and examine each study of the "drug problem" with skepticism as well as an understanding of the larger cultural forces which shape it. This allows data which appears to be the result a well-conducted, systematic study to remain useful to my work without denying the ways in which this systemization of knowledge contributes to the discursive processes which are the focus of my study.

The purpose of studying the rhetoric and images of these two periods is not simply to trace the genealogy of current discourses and fears around drugs, morality, violence, race, and public health; it is also an investigation of the power of that discourse, how it was produced and its effects. By looking for the (dis)continuities and (dis)similarities around the problem of the "drug wars," I hope to render visible the ways in which racialized drug rhetoric and policy have influenced Americans' sense of national identity, and their construction of those excluded from that identity throughout both eras of moral panic. Because both Chinatowns (and China herself) and the predominately black, urban ghettos where drug use is presumed to occur now are "contained" but "leaky" spaces, which Americans who do not inhabit them prefer to relegate to a "foreign" or "un-American" problem, policymaking which reinforces those ghettos serves as an example of what Smith's "ascriptive tradition" of American nationalism.

By making policy that in one case restricts Chinese immigration and in the other, facilitates the degradation of communities which are already some of the most impoverished in America, the enfranchised in America are creating a racialized space through policymaking and rhetoric which defines who is in America, and thus worthy of protection and who is not American, and thus inspires fear. John DiIulio wrote in his 1994 article "The Question of Black Crime," "America does not have a crime problem; inner-city America does" (DiIulio, 1994, p. 3). Historian Diana Ahmad has commented that

> When Chinese smoked opium, American were inclined to be somewhat understanding because most of them knew that Chinese families had remained in China, leaving the men with little to do in their spare time . . .But, when white Americans began smoking opium, the drug took on an immoral quality that the whites perceived as being Chinese (1997, pp. 145-147).

Language that relegates a systemic problem to spaces defined as "foreign," "other" and "un-American" allows most of America to see themselves as blameless and superior; it excuses them from seeing themselves as part of the problem.

Policy has often reflected these notions of "borders" and "quarantine." These racialized images, rhetoric and policy also distinguish between "good" Chinese and African Americans and their "bad" brothers and sisters. The racializing of certain spaces—Chinatowns/China and urban ghettos—performed a certain kind of containing function that allowed policymakers and the mainstream public to create a space which, although it was contained by American soil, was not itself American. By legislating that only certain classes of Chinese—merchants, teachers, students and travelers, all people of means—could enter America, and by distinguishing between tong members and good Chinese and claiming to be able to recognize the differences between the two, "experts" constructed a community divided among itself (United States Industrial Commission Report, 1901). African Americans are similarly divided into urban, ghetto-dweller criminals and those for whom affirmative action was intended. Thus DiIulio's spacial divide translates into a question of the deserving and undeserving as well as the divide between "inner city" and "American". Paradoxically, this split also led in both cases to a kind of essentialism which construed the "nature" of the minority groups in question as base and un-American, while providing for "exceptions" in the form of "worthy" members of the minority.

The notion of the Chinese as undesirable (with a few exceptions) helped lead to legislation outlawing narcotic traffic. Along with increasing physician power and desire to regulate medical practice and drug dosing (demonstrated by the passage of the Pure Food and Drug Act in 1906) Progressive Era policymakers and doctors became increasingly concerned with opium as a marker of deviance (Acker, 1995, pp. 118-123). John C. McWilliams dates the beginning of the drug wars to 1910, when Congressman David Foster and Dr. Hamilton Wright introduced a bill to restrict the use of opiates, cocaine, chloral hydrate and cannabis.[3] The Harrison Narcotic act was signed in 1914 amid a media campaign that stressed that drug use was not only unhealthy, but "un-American" (McWilliams, 1991, p. 361). The international context of this early discussion, which occurred on the heels of the Pure Food and Drug Act, would set a precedent that would continue to stress controlling drugs at their (presumably foreign) sources (Walker, 1991, p. 352). The next legislation, which occurred during the Prohibition Era, was the 1922 Narcotic Drugs Import and Export Act, was the next step in the "foreignization" of the drug problem (McWilliams, 1991, p. 363). During this era, a shift from a treatment model to a punitive model led to a drastic increase in incarceration for drug offenses such that by 1928, one third of penitentiary inmates were serving time for drug offenses (ibid., p. 364).

Recent years have seen a similar trend in incarceration of drug users. Although there are no statistics with racial data from the Harrison law period, it is well documented that African-Americans currently make up a disproportionate number of those imprisoned for drug crimes. Contemporaneous to the trends in rising incarceration and increasingly disproportionate incarceration of African Americans has been an increase in punitive models and decrease in rehabilitative models of punishment for drug offenders (Mauer, 1999, p. 46-49). For example, the "100:1" laws which punish drug users caught with crack with the sentence for one hundred times the amount if the drug had been cocaine, provide strict mandatory minimums for drug possession, and result in great racial disparity (88.3% of convictions for crack use are of black people) have repeatedly been upheld despite their disproportionate racial effect, their harshness, and their utter disregard for advances in drug treatment services.

These punitive models have been the result of a "law and order" mentality in recent political campaigns. The "law and order" election campaign successfully run by Richard Nixon in 1968 resulted in another crackdown on drug trafficking and use, the effects of which we are still feeling today (McWilliams, 1991, p. 372-373). Connecting the two time periods and racial groups which are the primary focus of this study was the tenure of Harry J. Anslinger as commissioner of the Federal Bureau of Narcotics from 1930 to 1970 (ibid., p. 364-5). He promoted punitiveness and published anti-marijuana literature promoting the image of African Americans and Mexicans as the primary users of this drug (ibid., p. 367). Through World War II and the 1950's, punitive measures against drug use continued and escalated (ibid., p. 370-71). Drug policy has fluctuated between a notion of drug use as a public health problem and drug use as a moral/legal problem. While these two concerns are not wildly divergent, (both, for example, result in a kind of exclusionist/containment discourse) changes in policy have reflected the prevalence of one or the other. I will argue that expert and popular discourse which attribute's blame for drug use to individual, moral causes rather than systemic causes contributes to an essentializing certain racial groups as "prone to crime."

Opium has its own history as a "Chinese" vice. The Opium War of 1839-1842 was fought after British smuggled opium illegally from India to Canton and eventually the rest of China, and thus the Chinese immigrants to America were familiar with it (Courtwright, 1996, p. 161). So, too, were white Americans. The Chinese opium trope as portrayed in popular discourse included images of both decadence and filth. One 1878 *New York Times* article describes "four wretched and dirty Chinamen . . . the opium . . . merchant in a squalid little room" ("Pining for Their Poison"). A missionary whose 1900 book *The Chinaman as We See Him* described his work converting immigrants described an opium den:

> To reach the subterranean dens one has to go down rickety stairs, along narrow passages where darkness reigns, and into low wretched rooms whose horrors no words can describe. Far away from the din of outside life the silence of death reigns supreme. The air is full of the stupefying smoke of opium. No ventilation ever reaches there, and not light penetrates the gloom except form the feeble flames of a few flickering opium lamps . . . some [of the smokers] are dried-up, sallow-colored sots; while others till retain much freshness and vigor, they having so far only indulged to a moderate degree (Condit, 1900, p. 58).

He further attaches the idea of "Chinese-ness" to the opium habit "The opium smoking habit was so well adapted to the Asiatic nature by its quieting, soporific, and yet gently exiting effect . . ." (ibid., pp. 57-58). The essential qualities of Chinese people were so tightly bound with their opium during this time that that the opium trope was constructed so that to be Chinese was to be an opium smoker.

However, it is clear that whiteness did not preclude opium, although a certain amount of whiteness was lost through the Orientalizing descriptors of white opium smokers. They are frequently described as "sallow" and "weak". One article provides an in-depth description of the ways in which white people became something else when they used opium.

> . . . the skin grows dry and harsh, and its natural color gives place to a tinge yellowish or bronzed; they eye loses its accustomed brilliancy, and assumes a dull, lusterless look . . . emaciation ensues . . . the strong become weak, the brave a coward, and all the nobler attributes of a vigorous manhood are swamped in the overwhelming rush of this . . . appetite (*The New York Times*, 1877, p. 8).

The "loss of manhood" was also mentioned by a proponent of Chinese Exclusion.

> . . . A confirmed opium smoker can be detected by a glance at his countenance. . . it knocks all the manhood out of a man, physically, mentally and morally; the victim loses all pride and conscience . . . to gratify his craving for the drug, he must lie on a filthy pallet in a miserable, nasty den, reeking with the foul odor of the vile drug" (*The New York Times*, 1881, p. 1).

The implication is of a loss of whiteness as a result of consorting with Chinese and using opium. One *Milwaukee Sentinel* article describes this process. "Even if they are Americans [during the use of opium] their countenances soon assume the celestial [Chinese] immobility . . ." (*The Milwaukee Sentinel*, 1888). The concerns with the loss of young, white men (particularly, although not exclusively) to opium use contributed to the moral panic around opium.

However, the transformation of a white person into an opium smoker involved a specifically Orientalist descriptors even when that person did not smoke in Chinatown, although the transformation was different. This is particularly evident in the *Times's* coverage of the wealthy who used opium. Wealthy white people did not go directly to the "dirty Chinese" and their opium dens for the pleasure of opium, but instead made their own spaces for smoking and relaxation. Here again decadence and filth composed a kind of magical, escapist space where the wealthy could indulge in colonialist fantasy.

One wealthy white woman who ran an opium parlor, which was described as being furnished with "Turkish and Persian rugs . . . Oriental luxury" was reported on in an issue of the *New York Times* in 1882. She claimed that "men do not interest the women who indulge in opium," suggesting that this space was not only a decadent refuge from the real world, but a compromise to Victorian female virtue that might have led to sexual "inversion" (*The New York Times*, 1882, p. 2).[4] Although opium consumption was legal at this time, the tone of the articles about it indicate that it was considered a moral failing, but a tolerated one when it was wealthy women who were indulging. Another article described an opium den run by a man identified as "Joe" Cohen was as similarly Oriental, but with primarily male patrons (*The New York Times*, 1899, p. 12). His "familiarity" with the Chinese (as well as white) opium traders and users and his opium parlor, which is described as "a luxurious establishment, fitted up in Oriental style . . . walls and ceilings were covered with red and gold cloth stamped with fleur-de-lis of gilt and the corners of the rooms were hung with bright-colored flimsy silks," indicated his status as a "leak" or "contamination" from Chinatown.

Carolyn Acker has established that attitudes towards (presumably non-Chinese) opium smokers emphasized the "vicious" opium smoker who sought thrills and adventure through the use of the drug (Acker, 1995, p. 123). Newspaper articles from the late nineteenth century demonstrate the image of the white opium smoker as a wealthy, debauched, man or woman who turned to the vice to try new adventures as well as the image of the fallen young male adventurer. Although these articles are about whites, they tell us about the concerns with "leaky" Chinatowns as well as Orientalist, upper-class thrill seekers. They illustrate the discursive processes which ascribed opium to Orientalism and delineated opium parlors as parts of the racialized space of China.

They also demonstrate a certain fascination with the decadence of the wealthy and their use of drugs. This is also present in contemporary media. The recent obsession with celebrity drug problems and the "heroin chic" craze are examples of fascination with drug use by wealthy people. For these contemporary images, it is not so much a loss of whiteness as part of a spectacle that the arrests and drug exploits of famous celebrities are repeatedly chronicled in such popular magazines as *Newsweek, Time,* and *People*. In interviews by Coco McPhereson of *The Village Voice* with various New York City residents about their views on scandal and celebrity drug abuse, most pointed to the entertainment value, "living vicariously" though the lives of drug addicted celebrities, and concerns with "image". The "heroin chic" craze has a specific genealogy in images of young women as passive objects which are used to sell products, but it is also part of the lurid fascination with drugs. This fascination is also present in the Exclusion Era, not only in the descriptions of wealthy people's drug parlors, but also in the descriptions of the "opium sensation" in several *New York Times* special articles on the opium problem.

However, the drug deaths of celebrities, including models famous for their "heroin chic" look, have contributed to moral panic and cued drug legislation which (along with the accompanying media frenzy) had the effect of punishing less celebrated drug users (Harold, 1999, p. 65). As Marc Mauer recounted, the 1986 death of rising basketball star Len Bias, reportedly from an overdose on crack cocaine, led to a Congressional reappraisal of drug sentencing, which resulted in "a series of mandatory sentencing laws prescribing stiff prison terms for a variety of drug offenses" (ibid., p. 62). This reaction, typical of the "moral panic" mentality of policymakers in this time period, exemplifies the ways in which the American polity reacts differently to the wealthy, elite, admired class's involvement with drugs. The answer, again, was "containment": put people in prison for longer sentences to remove the "drug problem" from threatening the rest of society.

In 1891, a twelve-year-old girl was sent to the Society for the Prevention of Cruelty to Children when it was discovered that someone in her house had sent her to an opium joint to purchase opium (*The New York Times*, 1891, p. 2). This girl's appearance in an opium den produced such a panicked response because it represented the worst fears of the middle class: that the decadence and filth represented by opium would infest their homes via innocent "vectors" such as this young girl. It also probably invoked fears of white slavery because she was a female child. However, the media representation of this problem neglects the agency of such "vectors," even when they are not children. One story of a New York man caught in a Chinese laundry buying opium is described as a "victim" of the habit (*Milwaukee Sentinel*, 1885).

Opium and other drugs are also threatening because, as Goode and Ben-Yehuda explain, they "take over", enslaving their users. The image of the "opium slave" is particularly salient to the question of moral panic during the Exclusion Era. Along with other arguments for Chinese Exclusion such as the anti-coolism, anti-drug discourse promoted the idea that Chinese could not integrate into democratic, American, society. For example, opium use was often described as "slavery," which implies that it "darkened" its users; it made white users less white. One lurid 1877 account of the ravages of opium abuse describes it as "silken threads . . . become iron chains which fetter [the user's] will and reduce him to the most abject of slavery" (*The New York Times*, 1877, p. 8).

Another article described white users as "slaves to the vice," implying that they were somehow more like coolies than American citizens.

Chinese prostitutes, who were slaves of the tong members who also smuggled or legally imported and sold opium, contributed to the belief that the Chinese were fit for slavery but not democratic government. These prostitutes were an important source of consternation to exclusion officials, who wrote in a 1901 report on Chinese immigration, "I think it is a conservative statement when I say that fully 90 per cent of all the frauds committed against the Chinese exclusion act in the bringing into the United States of slave girls and coolie laborers in inspired directly by these highbinder societies," (United States Industrial Commission, 1901, p. 763). Although some women came to the United States voluntarily, exclusion legislation made that difficult. According to interviews with these ex-prostitutes (all of whom told eerily similar stories) published in the report, slave women were generally from Canton, from large, poor families, and were either sold by their parents or tricked into accompanying a slave trader to Mexico, and from there to the United States.[5] They were sold from highbinder to highbinder and forced to give the wages from their prostitution to those highbinders (who essentially acted as pimps).

These women who were, like opium, often smuggled by highbinders, and used by white and Chinese men, were a source of great anxiety for exclusion officials.[6] Although opium is not mentioned explicitly in the questions or answers of the prostitutes interviewed for this report, because these women were a part of the Chinatown which white people feared as a source of decadence, filth and disease, they heightened fears about how to "contain" these threats. Presumably white men who visited them risked disease, not to mention the threat to racial purity that mixed-race babies who were American citizens by birth represented.

Women play a very different role in current understandings of the drug wars. The image of the crack addicted welfare mother has galvanized several recent policy decisions, one of which is chronicled by Dorothy Roberts. The 1989 precedent which allowed pregnant, crack addicted mothers to be prosecuted for child abuse and, according to one author, there is a continued tradition which devalues black motherhood. This precedent disproportionately affects poor black women, as their poverty and race make them more vulnerable, not more guilty. Health care officials have fewer qualms about invading their privacy, and social workers do not hesitate to confiscate their children because of the image of the black woman as an unfit mother. In addition, alcohol abuse, which is far more prevalent than crack use among white, wealthier pregnant women, is not criminalized although it also does damage to the fetus. The "social construction" of the relative harmfulness of drugs contributes to racial disproportion in prosecution of women for "fetal abuse."

Drew Humphries has shown in his study of media depictions of poor, crack or cocaine addicted black women that the media portrays them as uncaring women who are knowingly harming their fetuses while it portrays white women as repentant and desirous of help with their drug problems. Michael Tonry has demonstrated the way in which black female poverty and the specter of drug addiction and child neglect is used by politicians in his examination of the "myth of the welfare queen" (Tonry, 1995, p. 10). These treatments of black, poor women indicate a willingness to implicate individuals delineated by their race, gender and class in perpetuating medico-social problems rather than attempting to help them alleviate these problems. Like the fears about prostitute importation and white men's use of prostitutes, they contribute to the racialized space making and policymaking of a "drug war."

Anxiety about slavery, prostitution, and opium use was heightened by concerns with tong warfare, which peaked in San Francisco in 1917 and 1924. Tongs were Chinese American mutual protection societies which began to form sometime shortly after the Civil War. They sprang from the Chinese Six Companies, which some Chinese felt did not provide enough protection for Chinese immigrants to America in the face of white discrimination. The violence which resulted was probably attributable to the bachelor society of Chinese America and the discrimination immigrants faced. These "hatchetmen" as they were also called, brought fears of drugs, violence, collectivism (incompatible with American individualism), and slavery together.

Further, they were "recognizable" and different from "respectable Chinese." A policeman testified to the Industrial Commission:

> [when asked] Can you tell a highbinder from another Chinaman, when you see him? [answer] I can walk on the streets and pick them out and never make a mistake . . . [interviewer] Their hair is not so neatly kept—more fluffy—than other Chinamen, is it not? [answer] That is right; at the end of the cue [*sic*] where it joins the hair; and then they used to where different kinds of shoes and different kind of hats . . theme men . . .[carry] a little piece of red silk. On that silk was printed what society he was a member of . . . (United States Industrial Commission, 1901, p. 778).

Another interviewee, settlement worker Donaldina Cameron also claimed to be able to tell a highbinder from other Chinese people (ibid., p. 787).[7]

The "recognizability" of the highbinders probably contributed to a kind of "racial profiling" for the policeman who had the Chinatown beat. Gangs composed of poor people of color represent a kind of primitive horde to the American public who see them as examples of immorality and gratuitous violence rather than a response to the lack of protection from more "reputable" sources. Not unlike the fears of tong warfare are the fears of young African American gang members in their "colors," sporting weapons and babes, which (like the tong wars) have provoked extensive investigation.

These investigations are explicitly linked with fears about drugs and the migration of "urban problems." For example, a report posted on the "National Alliance of Gang Investigators Associations" says:

> [there has been an increase in] gang migrat[ion] to the suburbs and rural areas... gangs today are increasingly multicultural, multiracial and multiethnic ... It used to be young African-American males were the ones with their pants dropped below their waistlines, shoes untied, and hats flipped to the side. Today, street gangsters share this style and trend with the white youth of America... (National Alliance of Gang Investigators Associations, 2001, par. 5).

This report evinces great anxiety about the spread of gangs from the urban spaces where seemed to have once been contained. Like the descriptions of "highbinders" in the 1901 report on tongs and the various descriptions of opium addicts, the signifiers of gang membership, are assumed to be explicit and menacing. Their adoption by the "white youth of America" is seen as a kind of contamination of the mainstream and as a threat to "our" (as opposed to "their") children. Further the investigations compiled on this website center their concerns about gang membership on drugs and violence, which are similar some of the concerns that caused panic in the Exclusion Era. Although prostitution and immigrant smuggling are not salient issues for modern "gang investigators" as they were for Exclusion Era investigators, the discourse concerning drugs, violence, and "containment" is similar:

> We [presumably the investigators] are currently experiencing migration from different cities in California. The reason for this migration is narcotics-related... new subjects [gang members] come in and set up narcotics activity... Gang members are involved in narcotics are about 50 percent of the narcotics problem with the vast majority being involved in the trafficking of crack cocaine (ibid., par. 17).

The spread of drugs and violence are linked via these black and Hispanic intruders from the inner city, and with them comes violence to "average citizens" (implicitly white and middle class). "Although crime in general has decreased, gang crime may be increasing ... The most disturbing trend ... is the violent behavior towards the average citizen ... " (ibid., par. 23). The greater concern with the protection of "the average citizen" that characterizes this report furthers the notion that gang members are the "other"; they are foreign elements who introduce problems such as drugs and violence to the previously "uninfected" suburbs.

The government investigations of prostitutes, tongs, modern gangs and opium were part of a juridical constitution of the Chinatown and urban ghetto spaces as a racialized menace. The notion of the "investigation" implies a foreignness and an undesireablity in these spaces, while the concern with racialized social problems such as drugs, violence, and prostitution evinces an essentialism which allows the investigators to attach crime and violence inextricably to communities of color, and to justify excluding them. Similarly, investigations of threats to the public health which occurred in Chinatown are important to the constitution of the Chinese as essentially dirty, foreign and immoral. Investigations of opium use and gang warfare were often accompanied and echoed by investigations of contagious disease.

Nayan Shah's account of the creation of Chinatown in San Francisco as a racialized, dirty, foreign space through medical investigations of cholera (1854) and smallpox (1868-1869, 1977) demonstrates one kind of discursive "otherizing" carried on by public health officials (Shah, 1995, pp. 1, 16, 21). Medical experts of the Victorian Era conflated dirt, disease, criminality and lack of morality; Progressive Era reformers sought to clean up slums and Americanize their inhabitants (ibid., "Preface"). However, throughout the Exclusion Era, medical discourse contributed to notions of the Chinese as unhealthy foreigners, although the discourse eventually softened and became more focused on rehabilitation rather than exclusion/criminalization.

Concerns with disease were particularly centered around "secret diseases," obtained from Chinese prostitutes. Venereal disease and interracial sexual contamination were of particular anxiety to those who used arguments about Chinese morality to argue for their exclusion.[8] One proponent of exclusion described a Chinatown: " ... in 12 blocks are crowded, in indescribable filth .. . there is an "opium lay-out" in nearly every sleeping-room ... 35 dens of white prostitution, generally patronized by Chinese, and 69 of Chinese prostitution, patronized generally by whites .. so many children are afflicted with "secret" diseases, and... nine-tenths of it is traceable to the excessively cheap prostitution of 'Chinatown'" (Gilliam, 1998, p. 33). The traffic in women, and the possibilities that those women would help propagate Chinese wretchedness in America was conflated many things mainstream Americans attributed to the "other": dirt, sex, disease, filth, and drugs.

Although contemporary urban ghettos are not marked as "diseased spaces," part of the "urban drug dealer" trope includes disease. Recent popular depictions of African American drug users are more veiled in their racism, but similarly are concerned with the connections between venereal disease and drug use. The AIDS epidemic has increased the literature and images concerned with the spread of disease through needle-sharing in intravenous drug use and promiscuous, "unprotected" sex. In her work on media and the AIDS pandemic, Stephanie Kane has shown how the media transforms AIDS into a weapon used by criminals of color to wreck havoc on the innocent. This conflates criminality with disease, specifically sexually transmitted disease, and ascribes it to people of color.

Drug use itself is alternatively depicted as a moral or medical problem in the work of scholars concerned with the problem of drug dependency. This is determined by and determines the prevailing political discourse on drug dependency and the ways in which drug users serve as criminal images. Marc Mauer explains, in the 1988 election, George Bush beat Michael Dukakis by making him look soft on crime. By developing a campaign strategy focusing on Willie Horton, a black rapist who violated parole and killed a young couple, Bush exploited the public's need to feel safe by promoting himself as the source of law and order (Mauer, 1999, p. 63). This racist tactic has been used by many policymakers to influence public opinion, and drug laws continue to target the urban, poor and black. This was true during the Exclusion Era as well. Henry K. Norton argued that politicians had to appear anti-Chinese in order to get elected; history shows that they followed through on their campaign promises (Peffer, 1997, p. 34).

Further, policymakers who reify the racialized images of criminals also contribute to the discursive perpetuation of stereotypes through the media. By putting the drug problem in the ghettos and prisons of America, policymakers perform the same function they did in the Exclusion Era, which is removing the problem, and by extension, the people associated with the problem, from incorporation into the national identity. Drug sentences are a kind of exclusion, via disenfranchisement of felons and the delineation of a shameful space inhabited by African Americans. These punishments, and the exclusion of the Chinese, were made acceptable to Americans by the repeated images of drug users as "other" and "dangerous." These discursive rituals have been studied by scholars of media stereotypes. Gaye Tuchman's work on journalistic rituals foregrounds the importance of these rituals in generating "ready-made frames" which quickly become "stereotypes" for journalists who are writing about contentious issues (Tuchman, 1972, pp. 675-679). Further, Celeste Condit has suggested that when these rituals lead to discourse which polarizes a contentious issue (such as drug policy), faulty policy results (Condit, p. 327).

These images are not limited to political campaigns, but also pervade the daily news. Thus they influence public opinion not only around policy, but also as a production of a normative truth which institutionalizes the racism and otherising which is also reified by drug policy. David Jernigan and Lori Dorfman review and reproduce the work of many other scholars of the media drug wars who argue that television news emphasizes the "foreignness" of the war on drugs, with African American and Latin American people representing the "foreign" threat (Jernigan and Dorfman, 1996, p.169). Although current American policy does not explicitly force African Americans into the impoverished inner city, these media images contribute to policy which, like Chinese Exclusion, weakens communities. Removing productive adults for long periods of time from their families and communities helps perpetuate the cycle of poverty, yet policymakers and the American public continue to perpetuate this "solution" to drug problems.

They support these false solutions because of the enormous discursive power of the images of African American drug user. Franklin Gilliam Jr. and Shanto Iyengar found in a recent study that when people watched television newscasts about illegal drugs showing an African American or Hispanic criminal, they were more likely to support "get tough" crime policies. These policies emphasize punitive, individual solutions rather than systemic and rehabilitative ones, thus contributing to racist, essentialist ideas about crime.

However, in the Exclusion Era and today, there have been voices countering the mainstream depictions of the "drug criminal as other." The debates on the relative merits of rehabilitation and punishment in helping drug offenders come out of a certain kind of scientific knowledge that, while contested, is now privileged in a way that it was not for much of the Exclusion Era. The development of public health and sociology as fields of study have influenced drug discourse and in some cases provided alternatives to the "moral" discourse which condemns and otherizes drug users of color and their communities. These disciplines have had an increasing influence on policy and popular discourse, but have not escaped the "drug-criminal-foreign-black" metonymy.

Scholarship from the 1930's concerned with the problem of opium use and gang warfare was more "social problems" oriented and less "moralizing" than previous investigations. Unlike the earlier images of drug users, this discourse emphasized the ways in which the Chinese should be helped rather than excluded. It seems likely that this was a product of changing ideas about the Chinese as well as changes in "ways of knowing" about social problems, both of which would help lead to the end of exclusion in 1943. For example, Norman S. Hayner published a telling article in the *American Journal of Sociology*, tellingly titled "Social Factors in Oriental Crime." He attributed the high rates of crime in Chinatowns not to immoral decadence and un-American deviance but to "the extent to which they are incorporated in closely integrated family and community groups . . . Orientals [*sic*] living in aggregations of homeless men . . . with no stable nucleus of family life, tend to present more problems of maladjustment," (Hayner, 1938, pp. 908-909). He goes on to chronicle the problems of living without a family and with the temptations of prostitution, opium, gambling, and American goods (ibid., p. 914). His suggestion is that "criminality is low when a normal balance between the sexes makes possible a large amount of family life, and when a strong community organization maintains normal traditions . . ." (ibid., p. 919).[9] This contests Exclusion policies, which like contemporary drug policy weakened Chinese American communities by perpetuating gender disproportion and disrupted family cohesiveness with threats of deportation.

Tong warfare, too, was increasingly seen as the product of a racist society rather than an essential characteristic of the Chinese. A 1935 article entitled "The Chinese Tongs," which envisioned the violence endemic to tong culture as a reasonable response to the lack of protection by the police from crime. To protect themselves from the lawless amongst themselves and whites, to guard against their and desires for retaliation, fears, and hostility. Racial stereotyping by police and newspapers assisted them in vilifying the tong leaders and gunmen, and quite often the entire Chinese race. This understanding of what we would now term "racial profiling" and "racial stereotyping" added a nuance and sympathy to the social problems discourse which have previously been couched in racialized terms.

The move towards social science as way of understanding criminal behavior, which attributed criminality to socially determined rather than essential characteristics facilitates the rehabilitative, systemic rather than punitive and exclusionary model of drug control. Critiquing Americans' notions of the drug user as black and poor, and contributing to a discursive diversity around the "drug wars" are contemporary social scientists, some of whom are cited above, who study media and its effects. The presence of their scholarship indicates new possibilities for discussions of "who" is using drugs, why, and what should be done about drug abuse. Further critiques from the Left stress the need for alleviation of urban poverty and a refocusing on community and individual rehabilitation. For example, Marc Mauer, a leading proponent of alleviation of urban poverty as a "cure" for the inner city drug problem, decries the drug war and its racist effects his book *Race to Incarcerate*: " . . . as a national policy, the drug war has exacerbated racial disparities in incarceration while failing to have any sustained impact on the drug problem" (Mauer, 1999, p. 143). The recognition of the racist impacts of exclusion and drug policy was a counter discourse which added to the possibilities for solving the drug problem, and shifted the blame from individuals to larger social structures.

One of the most influential, radical, structuralist critiques of drug prison policies precipitated the Nixon Era "war on drugs." Eric Cummins identifies the radical prison movement of the late 1960's and early 1970's as a harsh critique of racist drug policy with foundations in the Black Power movement. By redefining all prisoners, particularly those incarcerated for drug offenses as political prisoners of an American caste system, the California (especially the Bay Area) Left countered explanations of crime that emphasized individual moral failing and punitive solutions to drug crime (ibid., pp. 142-143). Although this radical critique swiftly degenerated into what Cummins terms "crime fetishization," and failed to produce any substantive reforms in prison or drug policy, it did provide an alternative way of thinking about crime as the product of structural, rather than individual forces.

However, for every Berkeley leftist, there is a John DiIulio or a William Bennett. Bennett, one of the authors of *Body Count*, speaks as a policymaker and voice of the theory of "moral poverty." He argues that once a person is a victim of moral poverty, no social programs can save him or her (Bennett, DiIulio, and Walters, 1991, pp. 56-57). His problematic essentialist claims uphold what the evening news implies by its images; there are bad people out there, they aren't white, and they should be severely punished for drug use and prevented from hurting "innocent" people.

No radical voices like the Berkeley left appear from the Exclusion Era; however, the greater discursive diversity in the modern "war on drugs" does not necessarily mean better policymaking concerning drug offenders, or less racism, however that racism is coded. Both "drug wars" are characterized by an alienation and criminalization of people of color through individualist attributions of responsibility and images of those people as the dirty, immoral perpetrators of crimes. In the contemporary setting, more efforts are being made at prevention, more sophisticated science allows for more tools to combat drugs, but most of the combat still unfairly targets certain racial groups. Fears about drug use, gang violence, disease and the ways in which poor, racially defined urban spaces threaten to contaminate Middle America contribute to policymaking that perpetuates, rather than solves, the problem the "drug wars" claim to combat.

In this moment in time, as during the Exclusion Era, the American public is held captive to the notion of racialized drug use and crime. Even the voices which counter this notion cannot escape from it. At this fin-de-siecle, as with the last, detaching the fear of drugs from the fear of the "other" seems unlikely or impossible. However, as the current absence of a moral panic about opium and Chinese American drug use and violence makes clear, it is possible to eventually shift the discourse away from moral panic and "otherizing." If the anti-racist, anti-essentialist critique of current punishments wins the discursive power war, eventually the racial component of the discourse will be considered a relic of a less enlightened age and history will be transcended by the present. Until then, the recognition that the history of this present includes what we now understand to be racist, moralizing, otherizing arguments about drug use can foreground those aspects of contemporary drug policy.

Notes

1. While I recognize that the categories of "expert" and "popular" discourse are slippery and full of unfair value judgments about the quality of the work under discussion, I believe it is important to distinguish between the images and rhetoric confronted by *most* people *most* of the time and the images and rhetoric employed by those who study drugs professionally. Discursive power for the nonelite lies in the "normalization" of certain symbols and language. While elite discourse and popular discourse certainly influence each other and there is much slippage between them, it is nonetheless useful to distinguish between accepted ideology and rhetoric of the everyday and more specialized language.

2. Most often male, although occasionally young, female, sexually available and/or pregnant or with children (see further discussion of images of crack addicted mothers).

3. Historians periodize the drug wars in various ways. David Courtwright (1991) counts "four sustained legislative and governmental efforts against drug abuse. . . 1909-1923, 1951-56 . . . 1971-73 . . . [and] the Reagan-Bush [era]" (p, 394).

4. Inversion is often attributed to Orientalist vice. See Malek Alloula's *The Colonial Harem* (1986) for further explanations of inversion, sexuality, and colonial notions of the "Orient."

5. Although Bruce Grant claims in the 1930 book *Tong War!* that this report was, "pathetically hopeless, as the Chinese interpreters blandly made fools of the investigators," the translator appeared to have been a white, educated doctor, John Gardiner, so I am inclined to be less skeptical of this report than Grant. However, as a report compiled by white administrators, it is problematic even if there was no deliberate deception by the Chinese.

6. George Peffer chronicles anxiety and explains that before the more general Chinese Exclusion laws, the Page Law served to exclude women and uphold the pattern of bachelor society for immigrant Chinese.

7. Researchers' work rescuing prostitutes clarifies the ways in which this kind of "racial profiling" divided the Chinese community in the minds of whites into "good Chinese" and "bad Chinese." After rescuing prostitutes enslaved by high-binders, she would often see them married off to "respectable Chinese men," often merchants, who were desperate for wives because of the shortage of female Chinese (see Mildred Martin's *Chinatown's Angry Angel*).

8. Fears of racial contamination contributed to the discourse of "containment" in this era. A noted German degeneration theorist explains his logic in a chapter entitled "Fin-de-siecle". "A race which is regularly addicted ... to narcotics and stimulants in any form (such as fermented alcoholic drinks, tobacco, opium, hashish, arsenic) ... begats degenerate descendants who, if they remain exposed to the same influences, rapidly descend to the lowest degrees of degeneracy, to idiocy, to dwarfishness, etc" (Nordau, 1985, p. 34). These races, by interbreeding with other races, contaminated them with their degenerate characteristics, which are both acquired and heritable. Nordau's example is that mental illness, while primarily a French problem, has infected Germany. He relates this specifically with venereal disease, particularly syphilis, which was also of great concern to investigators of Chinatowns.

9. David Courtwright, a modern historian of bachelor societies, agrees both in the case of the Chinese and for white bachelor societies. "Although Chinese vice practices varied in their cultural details, the economic and social consequences were the same as those in white bachelor laborer communities: more debt, more death, and more disorder" (1996, 160).

References

Acker, Carolyn. 1995. From All Purpose Anodyne to Marker of Deviance: Physicians' Attitudes Towards Opiates in the US from 1890 to 1940. *Drugs and Narcotics in History*. Roy Porter and Mikulas Teich, (Eds.). Cambridge: University of Cambridge.

Ahmad, Diana. 1997. To Preserve Moral Virtue: Opium Smoking in Nevada and the Pressure for Chinese Exclusion. *Nevada Historical Review*, 41.3.

Alloula, Malek. 1986. *The Colonial Harem*. Minneapolis: University of Minnesota.

Bennett, William, John DiUlio, and John Walters. 1996. *Body Count*. New York: Simon and Schuster.

Condit, Celeste. Two Sides to Every Question: the Impact of News Formulas on Abortion Policy Options. *Argumentation*. 8.

Condit, Ira. 1900. *The Chinamen as We See Him*. Chicago: Fleming H. Revell.

Cose, Ellis. 1999. The Casualties of War. *Newsweek*. 6 September.

Courtwright, David. 1991. Drug Legalization, the Drug War, and Drug Treatment in Historical Perspective. *The Journal of Policy History*. 3.

Courtwrigth, David. 1996. *Violent Land: Single Men and Social Disorder from the Frontier to the Inner City*. Cambridge, Mass.: Harvard University.

DiIulio, John Jr. 1994. The Question of Black Crime. *The Public Interest*, 117.

Foucault, Michel. 1986. Disciplinary Power and Subjection. *Power*. Steven Lukes, (Ed.). New York: New York University.

Fredrickson, George. 2000. *The Comparative Imagination: on the History of Racism, Nationalism and Social Movements*. Berkeley: University of California Press.

Gilliam, E.W. 1886. Chinese Immigration. *North American Review* 143: 356.

Gilliam, Franklin Jr. and Shanto Iyengar. 1998. The Superpredator Script. *Nieman Reports*. Winter.

Goode, Erich and Nachman Ben-Yehuda. 1994. Moral Panics: Culture, Politics, and Social Construction. *Annual Review of Sociology* 20.

Harold, Christine. 1999. Tracking Heroin Chic: the Abject Body Reconfigures the Rational Argument. *Argumentation and Advocacy* 36(2).

Hayner, Norman. 1938. Social Factors in Oriental Crime. *American Journal of Sociology* 43.

Humphries, Drew. 1998. Crack Mothers at 6: Prime-Time News, Crack/Cocaine, and Women. *Violence Against Women* 4.

Jernigan, David and Lori Dorfman. 1996. Visualizing America's Drug Problems: An Ethnographic Content Analysis of Illegal Drug Stories on the Nightly News. *Contemporary Drug Problems*. 23.

Kane, Stephanie. 1998. *AIDS Alibis: Sex, Drugs and Crime in the Americas*. Philadelphia: Temple University.

Mauer, Mark. 1999. *Race to Incarcerate: the Sentencing Project*. New York: New Press.

McPherson, Coco. 2000. Stars and Bars. *The Village Voice*. 12 Dec.

McWilliams, John. 1991. Through the Past Darkly: the Politics and Policies of America's Drug War. *The Journal of Policy History*. 3.

Milwaukee Sentinel. 1885. In an Opium Den. 23 Aug.

Milwaukee Sentinel. 1888. The Opium Habit. 22 Jan.

National Alliance of Gang Investigators Associations. [online source] 2001. The National Gang Threat. 14 June, http://www.nagia.org/.

The New York Times. Chinese Treaties in the Nevada Legislature. 1881. *New York Times*. 21 Feb.

_____. Death in a Needle's Point. 1882. 19 Nov.

_____. The Opium Habit's Power: It's Extent in the United States. 1877. 30 Dec.

_____. An 'Opium Joint' Raided. 1891. 28 Sept.

_____. Opium Smokers Arrested. 1899. 11 Aug.

_____. Philadelphia's Opium Parlor. 1882. 29 Aug.

_____. Pining for Their Poison. 1878. 11 Aug.

Nordau, Max. 1895. *Degeneration*. New York: D. Appleton and Co.

Peffer, George. 1997. *If They Don't Bring Their Women Here: Chinese Female Immigration Before Exclusion*. Urbana: University of Illinois.

Shah, Nayan. 1995. San Francisco's 'Chinatown': Race and the Cultural Politics of Public Health 1854-1952. Diss. U of Chicago.

Smith, Rogers. 1997. *Civic Ideals: Conflicting Versions of Citizenship in U. S. History*. New Haven: Yale University.

Tonry, Michael. 1995. *Malign Neglect*. New York: Oxford University.

United States Industrial Commission. Immigration. 1901. *Report of the United States Industrial Commission*. Vol. 15. Washington, GPO.

Walker, William O. 1991. Introduction to the Special Issue on Drug Control Policy. *The Journal of Policy History* 3.

10

COMPARING JUVENILE DELIN-QUENCY IN FRANCE AND THE UNITED STATES

Susan Terrio

This chapter is part of a larger comparative ethnographic study of the processes whereby juvenile delinquents are identified and treated within the French and American juvenile justice systems. I was drawn to a comparison of these juvenile justice systems because, in spite of the many differences between them, both are undergoing enormous pressure for change in the wake of mounting public fears about youth violence. I want to start by suggesting areas of convergence and divergence in the US and France in the perceived nature, definition and evolution of the problem of juvenile delinquency before turning specifically to France. I began this research by closely examining the historic, national, and political contexts in which public debates on youth violence occur because this shapes not just government policy, criminal law, and judicial practice but also contributes to the emergence of the violent youth offender as a newly threatening social category. My goal is to make visible the multiple processes whereby social categories are constructed and naturalized as well as the ways in which various discursive domains—legal, political, and social scientific—work to stabilize 'facts' about law, justice, and deviance.

Media reports on rising juvenile delinquency rates have unleashed heated and recurrent debates in both France and the United States. In both nations there were significant increases in juvenile arrests for violent offenses between 1985 and 1995, despite marked differences in the nature and scope of the violence. In the US, juvenile homicide arrest rates doubled between 1985-93 fueled in part by crack epidemics, drug wars, and easy access to guns.[1] In France, arrests between 1986-93 for property destruction, aggravated theft, and assault and battery, rose sharply; in contrast to the US, juvenile homicide in France is extremely rare and the definition of aggravated theft is very wide encompassing everything from the use of arms to a push or a punch. Few of the aggravated theft cases I witnessed in the four months I spent observing the adjudication of penal cases in the juvenile court of the Paris Palace of Justice involved the use of a weapon, a trend reflected nationwide in France. In contrast to the US, the least common theft cases are those involving arms and because of strict gun control laws, the weapons of choice range from baseball bats to knives or razors.[2] Although juvenile arrest rates have decreased in the US over the past five years they have continued to rise in France. In the year 2000 overall arrests of juveniles rose 5.8%, the sharpest increase in 10 years.

Debates on delinquency in both countries have portrayed it as a crisis of national proportions. These debates were intensified by often sensationalist media coverage of particularly egregious and frequently unrepresentative acts of violence. Moral panics have been fueled by media predictions of a crime explosion by a new type of juvenile delinquent who was depicted as younger, more violent, more marginalized, and beyond reform. In both places these debates resurrected acrimonious disagreement on the merits of punishment versus rehabilitation.

Public fears of youth violence have politicized the topic of delinquency and engendered mounting concern with breaches of public order, prompted renewed calls for intensified surveillance and regulation of urban space, and created pressure for more repressive approaches such as longer and more severe sentences aimed not just at youth but also foreigners and illegal immigrants convicted of both crimes and misdemeanors. In response to accusations of laxism on the part of courts in general and juvenile or family judges in particular, in the 1990s both American and French public prosecutors acquired additional power to adjudicate juvenile penal cases.[3] New rhetorics of exclusion paralleled new forms of exclusion in the context of heightened socioeconomic polarization and challenges to the social welfare protections guaranteed by the state—although the extremes of poverty and segregation are far less extreme in French than American cities because of the still extensive social welfare benefits provided by the French state (Body-Gendrot, 2000). Over the past twenty years there has been a rapid expansion of prison populations in America and Europe along with emergent neo-liberal techniques for shifting responsibility for deviance, disruption, and failure away from institutionalized systems of discrimination and onto marginalized, minority youth and their families.

Whereas US collective fears of violence and loss of public safety focused disproportionately on African American and Latino minority youth in the ghettos of American cities, French anxieties centered on West and North African 'immigrant' youth in low income projects of French suburbs. The pervasive categorization of delinquents as synonymous with suburban 'immigrant' youth is particularly instructive since the majority of youth in question are not only French citizens but, in some cases, the *children* of immigrants.

Public debates on "juvenile predators" in the US tended to center on questions of morality breakdown and race; in France they were apt to focus on questions of cultural difference and citizenship. The most salient American category of belonging as reflected in the census is race/ethnicity, whereas in France it is nationality defined by a shared culture, language, and territory. In contrast to the US where the formal recognition of minority status and collection of census data on minority populations categorized by race have been the basis of affirmative action, in France the state recognizes no ethnic or racial minorities and the state body that conducts the census refuses to collect nationwide data on ethnic or racial origins. Both the American recognition of minority status and the French refusal to do so are justified according to the same logic—to prevent racism based on racial categorization and differentiation. Unlike the cultural pluralism of the prevailing American model, the French republican model seeks to erase ethnic/racial identity and to suppress cultural difference in the public sphere. This is meant to ensure that public space remains an abstract political arena in which all citizens are entitled, even required, to come together as equals. The term 'race relations' is taboo in France and there is no social science literature devoted to that topic. Thus, the celebration of cultural difference and the legitimacy of ethnic identity in the US is met with distrust by the French who link identity politics to ethnic conflicts, race riots and territorialized structures of inequality. "The notion of integration—preferred to assimilation by the French political and intellectual elites—has become the functional equivalent of race or ethnicity in the US and Britain" (Hargreaves, 1995, p. 2). But even when the cultural difference produced by immigration is implicitly recognized, the very terms of that recognition demand its elimination. The pervasive stigmatization and, even, criminalization of cultural difference—from the wearing of Islamic veils in public schools and the ritual slaughter of lambs at Islamic holidays in high-rise bathtubs to the criminal prosecution and tough sentences given to Malian women who perform female circumcision—cannot be separated from the disproportionate focus in French media on the problematic cultural difference embodied by violent 'immigrant' youth within the suburban projects.

In the US a century old juvenile justice system premised on the notion that children are less culpable and more amenable to rehabilitation is being progressively dismantled. The rise of serious juvenile crime between 1985-93 led to get-tough legislation at the state and federal levels—emphasizing more accountability, imposing mandatory sentencing guidelines and requiring the adult prosecution of juveniles charged with certain offenses. Since 1990 45 state legislatures have made it easier to prosecute juveniles as adults. Fifteen states, including the District of Columbia, now grant prosecutors the sole discretion to transfer juveniles to adult court. These laws depict the child criminal as capable of forming criminal intent and as morally responsible. Despite a sharp decline in US juvenile crime between 1995-1999, juvenile justice legislation before the 106th Congress retains its emphasis on punishment versus prevention. It bears reminding that these developments occurred in a context marked by the explosion of the US prison population from 380.000 inmates in 1975 to 1,860,520 in 1999 (Walmsley, 2000). In contrast to Western Europe where the death penalty has been abolished, up to recently the US remained one of only a few countries, including Iraq and Bangladesh, whose justice system permitted the execution of juveniles convicted of capital crimes.

Since 1945 the overall French approach to juvenile delinquency has privileged rehabilitation and social insertion rather than punishment and punitive isolation. The 1945 Ordinance, legislated by a leftist postwar government, substantially transformed a highly repressive pre-war juvenile justice system, the legacy of Roman law, local customary practice (the *Coutumes*) and the 1810 Napoleonic penal Code whose treatment of delinquents consisted mainly of confinement in houses of correction or reform work camps. These were infamous for their brutal disciplinary regimes, harsh living conditions, and exacting work rules. The 1945 legislation created for the first time a corps of specialized juvenile judges and separate courts in each French department for adjudicating penal cases involving both misdemeanors and crimes. This approach involved close monitoring, delayed judgment, and personalized sentences for troubled youth. It mandated thorough psychiatric, psychological, social and scholastic evaluations as well as the preparation of detailed family histories for all the minors brought before the court. Most importantly, it changed the 1912 legislation that had established 13 as the age for the capacity of criminal intent. It mandated the principle of reduced moral responsibility for minors aged 13-18 by creating national sentencing guidelines which automatically cut adult sentences in half except in exceptional circumstances.

Until recently the widespread consensus on prevention and prolonged juvenile justice—*justice dans le temps*—has been premised on a conception of the minor as a social and psychological work in progress. Thus, according to this logic rehabilitative interventions and judicial decisions necessarily evolve and adapt along with the emerging emotional and social maturation of the juvenile. However, the consensus on prolonged justice is giving way to increasing demands for justice in real time (*traitement en temps réel*). Politicians, prosecutors, investigating judges, law enforcement personnel, mayors, and even some juvenile judges are calling for more surveillance, immediate hearings, expedited judgment and harsher sentences for repeat juvenile offenders. Their justification for doing so has focused on the imperative of individual accountability and parental responsibility. At issue in this political discourse is the preeminence of the enlightenment contract implying both rights and obligations. This contract is based on the opposition between the individual and the group; universal human rights, democratic principles, and political enfranchisement are premised on the primacy of the individual freed from the constraints of collective cultural traditions and obscurantist customs. While the reality of institutionalized discrimination within public schools and workplaces facing youth of 'immigrant' ancestry is sometimes acknowledged, government ministers and elected officials on the left and the right now consistently invoke at-risk youth to take responsibility for their own lives by simply avoiding bad influences and staying in school. By admonishing young people in the projects to accept individual responsibility for their actions, as Justice Minister Elisabeth Guigou did in a 1999 interview (24-25 January, *Le Monde*), when she said, "It's your life, your future, your responsibility," political elites give voice to a liberal meritocratic ethos of equal opportunity and free choice that ignores entrenched structures of inequality and discrimination. It is telling that children of North African immigrants are under-represented in elite educational institutions that prepare for top private and public sector positions. They are also largely disenfranchised politically as few hold elective office at the local or regional levels and none have been elected to the National Assembly (Abélès 2000). Similarly, they are also under-represented in the judiciary, the bar or law enforcement.

In the 1980s widespread media attention was given to the appearance of what were described as "totally new phenomena" in France, that is, the rise of "problem" or "sensitive" areas in on the periphery of French cities, the *banlieue*, populated by concentrations of immigrant groups from West and Northern Africa. The French term suburb (*banlieue*) has a long history and dates back to the thirteenth century when it referred to the perimeter of one league (*lieu*) around the city. The centuries following the medieval period saw the rise of a stigmatized liminal space on the city periphery increasingly associated with social marginals, uncontrolled movement, and the territorialization of poverty. Emerging industrialization in the 19th century provoked a rural exodus which added a new class of factory workers to this unstable population living outside the city. It was a century marked by numerous worker uprisings and one in which the "fear of suburban faubourgs" marked by the immorality and crime of the "dangerous classes" replaced that of "sick neighborhoods in the city." In the 19th century as now, illicit activity in the "zone," as the suburb became known, was the topic of constant coverage in a rapidly expanding popular press (Boyer and Lochard, 1998, pp. 45-49). This created heightened fears for safety among the bourgeois and aristocratic elites in the 19th century city and intensified the demand for the spatial demarcation of social groups. Today, the French suburb is the functional equivalent of the American ghetto.

The alarm generated by what were deemed unacceptably high proportions of certain immigrant groups in housing projects, schools, and workplaces is at the heart of the widely evoked theory of the threshold of tolerance that posits the need to impose strict limits on these unassimilable "ethnic" islands. It is important to emphasize that the settlement and assimilation of immigrants populations in France has always been perceived as problematic. Moreover, the arrival of Southern and Eastern European immigrants in the interwar period engendered the creation of stereotypes and racialized images which closely resemble those applied to non-European, and particularly, North African, immigrants in the postwar period. During the earlier period European immigrant peoples were depicted as unassimilable and, therefore, less civilized because of their adherence to collective customs and religious beliefs. Their presence was said to constitute a threat to the French social body because they were associated with urban ghettos, violence, delinquency, pollution, promiscuous sexuality and political extremism (Withol de Wenden, 1991, pp. 99-102).

Since the 1950s when colonial and postcolonial migratory flows brought increasing numbers of North and Western African peoples to do the least skilled and most poorly paid work in French industry, construction, and agriculture, the line defining cultural proximity in contrast to cultural distance has shifted and become progressively Europeanized. North African immigrants and, to a lesser extent, Eastern European immigrants have been redefined as a social and economic problem. Their presence blurs the line between the metropole and former colonies (de Rudder, 1980), creating anxiety and fueling discrimination based on cultural not biological difference (Balibar, 1988; Taguieff, 1990).

Beginning in 1981, when young *beurs* (youth with a common North African ancestry) in the Lyonnais suburb of Les Minguettes rioted, burning cars, looting supermarkets and destroying public property, media attention has focused on the periodic "social explosions" occurring within the suburban projects. Government ministers, politicians, social scientists, prosecutors, investigating judges, and law enforcement have focused on what they present as a 'new' delinquency of exclusion associated with these liminal urban spaces. The much publicized increases in rates of youth violence beginning in the 1980s, produced a fundamental shift away from a previously accepted understanding of delinquency as a social and economic problem to one centering on delinquency as a cultural lack. These discourses on both the left and the right of the political spectrum revealed an emerging consensus on territorialized collective violence as the most relevant interpretive frame for understanding a new delinquency of exclusion (Collovald, 2000, p. 39). In 1990 a new Ministry of the City was created whose function was defined in identical terms: a territorialized approach to social exclusion.

The purported success of zero tolerance sentencing in reducing crime in American cities like New York, attracted attention in France in the 1990s. Both the left and the right have been absorbed by the issue of *fracture sociale* or mounting social fragmentation engendered by high youth unemployment and the potential unemployability of a large underclass of young people of non-European ancestry. This fragmentation is seen as the result of an ever widening gulf between the French middle classes enjoying full entitlement as political subjects with access to education, health care, and jobs, and their Others spatially marginalized in the projects, un- or underemployed and dependant on a parallel underground economy (Wiewiorka, 1996).

In the 1990s, public discourses have stressed threats to public order, safety, and national cultural values as well as the problem of integration posed by the cultural difference of 'immigrant' youth offenders, the majority of whom are French citizens. These discourses circulated through print and visual media have spatialized violence in 'immigrant' areas and depicted it as endemic to diaspora communities whether Maghrebi, African, or Antillian. Media coverage has centered almost exclusively on the most visible and violent incidents in the suburban projects, not working class inner-city neighborhoods. This coverage relies discursively and visually on the trope of "time bomb" and evokes an "intifada of the *banlieue*" perpetrated by "ghetto hoodlums."

Well publicized short-term but sharp increases in juvenile arrests in the early 1990s—the majority for violence directed at property not people—coupled with ubiquitous media reports on the "recidivist" (representing only 5% of all delinquents but according to various estimates account for between 60-80% of violent crime) moved the question of public safety to the top of the political agenda (Baranger, 2001). This prompted complaints about "laxist" juvenile judges and a new look at the long delays—from 6 months to two years—between arrest and judgment mandated by the 1945 ordinance. The return of center-right governments to power from 1993-1997 and the 1995 election of center-right president Jacques Chirac witnessed the first legislative amendments to the 1945 Ordinance voted in 1995 and 1996. These empowered presecutors and police to initiate expedited arraignment hearings and to request immediate judgment in certain juvenile cases (Rufin, 1996).

In the wake of the 1997 legislative elections that established a "cohabitation" government with a center-right president and a leftist cabinet headed by Socialist Prime Minister Lionel Jospin, the fight against youth violence became a priority for the left as well as the right. Jospin and the heads of powerful ministries such as Justice, Interior, and Education organized national symposia privileging social scientific expertise and commissioned state studies on the related topics of safety, delinquency and violence. Although a Socialist, Jospin, began to distance himself from the longstanding leftist positions on juvenile delinquency as stemming from pervasive social and economic inequality. He has advocated more repressive measures in the treatment of "recidivist juvenile delinquents" and created a Council on Domestic Security to target delinquency in newly classified "marginalized zones" in 24 French departments (*Le Monde,* 7 January 1999; 29 August 2001). His government devoted additional resources to fund neighborhood police and local anti-crime initiatives in both bad neighborhoods and problem schools. Following publication of Interior Ministry statistics showing a 10% increase in arrests for crimes and misdemeanors over the first trimester of 2001, Jospin once again shifted away from longstanding leftist policies on urban renewal. At the October 1, 2001 meeting of the inter-ministerial committee on cities, Prime Minister Lionel Jospin, accompanied by now Labor Minister Elisabeth Guigou, Culture Minister Catherine Tasca, and Urban Minister Claude Bartolone, announced a costly five-year plan for the rasing of "urban ghettos" in the suburban projects. For Jospin poverty and delinquency could only be eradicated by avoiding concentrations of low-income housing in "sensitive zones," a euphemism for the suburban projects (*Le Monde,* 1 October 2001).

To what extent and in what terms can a burgeoning delinquency of exclusion be understood or justified? Examination of available statistics reveals the problems surrounding both the definition and representation of delinquency. Since it is illegal to collect data on the racial or ethnic origins of French citizens, once the children or grandchildren of immigrants take on French nationality, they disappear from the official statistics of rates of arrest, prosecution, and incarceration. Thus assessing the true nature and scope of a 'new' delinquency of exclusion associated with 'immigrant' youth is difficult indeed. Similarly, the state statistics on prison populations only differentiate between French and foreign prisoners as well as minors and adults. It is true that non-European foreigners are over-represented in French prisons; two thirds of the 15,000 foreign prisoners in French prisons in 1995 were from North Africa (53%) and Sub-Saharan Africa (16%) (Tournier, 1997, quoted in Wacquant, 1999, pp. 103-105). It bears reminding that in France too, the prison population increased by 39% between 1983 (39,086) and 1999 (53,998). However the rates of incarceration in France and the US are vastly different. Out of 100,000 people, 680 people in the US versus 90 in France were in prison in 1999 (Walmsley, 2000).

Second, both social scientists and judges have issued caveats regarding the French national police/gendarmerie statistics routinely reported in the mass media. These are based on the numbers of minors arrested and/or questioned by the police not those formally charged and prosecuted (Aubusson de Cavarly, 1998; Baranger, 2001; Wacquant, 1999). This category of young people, if considered over a longer period of time, varied considerably and had over a 20 year period increased only moderately—in sharp distinction to the alarmist media coverage. Of the total number of arrests, the percentage of minors dropped from 15.2% in 1980 to 11.2% in 1986. This rose to 17.9% between 1993-1996 and then again to 19.4% in 1997 (Aubusson de Cavarly, 1998, p. 270).

Third, this 'new' delinquency has been associated in media reports and public perception with offenders who are said to be younger and younger. However, many judges report that younger offenders are not necessarily more violent than in the past but are more visible because they are more routinely reported to law enforcement authorities by school principals and social workers and more aggressively prosecuted now than in the past by public prosecutors under pressure to bring charges for offenses committed by young children from dysfunctional and violent homes (Baranger, 2001).

Fourth, the 'new' delinquency is depicted by mass media as increasingly violent. Since 1986 arrests for aggravated assault, assault and battery, aand malicious vandalism have risen from 11% in 1974 to 23.8% in 1996 (Aubusson de Cavarly, 1998, p. 271). However, over half of these arrests were for vandalism and the destruction of property, not physical attacks. For the period receiving the most media attention, 1993-1997, the highest increases in arrests were for drug use, carrying weapons (knives and razors), insulting and assaulting an officer, and destruction of property (Aubusson de Cavalry, 1998, p. 274). The increases in certain categories of offenses nonetheless sharply skewed the overall statistical profile of juvenile delinquency. If one considers the sentencing patterns in four juvenile courts representative of the whole (Paris, St. Etienne, Gap, and Rennes) from 1990-1994, only 7.5% of the sentences involved voluntary or involuntary acts of violence; in contrast 43% of the sentences were for simple thefts, 22% for car or motorbike theft, and 4% of vandalism (Blatier, 1999).

In 1999 then Interior Minister Jean-Pierre Chevènement appeared on national television to denounce "the soft line on delinquents" taken by then Justice Minister Elisabeth Guigou as "wrong-headed," even "anachronistic" when confronting what he termed, "those little savages" (*sauvageons*). He declared his outrage that "juvenile delinquency had doubled since 1992" and urged repeal of key provisions of the 1945 Ordinance so that violent repeat offenders could be tried as adults and incarcerated in closed juvenile detention facilities. Chevènement's controversial use of the epithet "little savages" unleashed a virulent public debate in which Justice Minister Elisabeth Guigou, many Parisian juvenile judges, and social scientists ardently defended the legal protections afforded juveniles in the Ordinance of 1945. The polemic was ostensibly resolved by the Jospin government's refusal to further modify the 1945 Ordinance. Another legislative initiative designed to reinforce repressive approached to juvenile delinquency, introduced by the center-right deputies in the National Assembly was again decisively rejected in a vote on October 11, 2001 (*Le Monde*, 11 October 2001). However, much less attention has focused on the unflinching support of Justice Ministry Minister Guigou's and her successor Marylise Lebranchu for the modifications in juvenile law first legislated in 1995-96.

In France, the 1990s saw more aggressive prosecution of juveniles accused of both misdemeanors and crimes, higher rates of incarceration—both preventive detention pending trial and imprisonment following sentencing—as well as longer prison sentences for juveniles convicted of criminal offenses. The percentage of minors in the overall prison population—although small—has doubled from 2.5% in 1993 to 5.6% in 1998. Based on a one-day visit I made to the juvenile wing of the huge Fleury-Mérogis prison that took me months to arrange, the only young men I saw that day were of North and West African descent.

The consensus in favor of prevention and rehabilitation is beginning to erode in favor of demands for more surveillance, accelerated sentencing and harsher punishment for violent offenders—a category understood to be synonomous with marginalized suburban youth of immigrant ancestry. Although some juvenile judges and social scientists have strongly opposed the repressive approach and highlighted the factors fueling violence such as institutionalized racism and political disenfranchisement, they have had to situate their texts within dominant discursive formations initiated and widely disseminated by the media. These are premised on a series of oppositions between social chaos and order, unemployment and work, gratuitous violence and legitmate defense, as well as immigrants and "*Français de souche*" (the pedigreed or true French) (Taranger, 1994). Political narratives strongly inform dominant discourses on the youth offender and focus on enlightenment values such as individual rights and obligations to the national polity such as basic civility, self-respect, individual accountability, and parental responsibility. These discourses give voice to the enlightment promise of civil rights and equal protection under the law but effectively mask the structures of inequality and discrimination faced by these youth.

These public discourses are dangerous because, as juvenile judges Thierry Baranger and Thierry Pech point out, they give rise to the ominous spector of urban thugs associated with a culture of poverty "without faith or law, with a premafia organization, secret solidarities, music and linguistic codes" (24 January 1999, *Libération*). This is a culture, they note, that is denied legitimacy by political discourse but one which is inextricably linked to the juvenile delinquent as a newly threatening social category—a category largely conflated with that of non-European populations spatially segregated in suburban projects.

Notes

1. For more on juvenile homicide rates, see Charles Doyle, "Juvenile Delinquents and Federal Criminal Law: The Federal Delinquency Act and Related Matters," *CRS Report for Congress* (2001).

2. For more on juvenile weapons of choice, see the 1998 report on juvenile delinquency commissioned by Socialist Prime Minister Lionel Jospin and in particular the analysis of the annual Interior Ministry juvenile delinquency statistics by a well-known criminologist Bruno Aubusson de Cavarlay published in appendix 4 to that report: Christine Lazerges and Jean-Pierre Balduyck, *Réponses à la délinquance juvénile. Mission interministérielle sur la prévention et le traitement de la délinquance des mineurs* (Paris: La documentation française).

3. See Cécile Prieur, "Prioritaire, la 'bataille de l'insécurité' ne doit souffrir 'aucun laxisme,'" in *Le Monde*, 29 August 2001 for an overview of the new approach on accountability launched by Socialist Prime Minister Lionel Jospin at the Villepinte conference on delinquency in 1997, shortly after the legislative elections of the same year that returned the left to power.

References

Aubusson de Cavalry, Bruno. 1998. Statistiques. Notes de Bruno Aubusson de Cavalry. *Réponses à la Délinquance des Mineurs. Mission interministérielle sur la prévention et le traitement de la délinquance des mineurs* (Christine Lazerges and Jean-Pierre Balduyck). Paris: La documentation française.

Balibar, Etienne. 1988. *Race, nation, classe: les identités ambiguës*. Paris: La Découverte.

Bailleau, Francis and Catherine Gorgeon (Eds.). 2000. *Prévention et sécurité: vers un nouvel ordre social?*. Paris: Les éditions de la Délégation interministérielle à la ville.

Baranger, Thierry. 2001. A quels enfants allons-nous laisser le monde? Unpublished paper.

Blatier, Catherine. 1999. Juvenile Justice in France. The Evolution of Sentencing for Children and Minor Delinquants. *British Journal of Criminology* (39)2.

Body-Gendrot, Sophie. 2000. *The Social Control of Cities? A Comparative Perspective*. Oxford: Blackwell.

Boubeker, Ahmed. 1999. *Familles de l'intégration*. Paris: Stock.

Boyer, Henri and Guy Lochard. 1998. *Scènes de télévision en banlieues: 1950-1994*. Paris: l'Harmattan.

Collovald, Annie. 2000. Violence et délinquance dans la presse. *Prévention et sécurité: vers un nouvel ordre social?* (Francis Bailleau and Catherine Gorgeon, eds.). Paris: Editions de la Délégation interministérielle de la ville.

de Rudder, Véronique. 1980. La tolérance s'arrête au seuil. *Pluriel* 21.

MacMaster, Neil. 1991. The 'seuil de tolérance': the uses of a 'scientific' racist concept, *Race, Discourse, and Power in France*. Maxim Silverman, (Ed.). Aldershot: Avebury.

Rufin, Michel. 1996. *Protection de la jeunesse et délinquance juvénile*. Paris: La documentation française.

Taguieff, Pierre-André. 1990. *La force du préjugé: essai sur le racisme et ses doubles*. Paris: Gallimard.

Talbott, Margaret. 2000. The Maximum Security Adolescent. 10 September, *New York Times Magazine*.

Wacquant, Loïc. 1999. *Les prisons de la misère*. Paris: Raisons d'Agir.

Walmsley, Roy. 2000. Research Findings No.116: World Prison Population List, second edition. United Kingdom: Home Office Research, Development and Statistics Directorate.

Wieviorka, Michel. 1996. Violence, Culture and Democracy: A European Perspective. *Public Culture* 8.

Wihtol de Wenden, Catherine. 1991. North African Immigration and the French political imaginary, *Race, Discourse, and Power in France*. (Maxim Silverman, ed.). Aldershot: Avebury.

11

JORGE LUIS BORGES'S "THE LOTTERY OF BABYLON" AS ALLEGORY FOR THE CRIMINAL JUSTICE SYSTEM

Michael Nieto García

Jorge Luis Borges is most famous for his short stories, which often embody philosophical principles, such as philosophical idealism, or otherwise treat themes in metaphysics. "The Lottery of Babylon" is one such story. This tale is from Borges's collection of short stories, *El jardín de senderos que se bifurcan*, published in 1941. The original title, "La lotería en Babilonia," is sometimes translated as "The Lottery of Babylon" and sometimes as "The Babylon Lottery." The symbolic nature of the story imbues it with meaning that resonates with contemporary reality, though this could not have been anticipated or directly intended by the author. The short story offers important lessons for citizens of modern states, especially those who are largely oblivious to the problems of the increasing rate of incarceration and the long-term effects of prison and criminal justice policy. The sequelae of ill-considered policy, or the way in which unintended effects can arise from noble intentions, is one such lesson; that the lives and futures of all citizens—on both sides of the prison bars—are interconnected is another.

It is hyperbolic to call "The Lottery of Babylon" an allegory. Like all of Borges's short stories "The Lottery of Babylon" defies summarization or totalizing synopsis. Any fiction that is deemed a direct allegory for anything else risks quickly becoming a dead metaphor—appealing to a very specific time, place, and society and failing to elicit more meaningful responses from future generations or more universal readers. To claim that "The Lottery of Babylon" is predominantly about the carceral arrangements of the fictional city-state would be a distortion of the text. The short story is usually read allegorically to represent humankind's absurd existence and the desire to impose order and structure on a meaningless and completely random universe. "The Lottery of Babylon" is, however, a highly symbolic text and can be read, on one level, as an allegory of the criminal justice system.

Borges, himself, has written of the way in which the meaning of texts varies greatly according to the linguistic, social, and historical context in which they are written and read. In another short story, "Pierre Menard, autor del Quijote," Borges's narrator argues that a verbatim copy of Miguel de Cervantes's *Don Quixote* transcribed in a different era is a completely different text. Borges first read *Don Quixote* in English (though Borges is Argentine his grandmother was English and he learned to read English at an early age) and when he later read the original in Spanish he said he thought that it was a bad translation. Somewhere between what is lost in translation by the culling of quotes from an English translation of "La lotería en Babilonia" and the apocryphal claim of direct correspondence that the term "allegory" suggests is a reading of this short story that addresses a contemporary social problem. What is intended here is not a hermeneutic reading of the text but merely to point out some parallels, similarities, and lessons to be learned from an important piece of fiction.

The randomness of the universe and the desire to impose order on it is a theme that Borges fictionalized more than once. Borges had a talent for abstraction. But, unlike the prisoner—reassured by his minister that, "Stone walls do not a prison make, nor iron bars a cage"—who said, "Well, they've got me hypnotized then; that's all" (Borges, 1941, p.20), the problem of prisons, or the prison industrial complex (PIC), is very real and immediate, and not nearly so abstract.

Borges's abstract fiction overshadows his biography as well as his other fiction but, in regard to Borges's possible views on incarceration, there are at least two items of interest. Firstly, Borges was a great lover of the detective genre and coauthored a collection of detective stories, *Seis problemas para don Isidro Parodi,* or *Six Problems for Don Isidro Parodi*, with his good friend Aldolfo Bioy-Casares in 1942. The protagonist of this collection of detective stories is falsely jailed by a corrupt criminal justice system. Don Isidro solves crimes from his prison cell, using pure ratiocination, in the spirit of Poe's Dupin. Because his mobility is limited to a small cell he cannot bumble onto the correct solution, as Columbo (Peter Falk) does, or beat up bad guys to extort information, or be beat up by bad guys who like to brag and reveal the information needed to solve the crime, as so often happens to Raymond Chandlers's Philip Marlow. After solving one of the crimes and identifying the culprit Don Isidro says, "Maybe it's because I've been living in this establishment [prison] for so long that I no longer believe in punishment. Everyone finds punishment enough in his own wrongdoings. It's not right that honest men be other men's executioners" (Borges, 1942, p. 108). Of course, we can never completely know an author's intentionality, nor would it be entirely useful if we did. Don Isidro's opinion may or may not be largely reflective of Borges's views about incarceration as punishment or a form of retribution. It is, however, likely that, in his personal views, Borges was more critical of prisons in later years, as the threat of his own incarceration became more real.

The second item is of biographical interest. Borges was openly critical of many of Argentina's political leaders—something that culminated in the Perón years—with the result that police informers almost invariably attended his lectures. Borges's sister, Norah, was jailed for political reasons in 1948, during the Perón era. Norah and her mother were arrested for taking part in a protest. Borges's mother was released to house arrest but Norah was jailed and chose to remain in jail rather than write a letter of apology to Evita Perón. These are events that happened after the authorship of *Seis problemas para don Isidro Parodi* and "The Lottery of Babylon" but the political context of fascism and the concomitant threat of incarceration that arose with it were already issues that no Argentine could ignore in the early 1940s. That Borges would, at some point in his life, personally experience the incarceration of a family member resonates deeply with the theme of the impossibility of immunity from the negative aspects of the interdependent social system portrayed in the "The Lottery of Babylon."

"The Lottery of Babylon" is narrated in a detached voice by a Babylonian who describes the historical emergence and eventual institutionalization of a state lottery. The lottery evolves from the rewarding of purely beneficial outcomes to the eventual meting out of punitive "adverse outcomes"—incarceration by lottery. The rate of incarceration in Babylon greatly increases because these new adverse outcomes make the lottery much more popular: "Pushed to such a measure by the players [citizens], the company found itself forced to increase its adverse numbers" (Borges, 1941, p. 132). The explosion of the prison population of the United States in the last two decades is similarly due in large part to pressure from the citizenry. Politicians use shibboleths such as "tough on crime" and "the war on drugs" for political expediency. But it is only because enough people believe that lengthening prison sentences and refusing to legalize certain drugs will make their world safer that such slogans are effective tools for winning elections and increasing funding for non-violent drug convictions.

The Babylonians pride themselves on their logic and soon find a lack of symmetry in the system to be illogical: the winners get monetary rewards, while the losers get jail. The Babylonian consciousness of this aspect of the system is strikingly parallel to the modern observation that "the rich get richer and the poor get prison." The discrepancy between punishment and reward in Babylon was institutionalized at an earlier stage in the development of the lottery and it is only later that they realize their distaste for the outcome. The lack of symmetry is never remedied; indeed, it doesn't seem possible though, in the very randomness of the lottery itself, the Babylonians maintain a sense of justice.

Of the agents of the lottery we find that "Their moves, their management, were secret" (Borges, 1941, p. 132), which is the most intolerable aspect of the Prison Industrial Complex: its invisibility and lack of transparency. Policy is made behind closed doors—removed from public scrutiny. The United States exists as a democratic form of government, at least moderately so. Good democracy is possible only when significant numbers of citizens are able to make intelligent decisions based on the availability of pertinent information. The making of informed decisions at the micropolitical level constitutes the national political culture in the aggregate. It is this which drives public policy, including prison policy, to the degree that the people maintain a balance of power with the state, keeping it and its multiple bureaucracies in check. The state no longer inflicts corporal punishment or holds public executions because American culture has changed, and no longer abides either act. Unfortunately, the opinion polls that drive political campaign platforms are not always a reflection of the thoughts and feelings of an *informed* citizenry.

The opinions that voters hold are often distorted because prison policymakers are not forthcoming with the information that citizens need to make informed judgments about the system. That prison policy is largely made by unelected officials who purposefully keep information about the prison industrial complex from the people is a mockery of democracy. In the absence of publicized information from within the prison industrial complex along with a dearth of investigative reporting from journalists—and the lack of more complex coverage of incarceration and its social effects in the media—there will continue to be less than the majority constituency needed for democratic change to come about.

The transparency and information problem is inherent in many bureaucratic institutions. When such institutions or agencies are running well people are far happier to not have to think about the social issues that the bureaucratic entities deal with. The success of bureaucratic governance ever poses the risk of sliding into a custodial state. The appeal of the luxury of not having to deal with politics and governance allows transparency to lapse so that when the agency is no longer fulfilling its social role in the best interests of the people no one is likely to sound the alarm and not enough people have enough information to make intelligent decisions or, even, to hold informed opinions on the matter.

The Babylonian Company, like most bureaucracies, has an ineffective communication system for denunciations or critiques of the system. In Babylon people place their accusations in the fissures of a dusty aqueduct, certain stone lions, or in a "sacred latrine called Kafka" (Borges, 1941, p. 133). Deliberately thwarting communication with the citizens it is supposed to represent, the Company never replies directly to complaints (Borges, 1941, p. 133). Communication between citizens of the United States and the prison policymakers is not much more effective than the Babylonian method of dropping notes in the fissures of a dusty aqueduct. One could count on one hand the number of New Yorkers who can call up the wardens or administrators at the New York State penitentiaries in Elmira or Auburn to critique the administration's interpretation of penal legislation and ACA (American Corrections Association) guidelines. Prisons do not even have public suggestion boxes, as even the smallest fast food chains do. There is simply no public forum for talking about how prisons should operate, what their long-term goals should be, or what their mission to society is.

Local sheriffs are elected officials but prison administrators are not. In most states only new parole board members and the top official, for instance, the Director of the State Department of Corrections, of the state prison agency are appointees of the Governor. They are subject to the people only when they make a decision that is so unpopular that the Governor feels that he must remove them from office or reprimand them because his own political popularity is at stake. The absence of real and regular discourse between prison administration and the public leaves the citizenry completely at the mercy of the prison industrial complex in the same way that the Babylonians are subject to the vagaries and tyranny of the Company.

Getting prison administrations to listen to constituents of the areas they serve is impeded by a lack of checks and balances—gubernatorial decrees, state approval of their budgets, and prisoner lawsuits—are too infrequent or, in the case of the latter, ineffective to make the administrators responsive to the society they serve. And even if the prison policymakers in one state were to increase communication with citizens and make successful reforms the improvement might not spread to other states. The prison culture and daily routine of each prison vary greatly, largely devolving from institutional choices made by the prison administration—how professional the staff will be, which prison programs and activities will be emphasized, the extent to which the prisoner's typical day will be routinized versus allow them to make personal choices. But the variation between prisons is also a source of reform as successful innovations or completely new models in one state or prison can be adopted by other prisons.

When curious citizens ask for information they are often told, usually by the prison's public relations officer (read: spin doctor), that keeping people in the dark is necessary because average citizens can't understand the complexities of the system and releasing too much information would only compromise security. The result is that most Americans know nothing about how short-sighted practices that are convenient for prison staff may have detrimental long-term effects for larger society. Most will know little or nothing of private sector business interests in maintaining current prison practices that benefit their special interests, even if they are harmful to larger society. The overmedication of prisoners is an example of both factors. This is a lucrative enterprise for the pharmaceutical industry—especially the makers of psychotropic medications, which are not targeted by the "war on drugs." Excessively medicating the prisoners is convenient for corrections staff but not a poisonous panacea for the prisoners, their families, and the communities they go back to when released from prison. Expensive mind-altering medications on which the former prisoners are often physiologically or psychologically dependent are stopped overnight—with predictably volatile consequences. Nevertheless, people are told to trust the experts: the prison administrators, their medicine-administering psychologists, and the rehabilitation and activities committees that determine the level of support for prison education.

In Babylon any reform of the system is supposedly so complex that it "cannot be understood except by a handful of specialists" (Borges, 1941, p. 133). But this logic of leaving everything to the experts can undermine democracy, whose founding principle is that the people are capable—intelligent enough to make sound decisions, when well informed—of ruling themselves. The major role of the experts should not be to take hold the reins of a custodial state but to help people understand the issues by disseminating information and publicly debating points and counterpoints, without forcing their own interpretations on people.

The United States is stuck in a vicious circle. Not enough people care about prison issues because not enough people have heard enough about it beyond superficial sound bites. There will be no change at the national level nor that of trendsetter states, such as New York and California, until enough people care enough to get politicians to open up prison policymaking to public scrutiny and to initiate reforms that consider the long-term goals and consequence of new policy. But not enough people will care about prison issues until there is more transparency from the policymakers and their institutions. Grassroots movements for prison reform will have to focus, first, on increasing transparency in policymaking and the administration of prisons so that a critical mass of newly-informed citizenry will demand change. Significant prison reform will not be denied when enough people see how the issue affects them personally.

"The Lottery in Babylon" begins with an allusion to the intertwined fates of all Babylonian citizens. Masters and slaves share the same fates—masters are slaves and slaves are masters. The transiently-privileged class is intimately aware of what it is like to be a member of the underclass. The first-person narrator intones, "Like all men in Babylon I have been a proconsul; like all, a slave; I have also known omnipotence, opprobrium, jail" (Borges, 1941, p. 130). Later in the story we see that the consequences of some seemingly innocuous actions mandated by the lottery can be utterly terrifying. Because everything is related to everything else such acts have direct consequences for all of the citizens of Babylon. Both winners and losers recognize that they are cast in the same boat on the chaotic sea of the Babylonian lottery.

One of the reasons for the continued rise in incarceration rates is that the middle classes and above—who exert the most influence on political power—do not imagine themselves ever being imprisoned. Their emotional instinct is that electing politicians who promise to be "tough on crime" is the commonsense solution to lowering the crime rate and keeping society civil. The perception of immunity from the crime punishment mechanisms that they endorse—or are oblivious to—tends to distort their sense of justice such that they are seduced by an unattainable ideal while their capacity to recognize the real outcomes of such policies atrophies. The immediate solution of locking up those accused of criminal acts gives a tangible sense of completion that belies the more complex reality of the further-reaching effects of such policy. Most people are less likely to see themselves as victims of these long-term effects than to see themselves as beneficiaries of the short-term solution. Locking someone up is a highly visible act but monitoring what happens behind the prison walls, keeping intact family connections and other social support nets for the prisoners and their families on the outside, assimilating released prisoners back into the community, and the financial and social costs of incarceration are less immediate, less visible, and less-frequently addressed parts of the problem.

The most convincing self-interest argument for reforming or abolishing the current manner and rate of incarceration is that stakeholders, voters, and policymakers will succumb, themselves, to whatever system they endorse or abide. To sacrifice the rights and civil liberties of any one individual jeopardizes everybody's rights and civil liberties, including one's own. In tolerating mass incarceration a person increases her own chances of being imprisoned. But the self-interest argument is only effective if everyone recognizes how prison policy affects them directly and indirectly.

The problem is that—for most of the decision-makers and those who are most politically influential—to be impacted directly is not very likely and recognition of the indirect effects of incarceration is unlikely to be of a significant level, failing to act as a catalyst to change. Like the winners in Babylon, the "winners" in modern societies tend to reap their benefits financially. The "winners" of society enjoy greater affluence and are unlikely to be incarcerated for property crimes, which account for the vast majority of the prison population. The affluent are also more likely to evade incarceration for drug offences—another huge sector of the prison population. And, when they are incarcerated, it tends to happen well into maturity, when they are no longer as impressionable and vulnerable as the vast majority of new arrestees, who tend to be minorities under the age of twenty five. All of this gives them the perception of insulation from the possibility of incarceration.

More powerful than a rational awareness of indirect consequences—such as reading statistics that show that that the rate of recidivism for former prisoners is unacceptably high or that stiffer sentencing does not have the desired deterrent effect on crime—is the emotional impact of being directly affected or threatened by the prison industrial complex. If the fictional case study of "The Lottery of Babylon" raises an awareness of the potential threats of absurd policies the promulgation of actual case studies of injustice and it-could-happen-to-you celebrity cases can disabuse those who don't think it can happen to them of their false sense of security. As it stands the bulk of the population is not aware of the extent of false imprisonment or legal imprisonment which, though technically legitimate, is unjust.

Most don't have a sense of the cruel ironies of how convictions are gotten. Still far too low is the level of awareness of the extent to which punishment often correlates less with commission of a crime than with who "cooperates" with prosecutors first and to what extent. Even aside from the snitch system—which works best when both the witness and the accused are guilty of some crime—many are "detained" (read: imprisoned) for no crime other than being unfortunate enough to witness someone else commit a crime. Far too often the perpetrator of the crime can be out on bail while the person who has committed no crime is held indefinitely as a material witness.

The risk of incarceration of innocent people is further increased because the system depends so heavily on the testimony of witnesses that an accusation is almost tantamount to conviction—to assume that the accused are frequently innocent would undermine the viability and effectiveness of witness testimony. There is an anecdote about a man sought by law enforcement authorities. Six different poses of the man were circulated as wanted posters, with the hope that the different angles and profiles of the man would make it easier to identify him. The chief of the local precinct calls headquarters later that night to report, "We've got five of them and the sixth is under surveillance." This story is a little less than fact but a lot more than fiction: Les Krantz (1993, p. 229) reminds us of a study in the U.S. by Dennis Cogan and Michael Radelet that found that since 1900, 23 innocent people have been executed and since 1970, 46 people on death row have been found innocent and been released. Krantz adds that: "most of those wrongfully convicted were poor and could not afford a defense attorney; half were black or Hispanic" (Krantz, 1993, p. 229).

A greater awareness of specific examples of such cases and the extent to which they occur would jolt many into realizing that their own willingness to abide the incarceration of others may prove instrumental in securing their own "detention"—even if they have not committed a crime. By changing the attitudes and opinions of a significant number of citizens the national culture can be changed—and that, in the United States, is a prerequisite for getting the legislators, criminal justice institutions, and policymakers to reform unacceptable practices, attitudes, and policies.

The ratio of false imprisonments to legitimate convictions that is considered an acceptable number in the name of maintaining law and order will vary from person to person. Invariably a very high number is tolerated by most people, provided they are not personally and directly affected. Apathy tends to win out over rational evaluations of even the most important political issues. Policy reform is seldom initiated by pure ratiocination—the way Don Isidro Parodi solves crimes—but by felt experience. Few who have not spent significant time in jail or prison will be motivated to change a system that is only cognitively intolerable.

When members of the criminal justice system—police officers, prosecutors, judges and others who never expected to be convicted of a felony—end up in prison their attitudes about incarceration change overnight. Even when they admit to having committed the crime that they have been imprisoned for—and feel that they should be punished—they quickly join the other prisoners in denouncing the punishment as excessive, inappropriate, and doing more harm than good to society and humanity.

Almost none of those who do the sentencing and those who manage the prisons have ever been behind bars. They lack the epistemic privilege needed to create just policies. If legislators, judges, prosecutors, and police officers did time there would be lot fewer people in prison and they would be serving much shorter terms. One aspect of the criminal justice system is that convicted felons are not allowed to work in it. Unlike the former proconsul in "The Lottery of Babylon," none of the key prison perpetuators are former slaves or prisoners—and those who do experience prison will not be allowed to return to their former positions.

In Isaac Asimov's short story "The Winnowing" (1976) a covert First-World think tank plots to employ triage as a preemptive strike to curtail overpopulation.

They plan to distribute a drug that is lethal to the majority of the world population—varying randomly with genetic makeup—in relief food supplies. The schemers are rationally convinced that their plan is the most humane solution to the threat of overpopulation, which would cause even greater suffering. That they do not know, beforehand, who will be affected by the drug and who will be immune to it absolves their consciences of all sense of personal responsibility.

The scientist who manufactured the drug is morally incensed when he realizes the plan and invites the conspirators to a parley to discuss the status of the project. The scientist remains unconvinced by their rationalizations but at the end of the session he agrees with them—so much so, he tells them, that they should not object to the fact that he has contaminated the sandwiches that they all just ate with the drug (Asimov, 1976). Needless to say, the insidious solution is never carried out.

In Borges's Babylon every proconsul will remember his experiences as a slave when deciding on the treatment of slaves. But in the United States there is no way to get the prison policymakers and criminal justice system players to eat the prison sandwich. Imagine the changes that would come about if every prison warden, every prosecutor, and every judge had to spend a year in prison before assuming their positions in the criminal justice system.

Such a solution to the prison problem is unlikely, as is innovative experiment of the magnitude that the Babylonians engage in. Power is diffuse enough in the United States that no single person—from legislators to federal judges to prison wardens and governors—has enough power to easily correct obvious problems in the system. Passing the buck is the closest that many bureaucrats come to social responsibility. It would currently be political suicide for most politicians to do the right thing since many of the most reliable voters have strong ideological opinions—seeing everything in black and white—unmitigated by the type of public education about prisons that would help many citizens to form more accurate views on the issue.

It is imperative to democracy that issues as complex as the prison problem not be easily solvable by a single person or small group of insiders. American governance was structured to separate and balance institutional powers so that a single mandate cannot solve an issue that has roots in several different sectors of the economy, society, and society's institutions. But the test of democracy's effectiveness is in being able to solve societal problems, such as the rise of the prison industrial complex, from a groundswell of public opinion or even from the impetus of a minority group of informed citizens.

The prison problem must be dealt with from many different sectors of society. Existing prison volunteer projects, alternative education programs for prisoners, spiritual and psychological guidance, and other such prison programs are a vital part of the solution. In addition to the prison reform movements that critique American prisons from the outside working from within the existing system will be vital. Even if the existing institution of prison were abolished overnight many of the key players in the criminal justice system would maintain their old networks so that reform that does not come, at least partially, from within can be no true reform at all. Lobbying by influential interest groups is, taking the bad with the good, part and parcel of American democracy and a likely precondition for any significant reform. For more sweeping changes to be made prison reform movements will have to accrete significant numbers of supporters from across all strata and sectors of society.

The prison issue is one on which no one can afford to remain neutral. In Henry Adams's novel *Democracy*—a mordant condemnation of the corruption of the Grant administration—a fictional government appointee and historian, Mr. Gore, expounds upon democracy as a form of government. Implicit in his assessment is the need for an informed public. When Mr. Gore is asked if he thinks that Democracy is the best government he replies,

> I believe in democracy. I accept it. I will faithfully serve and defend it. I believe in it because it appears to me the inevitable consequence of what has gone before it. Democracy asserts the fact that the masses are now raised to higher intelligence than formerly. All our civilization aims at this mark. We want to do what we can to help it. I myself want to see the result. I grant it is an experiment, but it is the only direction society can take that is worth its taking; the only conception of its duty large enough to satisfy its instincts; the only result that is worth an effort or a risk. Every other possible step is backward, and I do not care to repeat the past. I am glad to see society grapple with issues in which no one can afford to be neutral. (Adams, 1952, p. 50)

The narrator of "The Lottery of Babylon" ends by concluding that everything in Babylon is an infinite game of chance but the prison industrial complex did not arise by disinterested chance and no nation can afford to passively accept their conversion into a prison nation. Public education about prisons is necessary. Cultural attitudes concerning prisons will not change until enough people known a lot more than is currently commonly known about the prison industrial complex and what being incarcerated is really like. Until then there will be no critical reassessment of prisons in theory or in praxis—both of which must carefully consider and monitor the long-term effects of policy. Most importantly, citizens must realize and feel that they are subject to anything they allow to be perpetrated on any other individual, sector of society, or society—as each person's fate is interconnected in a complex society and in a world of interdependent societies and economies, as is everybody's in Babylon.

References

Adams, H. 1952. *Democracy: An American Novel*. NY: Farrar, Straus, and Young.

Asimov, I. 1976. The Winnowing. *The Bicentennial Man and Other Stories*. Garden City, NY: Doubleday.

Borges, J. L. 1983. *Ficciones*. Barcelona: Seis Barral.

Borges, J. L. 1981. The Lottery in Babylon. Trans. A. Kerrrigan. In E. R. Monegal and A. Reid (Eds.), *Borges: A Reader*. New York: Dutton.

Borges, J. L., & Bioy-Casares, A. 1981. *Six Problems for Don Isidro Parodi*. Trans. N. T. di Giovanni. New York: Dutton.

Krantz, L. 1993. *America by the Numbers: Facts and Figures from the Weighty to the Way-out*. Boston: Houghton Mifflin.

PART III

African and Comparative Perspectives on Penal Law and Prisons

12

DEVELOPMENT CRISES, PREDA-TORY REGIMES, AND PRISONS IN AFRICA: AN IMPEDANCE-FACILITA-TION PERSPECTIVE

Seth N. Asumah

INTRODUCTION

In the post independence era, African nation states continue to be submerged in the crises of development. These nation states are still struggling with developmental goals of economic growth, equity, stability, democracy, and autonomy. Most of these goals were defined by the North (European and North American nation states) for African countries in the post-colonial era. The first two goals are economic goals—economic growth and equity. Stability and democracy are political goals, whereas autonomy is both an economic and a political goal. In order to attain these goals, prison models, also from the North, have been borrowed by African leaders as instruments of impedance and/or facilitation to enable them to reach sustainable development.

Governments and regimes in Africa desirous of transcending development crises have capitalized on Euro-American models of prisons as institutions and implements for impedance and facilitation in political participation and human rights. Yet, because of the levels of underdevelopment in African countries, the process of acquiring alien institutions in the form of prisons has created a policy cul de sac for most African governments owing to the fact that they have insufficient resources to maintain these prisons while the prison population continues to grow.

It was surprising that the first Pan African Conference on "Prison Conditions in Africa" organized in Kampala, Uganda in 1996, tackled prison and penal reform by addressing major themes such as prison conditions, treatment of prisoners, good prison management, the reduction of the use of imprisonment, the role of civil society in penal reform, and the reintroduction of African models of prisons. Nonetheless, none of the themes made any direct connection between development goals and prison reform. Nevertheless, it was unforgivable that the September 2002 "Pan African Conference on Penal and Prison Reform in Africa" hosted by Burkina Faso and held under the guidance of the African Commission of Human and People's Rights (ACHPR), with support from Penal Reform International (PRI) and the African Penitentiary Association (APA), again failed to endeavor to create a platform for a discourse on development goals and prisons. Although the 2002 Conference produced a fairly strong "Ouagadougou Declaration on Accelerating Penal and Prison Reform in Africa," it is certainly arguable that such reforms cannot be sustained without a thorough discussion and analyses of the relationships between development goals of African nation states and prison reform.

In this chapter, I argue that predatory regimes in Africa, in their frustration in dealing with development crises and absent concrete development goals, have kowtowed to prison models from their former colonizers to violate human rights, through facilitation and impedance for sustenance of predatory hegemonic power, therefore making penal and prison reform a policy cul de sac. The interesting thing about this study, for me, is the ability to analyze development goals and efforts of different African regimes using prisons as the primary tools for their socio-political processes of facilitation and impedance.

By facilitation, I am referring to a socio-political process by which regimes maintain their hegemony and attain their development goals by utilizing penal and prison systems through detaining opponents or perceived socio-political deviants to increase the rate of success. Impedance, on the other hand, refers to how predatory regimes use penal and prison systems as tools for thwarting the efforts of their opponents and perceived socio-political deviants by detaining or putting them in penitentiaries. If most African regimes are increasing their prison populations, but that practice is devoid of development goals that facilitate prison reforms, then scholars and policy makers should revisit the theories and concepts of development and underdevelopment in order to fine-tune their effects on prison reforms.

DEVELOPMENT REDEFINED

What therefore is development? Development is a process of reaching self-sufficiency, self-reliance, and advancement. Development may include growth, but growth itself is not a necessary condition for development. Growth is an increase in productivity measured in gross national product (GNP), gross domestic product (GDP) or physical quality of life index (PQLI). If the general populace is growing and developing but prison infrastructures are lagging behind such growth and development, what does that discrepancy represent? If in many African nation states imprisonment remains the cornerstone of reformatory and correctional penal systems but this process remains far behind the galloping rate of other processes of development, then what should African countries do to create a state of equilibrium between prison reform and other development goals? I will address these questions after clarifying some of the conceptual framework needed for analyses in the article. The nature and style of governance of regimes in Africa are pertinent to the processes of facilitation or impedance and the usage of prisons. Many of the governments that have ruled African nation states can be considered predatory regimes because of the intensity and scope of their power dimensions and reliance on prisons to sustain their hegemony.

PREDATORY REGIMES AND PRISONS

What types of regimes are called predatory regimes? Predatory regimes are ferocious, and they prey on their own people. Most of them dwell in a state of domination and subjugation. Predatory regimes are involved in the politics of anti-politics and political pornography—an obscene and distasteful practice in politics. Predatory regimes create vampire states by using prisons as their most effective institution for dealing with problems and issues within the body politic. South Africa, during apartheid, Uganda, Sierra Leone, Morocco, Liberia, Nigeria, Zimbabwe, and Tanzania are all examples of predatory regimes with vampire elite in Africa. It is important to note that even though there have been regime changes in some of these nation states, the lingering effects of predatory politics continue to affect the prison infrastructures and population today. Below are selected African countries with official prison capacity and total population that reflects the endeavors of the vampire elite in those nation states.

Table 1: Official Capacity and Total Prisons' Population

	Country	Official Capacity	Prison Population
1	Botswana	3,198	6,413
2	Kenya	10,000	28,064
3	Lesotho	2,200	2,552
4	Madagascar	12,962	20,109
5	Malawi	5,500	7,341
6	Morocco	35,000	48,600
7	Nigeria	41,851	44,797
8	South Africa	99,534	162,638
9	Tanzania	21,118	45,611
10	Zimbabwe	16,000	19,256

Source: United Nations African Institute for the Prevention of Crime and the Treatment of Offenders (UNAFRI) 2001.

Common characteristics of African prisons include the absolute neglect in development goals and the galloping rate of increase of the inmate population because of the activities of predatory regimes and the processes of impedance and facilitation. Kibuka (2001) carefully notes,

> ...in many African countries, evidence abounds of harsher penalties being imposed in the form of lengthening periods of imprisonment. In many countries, despite noticeable rapid growth rates in national populations over the past twenty years or so, and the widespread increasing incidence of crime rates [which is concomitant with development and urbanization] leading also to escalating numbers of individuals being sent to prison, there is hardly any evidence of new penal institutions being constructed in the same time period (Kibuka, 2001, p. 1).

This is obviously a problem of development goals devoid of any consideration for improvements in prison infrastructures and human rights conditions.

Also, in the same vein, Ayittey (1998), who is assessing the quality of "vampire" regimes and how they have destroyed most political institutions, except the penal systems and prisons, asserts,

> the inviolate ethic of the vampire elite is the self-aggrandizement and self-perpetuation in power. To achieve those objectives, they subvert every key institution of government: the civil service, judiciary, military, media, and banking. As a result, these institutions become paralyzed. Laxity, ineptitude, indiscipline, and lack of professionalism thus flourish in the public sector. Of course, Africa has a police force and judicial system to catch and persecute the thieves. But the police themselves are highway robbers, under orders to protect the looters, and many of the judges are themselves crooks. As a result, there are no checks against brigandage (Ayittey, 1998, p. 153).

The irony of this statement is that while most state agencies are suffering from a paralysis of underdevelopment, prisons become the major instrument and institution for sustaining the hegemonic power of the vampire elite in these predatory regimes.

Since I am more interested in political developmental crises and how prisons have served as facilitators or impedance, I will briefly itemize the crises of political development. These include identity, legitimacy, penetration, participation, and distribution crises. In order to reach a point of sustainable development, African regimes must transcend these development crises by creating and attaining development goals that should be inclusive of penal and prison reforms. Political leaders in Africa have continued to struggle with all the above-mentioned crises, and in their frustration, prisons that are supposed to be used to confine serious criminals are being used to silence political opponents and perceived socio-political deviants.

Identity crisis refers to how the general populace identifies with the nation state. Here, the general populace would have to transcend tribalism, cronyism, and nepotism as they relate to clans, tribes, and nations in order for development to take place. Many predatory regimes are not well equipped with institutions of civil society to deal with identity crises. These regimes have no patience in identity polities, so they either impede the process of identity formation or facilitate the creation of superordinate groups by imprisoning subordinate ones. In this connection, prisons have been used as instruments for silencing tribes or clans who refuse to identify with the state or conform to the political whims of predatory regimes.

Penetration crises include how regimes uphold the rule of law in a particular country. How does the regime enforce rules, regulations, and law without the threat or use of force in prisons? Many predatory regimes are not law-governing nation states. Their only cannon is a corrupt criminal justice system backed by inhumane prison systems. Predatory regimes have legitimacy problems. To compensate for their lack of legitimacy in providing a framework for a law-governing nation state, they overly depend on a process and institution of incarceration to realize their development goals.

Participation crises involve both autonomous and mobilized participation. Mobilized participation involves force, coercion, and quid pro quo actions. Predatory regimes utilize facilitation and impedance in the participatory process. Prisons are utilized as the catalyst for both facilitation and impedance in political participation. Opposition parties always end up in prison. Non-conformists or perceived socio-political deviants also find themselves in jails that are underdeveloped, overcrowded, and infested with diseases.

The last, distribution crises, include the dispersion of power and resources. Hegemonic, predatory regimes maintain power for themselves. Power and resources are amassed for self-gratification. Here again, penitentiaries and their harsh conditions serve not as instruments for behavior modification, but a harbinger for cruel and unusual punishment for the masses and political opponents who must share power and resources with the vampire elites if these nation states are to reach a stage of sustainable development.

COLONIAL PRISON SYSTEMS IN THE POST COLONIAL ERA: THE EVIDENCE

During colonialism and the pre-independence periods, the British, French, Portuguese, Belgians, Dutch, and Germans all utilized prisons as instruments and institutions of impedance in the political process by detaining African leaders, such as Kwame Nkrumah of Ghana, Jomo Kenyatta of Kenya, and Nnamdi Azikiwe of Nigeria for demanding independence immediately. It was rather ironic that after these African leaders secured their independence from the colonizers and maintained power, they became dependent upon the same colonial penal and prison systems and used them against their own African people.

Kwame Nkrumah, for instance, propounded the Protective Detention Act, which put in prison anyone who challenged the audacity of the president. Nkrumah silenced his opposition by locking them up. Predatory leaders such as Mobutu Sese Seko, Kamusu Banda, Idi Amin Dada, and Sekou Toure, who accused the British and the French for using prisons to impede the political process, found themselves doing exactly what the colonizers did—capitalizing on the prison systems by making it known to the masses that there was no room for opposition during developmental crises. The facilitation—impedance approach for utilizing prisons for political gains has continued to the present time. Successors of these founding fathers of African nation states have continued to use the archaic prison system even today for facilitation and impedance.

The Executive Director of the African Division of Human Rights Watch, Peter Takirambudde, puts it succinctly, "Eritreans, who struggled valiantly to become free and independent, deserve to have their human rights respected, unfortunately the government continues to deny them that opportunity.... [by putting them in jail]" (Takirambudde, 2003, p.1). Unfortunately, for many

African nation states since independence, the courts and other institutions in Africa have increased, but the functions and number of prisons remain the same—causing overcrowding, infections from diseases, and human rights abuses.

Prisoners in vampire states in Africa who refuse to compromise their political principles are treated with cruelty, and their families are denied access to communicate information of their conditions to the outside world. In Burundi, some 9,000 people were in jail in the year 2000, some of them were Hutus who were accused of crimes related to the 1993 massacres but have not yet been tried (Human Rights Watch, 2003, p.1). Similar situations could be found in Ethiopia where 3,537 new detainees are held for national security reasons (ibid, p.2). The objector may argue that even in the United States these days many people are kept in jails for national security reasons. That point is quite correct, nonetheless, Ethiopia has not yet suffered a terrorist attack as monumental as that of September 11, 2001. As much as I do not condone imprisonment without conviction, I think the rule of law and prison systems in many African nation states desperately need overhauling. Tunisia has one of the highest per capita incomes in Africa, but one of the worst prison records. Beatings by guards are frequent and disciplinary measures are degrading and cruel. Political prisoners are shuttled incessantly among prisons—forcing families to travel great distances for visits.

In Egypt, the Egyptian Organization for Human Rights (EOHR) and the Human Rights Center for the Assistance of Prisoners (HRCAP) reported recently the over 2,000 Islamist prisoners were detained without charges and most of them are sick because of prison conditions in Fayoum Prison. Medical care for prisoners is grossly inadequate. Inmates have to stand with their hands raised above their heads facing the wall when talking to doctors to determine their illness. Doctors examine prisoners as far as 10 yards away and insult most of them for faking their illness (Human Rights Watch, 2001).

South Africa presently has about 179,000 prisoners, making it second only to the United States in the number of inmates per capita (Reuters NewMedia, 2003, p.1). Under apartheid, the South African government declared many political offences as criminal ones. By 1991, the African National Congress (ANC) claimed that there were over 5,000 political prisoners incarcerated in that country (Savage, 2000, p.2). Even after the Indemnity Act, which facilitated the release of many prisoners, was enacted, the legacy of the predatory apartheid regime continues to haunt the present government. South African prisons have become even more dangerous because prison gangs with HIV have adopted a new form of punishment labeled as "slow puncture," a practice in which HIV-positive prisoners rape disobedient prisoners or those with divergent political viewpoints. South Africa has the highest number of people living with HIV in the world and with a population of 42 million people, the country accounts for 4.8 million people with HIV/AIDS (Reuters, 2002, p. 1) Overcrowding is a common phenomenon in South Africa's prisons. The prison population suffers worse atrocities because in 2000, for instance, 63,965 inmates who have not been charged or convicted still accounted for over 75 percent of the overflow population in prison (Human Rights Watch, 2003, p.5).

In Ghana, overcrowding at the Sekondi Central, Ekuase, and Nsawam prisons has led to the spreading of yellow fever, diarrhea, typhoid fever, pneumonia and cerebral spinal meningitis among inmates. In the same country, political prisoners who were pardoned by the new regime in December 2001 are still in prison today—they lock them up, but they do not rehabilitate prisoners in Africa. In Uganda, a prisoner claims, "we used to have breakfast and blankets, now we have nothing" (Human Rights Watch, 2001).

Most of the African prisoners in vampire states eat only once a day and are treated like animals, while the predatory elite eat everyday and suck the economic blood of their nation states. In Rwanda and many other African nation states that are struggling with development crises, the predatory regimes have called upon families of inmates to bring food to their family members. Nonetheless, proximity is not in favor of these families who have to walk or travel for many miles before reaching their destination if they are lucky enough. These accounts are just a few of the plethora of prison cases in predatory regimes struggling with developmental crises.

CONCLUSION

It could be deduced from the discussion above that the marginal propensity to transcend development crises in Africa directly affects the marginal propensity to maintain standard correctional facilities and human rights provisions. It is obviously not enough to merely reach sustainable development by neglecting human rights and prisons infrastructures. Development, industrialization, Westernization, and urbanization are all concomitant with increments in crime rates and political divergence. These processes in and by themselves call for new visions for penal and prison reforms in Africa. Should developing nations and African nation states, in particular, struggling with development crises borrow prison models from the North even though they do not have the facilities and capacity to make them work? Perhaps African countries may want to revisit their ancestral ideas of reforming and rehabilitating offenders into good citizens instead of inheriting a colonial legacy of locking prisoners up without lifting them up.

Note

I am deeply indebted to Ms. Sandra Long, Tully High School Social Studies Department, for her insight, patience and assistance in the research process for this chapter.

References

Ayittey, George. 1998. *Africa in Chaos*, New York: St. Martin's Griffin.

Human Rights Watch, December 2003. Prisons in Africa. http//www.hrw.org/prisons/africa.html

Human Rights Watch, December 2001. Prisons in Africa http//www.hrw.org/prisons/ Africa.html

Kibuka, Eric. 2001. *Prisons in Africa*. United Nations Programme Network Institutes on World Prisons Population: Facts, Trends and Solutions. Vienna, Austria.

Reuters NewMedia, November 21, 2002. South Africa Prison Gangs Use AIDS Rape as Punishment. Reuters Limited, Johannesburg, South Africa.

Savage, Kate. 2000. Negotiating the Release of Political Prisoners in South Africa. Center for the Study of Violence and Reconciliation. Harvard University.

Takirambudde, Kate. 2000. Negotiating the Release of Political Prisoners in South Africa. Center for the Study of Violence and Reconciliation. Harvard University.

13

RACE AND ROBBEN ISLAND: THE POLITICS OF PENAL ORGANIZATION AND ITS RELATIONSHIP TO APARTHEID

Rashad Shabazz

From the 1960's until after the end of apartheid, Robben Island prison held numerous anti-apartheid political activists. It was the capital for political incarceration in South Africa, as it had been since the late eighteenth and early nineteenth century. Although it has been described in categorically different ways—as a "university", "hell-hole" and site for political struggle and torture—and is difficult, if not impossible, to make sense of Robben Island in a fixed way. The way it overlaps with the historical realities of colonialism, capitalism, and white supremacy, for example, makes Robben Island as much tool for domination as an institution for safety. I would like to suggest that one of the central ideologies that informed the day-to-day practices on the island was racism. Racism was at the heart of the island's function, and at least according to one scholar, the island deeply informed the identity of the nation. Literature by political prisoners offers important insights into uncovering or getting at the underlying more abstract elements that govern the island. Racist ideology deeply informed the organizational and punitive aspects of the island.

One of the most dramatic and memorable scenes depicted in the memoirs of political prisoners was the arrival to the island. Because the prison was on an island, most new prisoners were taken by boat. As I read them, I was stuck by the fact that they read more like eighteenth century accounts of slaves arriving to the new world, than what one might consider to be a convention introduction to prison. Granted they talked about administrative elements that are found in many narratives about prison—cell assignment, distributing clothing, handing out prison numbers. However, their transportation to the island evokes memories of slave trafficking. Take, for example, Indres Naidoo's telling of his arrival to the island:

> We could see the splashing outside, a little bit rough, and the boat rolled from one side to the other. It was frightening for many of the prisoners, especially as the waves hit the portholes and as we felt the chains have on use, trapped in the hold. Some of the prisoners trembled, others became seasick and made a dash to the toilet, dragging their partners with them, their chains rattling loudly (Naidoo, 1983, p. 61).

If one took out the word "prisoners", it would be difficult to distinguish this scene from musing by slaves arriving to the new world. Moses Dlamini, who was a member of Pan African Congress and was imprisoned on the island for most of the nineteen sixties, writes in his memoir *Robben Island Hell-Hole,* of his account of his first introduction to Robben Island:

> The boat went up and down as it cut through the waves. After what seemed like a long time, it was slowed down and ultimately docked. We had arrived at Robben Island. We were taken out of the boat with insults and yells onto two waiting trucks where we were packed in like sardines (Dlamini, 1984, p. 21).

Poet and activist Dennis Brutus writes in a poem entitled "cold" of being taken to the island for the first time:

> Overhead
> the larger frosty glitter of the stars
> the Southern Cross flower low;
>
> the chains on our ankles
> and wrists
> that pair us together
> jangle.
>
> glitter
> we began to move
> awkwardly. (Brutus, 1973, p. 53)

Again, these descriptions evoke visual memory of human bondage. The image of black bodies chained together, being shipped to an unfamiliar location, and "packed like sardines" makes it difficult to not see the parallels. However, these glaring similarities should not be read as a suggestion that slavery and twentieth century incarceration is the same thing. Though they emerge from the same seed, the historical and political periods they took shape under, are different. Seventeenth and eighteenth century slavery was a brutal practice that exploited the labor of blacks, and reduced them to mere commodities, which gave owners currency to treat slaves in any way they felt. It was a visceral and open white supremacy that needed no legal or moral sanction. The idea that blacks and other people of color constituted a group that could be publicly violated informed the practice penitentiary punishment (as well as more generalized forms of punishment found throughout the society) during the nineteenth and twentieth century. As a matter of fact, this thinking not only affected penitentiaries, it deeply permeated all institutions and social relations between blacks and whites. However, it did not operate in the same way slavery did. Slavery used explicit forms of white supremacy; nineteenth and twentieth century penal punishment used forms of racism injected into legal frameworks. It relied heavily on the notion idea that "blackness" equals "criminal", "other", "that which is to be contained" and kept away from the purity of "whiteness."

This in turn gave currency to legal and extralegal forms of domination. There is, nonetheless, a direct link between the South African penitentiary in the twentieth century and slavery.

Even with the outlawing of slavery in South Africa at the beginning of the nineteenth century, new institutions emerged to control Africans. Scholars, like Harriet Deacon (1996), have noted the role of penitentiaries—specifically, Robben Island—in reestablishing controls over black labor. Yet, we would be wrong in saying Robben Island was slavery in another form. Instead, it would be more accurate to suggest it has "congealed forms of antiblack racism" that existed under slavery incorporated its institutional framework. (Davis, 2003) One of the ways punishment was manifested, for example, was to make distinctions between black, Indian and white. To put it simply, to be punished on the island was to be, primarily, racialized.

Once on the island, prisoners were quickly reminded that, although they were not on the mainland, apartheid still ruled. In his memoir *Long Walk to Freedom*, Nelson Mandela recalls leaning of the racial hierarchy on the island. Despite being there for a short period just two years before (1963), he notes Robben Island had become:

> "the hardship station" for penal punishment throughout the country and a bastion of white supremacy. Gone were the black and colored warders, as well as their sympathies for the prisoners along with them. The new regime was all white, mostly Afrikaner speaking; they demanded a "master-servant relationship" between warders and prisoners. The racial divide on Robben Island was absolute: there were no black wardens and no white prisoners. (Mandela, 1994, p. 387)

Like the mainland's prison regulations, everything, from diet to clothing, was based on a rigid color system. For example, Colored and Indians received slightly better treatment than blacks did. Upon their arrival to the island, African National Congress (ANC) members like Mandela, Walter Sisulu, Govan Mbeki and other blacks were ordered to wear shorts as part of their prison uniform. "All of us, except Kathy (Ahmed Kathrada)", says Mandela, "received short trousers, an insubstantial jersey and a canvas jacket. Kathy, the one Indian among us, was given long trousers." According to Mandela, "Short trousers for Africans were meant to remind us that we were 'boys.'" (Mandela, 1994, p. 383) Naidoo echoes a similar point in an exchange he had with a warder. "What's the matter with you Indians", said the warder, "You've got a long history of civilization, you wore silk long before the white man, and here you are jumping from tree to tree with these barbarians. " (Naidoo, 1983, p. 41) Although it may seem minor, this reveals the way race comes into play. Race is used to create distinctions for the purpose of punishment; and just as important, it is used as tool to organize all aspects of life on the island. Even the physical examination was an exercise in racism.

In most prisons, a physical examination is performed when a new prisoner is brought in. This was also the case on Robben Island. However, the practice had an extra dimension of racist subjugation incorporated into it. The recital exam—which is in and of itself cruel and degrading, and according to Davis (2005, p. 47) is admissible precisely because it is done in prison—provides a disturbing insight to the way racism is part of the workings of the penal system. According to Moses Dlamini, the prisoners were treated like "hogs." When he arrived, he, along with several other prisoners was ordered by white warders to strip. Standing naked, they were "examined." An Afrikaner, with a thick glove took his finger and pierced the anus of mostly black political prisoners. In an ugly scene of sexualized racism, Dlamini describes his examination:

> Soon the doctor stood behind me. He first patted my buttocks and while I was concentrating on that, he abruptly thrust his thick gloved middle-finger into my rectum and with the finger half-bent, he turned it round and round form almost a minute. Dizzy with pain, I winced and winced to no avail. By the time he proceeded into the next man, my rectum was so painful that I though it was bleeding internally. (Dlamini, 1984, p. 19)

This act was precipitated by the warders suggesting the size and shape of the prisoner's buttocks would be liked by the doctor: "Hy's 'n vegat" (he's big buttocked)…"the doctor is going to enjoy himself with this one." (Dlamini, 1984, p. 18) The episode was so horrible it forced Dlamini to wonder, "if the Nazis ever did this to their victims who were their political opponents." (Dlamini, 1984, p. 18) Again, this is another example of how anti-black racism is part of the penal system. As debates rage about is abject dehumanization and what is not called torture (ironically in the United States), we should think about whether this treatment is necessary for "safety" or whether it simply reproduces racist violence.

The physical torture described above was not uncommon. The warders played a central role in administering theses acts. To many, the warders were outright "ruthless." Although there were moments of humane treatment between prisoners and warders, this was often not the case. Reverberating the sentiments articulated above by Mandela, Monhde Colin Mkunqwana, a member of the ANC's armed wing, Umkhonto weSizwe, states, "the brutality of the warders was clearly meant to instill the idea that the white man was superior." (Coetzee, 2000, p. 60) Johnson Philip Malambo, a member of the Pan African Congress (PAC) describes in detail the humiliating physical torture performed by warders on political prisoners. After having to dig a deep hole in the sand, Mlambo, was "buried alive." He was given what warders called "island vodka." Says Mlambo, "I was made to stand in a hole and a sadistic prison warder urinated on my face." (Pheko, 2002, p. 35) It is precisely for these reasons Ahmed Kathrada called life on the island "veritable hell." But it is important to keep in mind that physical torture was part of a larger form of punishment. The structure of the penitentiary was created for the purpose of punishment. And out of this emerged new ways to articulate punishment. The connection between structure and punishment is most eloquently captured by Dennis Brutus in a poem called "On The Island":

Cement-grey floors and walls
cement-grey days
cement-grey time and a grey susurration...

A barred existence
so that one did not need to look
as the doors or windows
to know that they were wee sundered by bars (Brutus, 1973, p. 71)

Brutus is not only describing the horrible conditions of the prison, but even more, he is suggesting that they are in and of themselves, punishment. But it is not punitive only in the sense that it physically affects prisoners; it is punitive, also, in the sense that it psychologically punishes prisoners. Punishment, then, is not only "cement-grey floors and walls", but it's also "cement-grey days" "time", an existence that is "barred" physically and psychologically.

Mental punishment, however, was not tied to the prison structure. The fact that Robben Island was a colonial institution demanded it be 'democratic' in this respect and come into contact with other elements in the prison. Therefore, it was discursive, but, because it a colonial institution, it was concerned with race, particularly, with imposing cultural hegemony over people of color. In what he describes as the "the chains [being] bound", Indres Naidoo, is told by a warder that speaking indigenous languages on the island is not wise. The warder threatens, "If you know what's fucking good for you, you will learn to speak Afrikaans bloody fast." (Naidoo, 1983, p. 66) Prisoners, like Mandela and Dlamini, echo similar experience in their prison narratives.[1]

It should be noted that although racism played a major role in the way the function of the island, it was not the only form of domination used. Methods to deny and disrupt organizing by political prisoners were constantly employed by prison authorities. One of the most interesting methods used was instituting a policy of denying the use of the pronoun 'we' in written documents to prison authority or letters of family and friends. Says Michael Dingake, the use of "'We' meant one had assumed, unlawfully, the role of spokesman of other prisoners," which was forbidden. (Dingake, 1987, p. 167) And as a result, all aspects of the prison experience, particularly with respect to punishment, was directed at making the prisoner—specifically political prisoners—autonomous individuals. This affected everything from not being able to share food with other prisoners, all the way to the construction of individual cells.

These kinds of subtle, but, yet, extremely damaging forms of punishment described above were found throughout the island. For example, many political prisoners write in their memoirs of the fight for the right to study. It was a major source of contention between the prisoners and the prison administration. The isolation and boredom of prison life—"cement grey days" and "cement-grey time"—made education important to the prisoners. Prison officials used the pursuit of education as a means to keep prisoners in check, and denial of the right to study was used as a form of punishment. According to Michael Dingake, study was used by Robben Island officials to make prisoners "more amenable to prison discipline or alternatively turn the privilege into a psychological instrument of torture."

These forms of punishment are rightly understood by Joseph Faniso Mati and Nelson Mandela as attempts by prison officials to destroy not only the body of the prisoner, that is, to make him submit, to the authority of a white state apparatus, but, more importantly, to destroy the spirit and the hope for a free South Africa. Says Mandela, "prison is designed to break one's spirit and destroy one's resolve." (Mandela, 1994, p. 390) This was a major reason for the brutality on the island; and is precisely why the penitentiary was central to apartheid. The penitentiary was to be a way to remove the 'threat' of anti-racism, as well as to organize the entire society.

In reading the literature of political prisoners on Robben Island, one is able to glean from their writings that the island was much more than prison. Although it served the purpose of detaining social and political prisoners, it had other, sometimes more pressing, agendas. The descriptions given above uncover some of these important functions. Using racism as a tool to organize and punish was only part of its function. Racism on the island was also, and I think most importantly, used as a pedagogical tool. In other words, racism was used to reinforce white domination, and teach Africans, Indians, Colords and Afrikaners the logic of white supremacy. Most importantly, it was used to normalize the system of racial hierarchy that existed on the mainland; and the techniques use to organize and punish racial subjects. I think the literature of political prisoners articulates this point explicitly. However, I want to take this point even further and suggest that the practices of racialized punishment and how prisoners organized on the island informed apartheid's ability to organize society and carry out wide ranging and "layered" forms of punishment. This is the case, particularly, in three key areas: 1) the use of racial categories to separate people; 2) maintaining this separation by creating mechanisms to police lines of racial demarcation; 3) using race as a factor in determining how and who gets punished. This is why scholars like Harriet Deacon and Paul Gready agree that Robben Island had a profound affect on twentieth century South Africa; says Deacon, "Seldom has one small piece of land been so heavily imbrued with a symbolism which remains, like understanding of its past and hopes for its future, so deeply contested." (Marbark, 2004) Gready suggest the practice of confinement was "Central to apartheid's design were layered spaces of confinement and exclusion: lives were lived within an evolving crosshatch of mutually enforcing insides and outsides, behind bars and borders." (Gready, 2003, p. 1)

Michael Dingake, who was incarcerated on the island for two decades, suggests there is special relationship between South Africa and the penitentiary, as well. According to Dingake, "the whole of South Africa is a prison." Echoing this same point, Oliver Tambo takes this point even further by suggesting "the tragedy of Africa, in racial and political terms, [has been] concentrated—in South Africa... and, in a special sense, on Robben Island." (Coetzee, 2000, p. 1) This focus on the role of the penitentiary, specifically, Robben Island as it relates to the nation is not so surprising if we examine the history the twentieth institution rests on. Since the nineteenth century, it has been one of the, if not the single most, important institution for organizing society. That is to say, it has been employed to resolve the "contradictions" of life in a multiracial society.

Controlled by the Dutch during the seventeenth and eighteenth centuries, Robben Island became the flagship prison in South Africa's penal system during the early part of the nineteenth century. It was used primarily as place to detain political opponents, those 'criminals' considered "dangerous" and for those suffering from mental illness. (Deacon, 1996, p. 36) By the early nineteenth century, the island was under British authority. In 1828, the prison authority set up ridged lines for carrying our racially exclusive punishment. It was argued by British colonial authority "black convicts responded less well to reformative effects of imprisonment than to physical punishment." (Deacon, 1996, p. 36) Therefore, it was believed that physical punishment—public whippings, and other forms of corporal punishment—was not only 'effective', but, even worse, morally appropriate for Africans. Despite the fact that South Africa was influenced by European and North American prison reformers, who demanded less punitive measures in favor of moral and spiritual reform, British officials did not feel this was applicable to Africans.

Ironically, it was during the period the island was also used mostly as an insane and leprosy asylum that the practice of infusing race into the organizational and punitive elements of the prison was carried out. As a result, a host of techniques and practices were developed. Most notably among them was the use of racial segregation (this was also performed according to class and gender), the rise of techniques to separate the races, the creation of fraudulent scientific racial categories, which gave rise to the creation of racially appropriate techniques of punishment and discipline, and technologies for racialized punishment. Each one of the techniques made it possible for an organized, efficient and sanitized racism to take shape.

This kind of racialized punishment continued well into the twentieth century. However, after the end of the Second World War, there was a shift in the direction of racialized punishment on the island. This was the case in part because of the direction of the new South African government. The victory of the Nationalist Party in 1948, brought with it sweeping new laws that would reshape all of South Africa. The policy of apartheid or the development of racial grouping along "their own lines" affected all aspects of life in South Africa and the prison was not absolved. Although race had always been central to the formation of the penitently, the official policy of white supremacy changed the penitentiary's relationship to South Africa. The post-war penitentiary played an important role in the application and form of apartheid. It was a blueprint for organizing social relations between Africans and whites. And it provided practical ways for dividing living space between racialized groups, creating racial categories to organize, and creating mechanism to reinforce lines of racial demarcation; and instituted the racialization of punishment.

In part, the writings by political prisoners help us to see clearly the logic that dominated Robben Island: white supremacy. At the same time, their literature suggests more than this somewhat obvious fact. More importantly, this literature reveals the ways in which the continued legacy of colonial racism persists in the penitentiary's current form. It also reveals how important the penitentiary is to the nation, how it directly influences apartheid policy.

There is an overwhelming sense in their literature that apartheid and the penitentiary are connected. It is important to take note of how the various methods used to organize the prison around the logic of white supremacy allowed for the creation of multiple sites of racist punishment. Although they appear as 'objective' mechanisms to organize the prison, an analysis of them reveals there is more to them than this. In describing the commodity, Karl Marx suggests, although it appears as "an extremely obvious, trivial thing" a close examination reveals it to have "abounding in metaphysical subtleties." (Marx, 1977, p. 163) Similarly, the organizational techniques on Robben Island may appear as "trivial" and "obvious", but the literature of political prisoners illuminates the subtly, and, yet, brutal ways organization and punishment are one in the same.

In light of the fact that Robben Island is now a museum and "national monument", it is important to think about what this means to South Africa. If anything, it should force us to undo our ridge notions of those associated with the penitentiary. It should prompt us to rethink the notion that those who are incarcerated are worthless or beyond help, and that they are of no use to society. Although there are other positions to negotiate on this topic, I would like to end by saying a more complicated reading of the penitentiary is long overdue. We can learn much from this institution and the role it plays in (most notably) democratic societies. The dictum from Dostoyevsky is correct; we can tell so much about a society by how it treats its poor, its "wretched of the earth", by how it treats its prisoners. We should not be surprised, therefore, that the post-apartheid leadership emerged from prison. In fact, it is fitting.

Notes

1. Punishment at Robben Island is in step with the practice of white supremacy throughout the country. Afrikaans was made the national language in the early part of the twentieth century. Although Africans spoke their own languages within their communities, the public language was Afrikaans. Being an apartheid institution, we should not find it surprising that prison officials demanded prisoners speak Afrikaans. However, despite the attempts by warders to blunt organizing by politically prisoners, they were still able to make several changes within the prison for the betterment of all prisoners. One scholar goes as far as to suggest that during the 1970's with much of the political leadership in prison, Robben Island was the

most politically organized space in the country. See Fran Buntman, "Resistance to Robben Island 1963-1970, in Deacon, 1996.

References

Bernault, F. (Ed.). 2003. *A History of Prison and Confinement in Africa*: Portsmouth, NH: Heinemann.

Brutus, D. 1973. *Simple Lust*. London: Heinemann.

Coetzee, J. K. 2000. *Plain Tales from Robben Island*. Hatfield: Van Schaik.

Davis, A. Y. 2003. *Are Prisons Obsolete?* New York: London: Seven Stories; Turnaround.

Davis, A. Y. 2005. *Abolition Democracy: Beyond Empire, Prisons and Torture*. New York: Seven Stories Press.

Buntman, F. 1996. *The Island: A History of Robben Island, 1488-1990*. Bellville, South Africa: Mayibuye Books, University of the Western Cape.

Dingake, M. 1987. *My Fight Against Apartheid*. London: Kliptown Books.

Dlamini, M. 1984. *Hell-hole, Robben Island: Reminiscences of a Political Prisoner in South Africa*. Trenton, N.J.: Africa World Press.

Gready, P. 2003. *Writing as Resistance: Life Stories of Imprisonment, Exile, and Homecoming from Apartheid South Africa*. Lanham, Md.: Lexington Books.

Mandela, N. 1994. *Long Walk to Freedom: The Autobiography of Nelson Mandela* (1st ed. ed.). Boston: Little, Brown.

Marbark, R. 2004. The Rhetorical Space of Robben Island. *Rhetorical Society Quarterly*.

Marx, K. 1977. *Capital: A Critique of Political Economy*. New York: Vintage Books.

Mashinini, E. 1991. *Strikes Have Followed Me All My Life: A South African Autobiography*. New York: Routledge.

Naidoo, I. 1983. *Robben Island: Ten Years as a Political Prisoner in South Africa's Most Notorious Penitentiary*. New York: Vintage Books.

Pheko, M. 2002. *The True History of Robben Island Must Be Preserved*. Johannesburg: Tokoloho Development Association.

Reddy, T. (2000). *Hegemony and Resistance: Contesting Identities in South Africa*. Aldershot: Ashgate.

Suttner, R. 2001. *Inside Apartheid's Prisons: Notes and Letters of Struggle*. Pietermaritzburg, South Africa: Ocean Press; University of Natal Press.

Visser, W. 2004. The Production of Literature on the 'Red Peril' and 'Total Onslaught' in Twentieth-Century South Africa. *Historia 49*.

14

INTERNATIONAL HUMAN RIGHTS PROTECTION FOR PRISONERS: A SOUTH AFRICAN PERSPECTIVE

John C. Mubangizi

INTRODUCTION

Prisoners' rights are human rights first. Any discussion of the protection of such rights has to be viewed in that context. Protection of human rights generally takes place at two levels: the domestic level and the international level. Most of the discussion concerning human rights in South Africa today is focused on the protection of such rights through a Bill of Rights. At a different level, there is the international dimension of human rights protection. It is this dimension, with specific reference to prisoners' rights that this paper is essentially concerned with. The paper therefore looks at how prisoners' rights are protected through the system of international law and briefly indicates the direction taken by South Africa in trying to provide for such protection.

It should first be noted that international law does not prohibit imprisonment as such except where the incarceration is effected in violation of internationally recognized human rights and fundamental freedoms. It is a basic principle of international human rights law that convicted prisoners do not thereby lose their fundamental rights, except those which are incidental to their lawful detention (Naldi, 1992, p. 716). Accordingly, provision is made under Article 10(1) of the International Covenant of Civil and Political Rights (ICCPR) that:

> All persons deprived of their liberty shall be treated with humanity
> and with respect for the inherent dignity of the human person

Article 5(2) of the American Convention on Human Rights provides, *inter alia* that:

> All persons deprived of their liberty shall be treated with respect for
> the inherent dignity of the human person.

These instruments, together with a host of others including the Universal Declaration of Human Rights, the European Convention on Human Rights, the African Charter on Human and Peoples' Rights, the UN Convention against Torture and other Cruel, Inhuman or Degrading Treatment or Punishment, all prohibit torture, and cruel, inhuman and degrading treatment. Other specific international instruments have implicitly or explicitly included these notions in their provisions. Before determining which way South Africa is headed we shall first look at the development and content of certain specific international instruments and see how these instruments have been applied and interpreted to protect specific rights of prisoners.

INSTRUMENTS PROVIDING FOR INTERNATIONAL HUMAN RIGHTS NORMS FOR PRISONERS (UNDER THE UNITED NATIONS SYSTEM)

The United Nations Standard Minimum Rules for the Treatment of Prisoners

As early as 1926 the International Penal and Penitentiary Commission was working on a draft set of standard minimum rules for prisoners. The activities of the Commission mainly between 1929 and 1933 resulted in the drafting of a set of such rules in 1934 (Van Zyl Smit, 1992, p. 80). In 1950 the United Nations became involved in the process and in July 1951 at its last session, the International Penal and Penitentiary Commission approved a revised draft of the Standard Minimum Rules for the Treatment of Prisoners (ibid.). In 1954 a set of these rules was approved by the First United Nations Congress on the Prevention of Crimes and the Treatment of Offenders. The United Nations Economic and Social Council endorsed the text in 1957 and in 1977 an additional article (rule) 95 was added to ensure that persons arrested or detained without charges should benefit from most of the provisions of the Standard Minimum Rules (ECOSOC, 1957 and 1997). These Rules are reviewed on an on-going basis by the Committee on Crime Prevention and Control of the Economic and Social Council. In so doing, the United Nations tries to keep pace with current penological thinking in an effort to achieve greater success with respect to adoption and implementation of the Rules (Strydom, Pretorius, Klinck, 1997, p. 121).

The main objectives of the Standard Minimum Rules is stated in the Preliminary Observations thus:

> The following rules are not intended to describe in detail a model system of penal institutions. They seek only, on the basis of the general consensus of contemporary thought and the essential elements of the most adequate systems of today, to set out what is generally accepted as being good principle and practice in the treatment of prisoners and the management of institutions (Standard Minimum Rules for the Treatment of Prisoners).

The Rules are contained in two parts. Part I containing 55 articles provides in specific detail for rules of general application regarding the following matters; separation of categories of prisoners, accommodation, personal hygiene, clothing and bedding, food, exercise and sport, medical services, discipline and punishment, instruments of restraint, information to and complaints by prisoners, contact with the outside world, books, religion, retention of prisoners property, notification of death, illness, transfer, removal of prisoners, institutional personnel and inspection. Part II containing articles 56 - 95, provides for rules applicable only to special categories of prisoners. These include rules applicable to prisoners under sentence, rules regarding insane and mentally abnormal prisoners, rules regarding prisoners under arrest or awaiting trial, rules regarding civil prisoners and rules regarding prisoners under arrest or detained without charge.

The Basic Principles for the Treatment of Prisoners

In an effort to give greater meaning to the significance of the Standard Minimum Rules for the Treatment of Prisoners, the General Assembly of the United Nations adopted the Basic Principles for the Treatment of Prisoners in 1990. These "were specifically designed to facilitate the full implementation of the Standard Minimum Rules by articulating the basic principles underlying them" (Van Zyl Smit, p. 80). This objective is clearly reflected in the preamble to the resolution adopting the principles (UN GA Res. 45/111, 1990). Among other things, the Principles confirm certain fundamental prisoners' rights and stipulate that all prisoners should be treated with due respect for their inherent dignity and value as human beings, without discrimination of any kind (Strydom, Pretorius and Klinck, p. 134). Prohibition of discrimination on various grounds is provided for under Principle 2. Principle 5 declares that:

> Except for those limitations that are demonstrably necessitated by the fact of incarceration, all prisoners shall retain the human rights and fundamental freedoms set out in the Universal Declaration of Human Rights, and where the state concerned is a party, the International Covenant on Economic, Social and Cultural Rights, and the International Covenant on Civil and Political Rights and the Optional Protocol thereto, as well as such other rights as are set out in other United Nations covenants (UN Declaration, Principle 5).

Principle 6 provides for the right of prisoners to take part in cultural activities and education aimed at the full development of the human personality. Principle 7 regards solitary confinement and the restriction or abolition thereof. Principle 9 provides for access and availability of health services and finally Principle 10 stipulates that favorable conditions should be created for the reintegration of the ex-prisoner into society under the best possible conditions.

It has to be emphasized that the Basic Principles for the Treatment of Prisoners, just like the Standard Minimum Rules, is not *per se* legally binding. Both these instruments do not constitute international treaties. They are nevertheless, unanimously accepted by a large international community of countries to which South Africa belongs. "Indeed," says Van Zyl Smit, "the official South African response to the Rules was enthusiastic and there is considerable evidence that the South African Prisons Act of 1959 was drafted as a conscious response to these Rules" (Van Zyl Smit, p. 80). Both the Rules and the Principles also provide guidance in interpreting general rules applicable to prisoners, and serious or widespread non-compliance may well be seen as violation of prisoners' rights.

Body of Principles for the Protection of All Persons under Any Form of Detention or Imprisonment

This instrument was a result of a study undertaken by the United Nations Commission on Human Rights whose findings were initially published in 1962 (UN publication No 65 XIV2, 1962). The study dealt with the right to be free from arbitrary arrest, detention and exile (ibid.). The conclusions of the study gave rise to a draft document, which after several years was finalized by a Working Group appointed by a Committee of the General Assembly. In 1988 the final draft of the Body of Principles for the Protection of All Persons Under Any Form of Detention or Imprisonment was approved and adopted by the General Assembly (GA Res. 43/173, 1988). The Body of Principles is prefaced with a 'scope' which says:

> These principles apply for the protection of all persons under any
> form of detention or imprisonment (ibid.).

The Principles (39 in number) range from very general formulations of the human rights of persons under any form of detention or imprisonment, to more specific guarantees of a procedural nature, to provisions on particular rights to be ensured in places of detention or imprisonment (Strydom, Pretorius and Klinck, p. 130). A random classification of the contents of the instruments would see the principles fall into the following categories:

a) general provisions on human rights of detained or imprisoned persons (Principles 1-8)
b) procedural safeguards (Principles 9-14)
c) treatment of detained or imprisoned persons (Principles 15-39)

A general clause providing that nothing in the Body of Principles shall be construed as restricting or derogating from any right defined in the International Covenant on Civil and Political Rights concludes the instrument.

The United Nations Standard Minimum Rules for the Administration of Juvenile Justice

This is one of two important UN instruments specifically formulated for the detention of juveniles. It was felt that there were compelling reasons for treating adults and juveniles differently, and it was therefore decided that a complementary set of standards be designed to provide special safeguards for young offenders. The result was the United Nations Standard Minimum Rules for the Administration of Juvenile Justice (also known as the Beijing Rules) adopted by the United Nations General Assembly in 1985 (UN Res. 40/33, 1985).

Although the Rules discourage the use of institutionalization for juvenile offenders, they set out certain essential elements for the protection of such offenders who are placed in institutions. These elements cover matters such as minimum age of criminal responsibility, the objectives of juvenile justice, the features of effective, fair and humane juvenile justice administration and human rights principles to be applied (Strydom, Pretorious, and Klink, p. 138). The Rules also deal with the relationship between themselves and the Standard Minimum Rules for the Treatment of Prisoners, detention pending trial and objectives of institutional treatment.

The United Nations Rules for the Protection of Juveniles Deprived of their Liberty

This is the other UN instrument dealing with juvenile detention. It was formulated in response to the fact that the Standard Minimum Rules for the Administration of Juvenile Justice did not fully address the conditions in which juveniles deprived of their liberty were detained (ibid., p. 144). The Rules were adopted by the General Assembly of the United Nations on 14 December 1990. The main objective of the Rules is stipulated in Rule 3, which states:

> The Rules are intended to establish minimum standards accepted by the United Nations for the protection of juveniles deprived of their liberty in all forms, consistent with human rights and fundamental freedoms, and with a view to counteracting the detrimental effects of all types of detention and to fostering integration in society (UN Rules for Protecting Juveniles, 1990).

Rule 1 also reiterates the least possible use of institutionalization for juveniles. Imprisonment should be used as a last resort, says the Rule.

The instrument is divided into four parts; fundamental perspectives, scope and application of the Rules, juveniles under arrest or awaiting trial and the management of juvenile facilities. Regarding the conditions of detention, provision is made by the Rules for juveniles to have the right of legal counsel and be enabled to apply for free legal aid, where such aid is available, and to communicate regularly with their legal advisers. Juveniles should also be provided, where possible, with opportunities to pursue work, with remuneration, and continue education and training (ibid.).

Regarding management of juvenile facilities, the Rules provide in specific detail for the proper keeping of records, admissions, registration and transfer. Provision is also made for classification and placement, accommodation, education, vocational training and work. The Rules also set out juveniles rights in regard to recreation, practicing of religion, medical care, contacts with the wider community, disciplinary procedures and procedures for returning to the community.

Other instruments under the United Nations System

There are a number of other instruments under the United Nations system for the protection of prisoners' rights. These include; Principles of Medical Ethics Relevant to the Role of Health Personnel, Particularly Physicians, in the Protection of Prisoners and Detainees Against Torture and Other Cruel, Inhuman Degrading Treatment or Punishment. The purpose of these six Principles is to prohibit health personnel from using their knowledge and skills in assisting in the interrogation of prisoners and detainees in a manner that may adversely affect their health. Principle 2 specifically states that it is "a gross contravention of medical ethics, as well as an offence under applicable international instruments, for health personnel, particularly physicians, to engage, actively or passively, in acts which constitute participation in, complicity in, incitement or attempts to commit torture or other cruel, inhuman or degrading treatment or punishment." Another United Nations instrument is the Declaration on the Protection of All Persons from Being Subjected to Torture and Other Cruel, Inhuman or Degrading Treatment or Punishment. Adopted in 1995, the Declaration seeks to prohibit torture and other forms of ill treatment. It has its genesis in the UN Convention against Torture and Other Cruel, Inhuman or Degrading Treatment or Punishment. These two instruments provide the basis for standard setting and implementation as far as torture and ill treatment of prisoners is concerned.

Another important instrument is the Principles for the Protection of Persons with Mental Illness and for the Improvement of Mental Health Care. It deals with treatment of mentally ill persons and requires that such treatment should be based on humanity and respect for the dignity of the human person. Of particular relevance is Principle 20, which deals specifically with persons serving sentences of imprisonment for criminal offences, or who are otherwise, detained. It requires that such persons should receive the best available mental health care. Finally, the Model Agreement on the Transfer of Foreign Prisoners and Recommendations on the Treatment of Foreign Prisoners requires states to co-operate in facilitating the transfer or return of persons convicted of crimes abroad to their country of nationality. Provision is also made for the rights of such foreign prisoners and how they should be treated.

INSTRUMENTS PROVIDING FOR INTERNATIONAL HUMAN RIGHTS NORMS FOR PRISONERS (UNDER REGIONAL SYSTEMS)

European Standard Minimum Rules for the Treatment of Prisoners

These Rules are basically a European version of the United Nations Standard Minimum Rules for the Treatment of Prisoners. They were adopted by the Council of Europe's Committee of Ministers by Resolution (73)5 of 9 January 1973. These rules (like the United Nations Rules) are also divided into two parts. Part I deals with rules of general application while Part II deals with rules applicable to special categories of prisoners. Under Part I the Rules provide for matters relating to registration, distribution of prisoners, accommodation, personal hygiene, clothing and bedding, exercise and sport, medical services, discipline and punishment, information to and complaints by prisoners, contact with the outside world, and such other matters. Under Part II the categories of prisoners considered include; prisoners under sentence, insane and mentally abnormal prisoners, prisoners under arrest or awaiting trial and civil prisoners.

There are a few noticeable differences between the European Standard Minimum Rules for the Treatment of Prisoners and their United Nations counterparts. First, while the latter talks of separation of categories of prisoners (under rule 8), the former speaks of 'distribution' of prisoners (under rule 7). Under the European version, Rule 22 provides that prisoners may not be submitted to medical or scientific experiments, which may result in physical or moral injury to their person. This prohibition is missing in the United Nations Rules. Rule 37 of the European version provides that; "Prisoners shall be allowed to communicate with their family and all persons or representatives of organizations and to receive visits from these persons at regular intervals ..." The reference to "all persons or representative of organizations" is absent from the equivalent provision of the United Nations Standards (Rule 37) (Strydom, Pretorius, Klink, p. 152). Finally another noticeable difference is the omission by the European Rules of the provision regarding privileges. Under the United Nations Rules this is dealt with under Rule 70, which provides that:

> Systems of privileges appropriate for the different classes of prisoners and the different methods of treatment shall be established at every institution, in order to encourage good conduct, develop a sense of responsibility and secure the interest and co-operation of the prisoners in their treatment (UN Rule 70).

The European Rules do not have a regional equivalent.

Revised European Standard Minimum Rules for the Treatment of Prisoners

The purposes of these Rules are set out in the preamble as, *inter alia*, to establish a range of minimum standards for all those aspects of prison administration that are essential to human conditions and positive treatment in modern and progressive systems; and to serve as a stimulus to prison administrations to develop policies and management style and practice based on good contemporary principles and equity. Also according to the preamble, the rules place renewed emphasis on the precepts of human dignity, the commitment of prison administration to humane and positive treatment, the importance of staff roles and effective modern management approaches.

Contained in 5 parts, the Revised European Rules "reflect a re-assessment of penal philosophy and prison administration." They also reflect a "shift in priorities and emphases, whilst maintaining the basic principles and norms of the United Nations Standard Minimum Rules" (ibid). Under Part I, the usual basic principles are laid down, Part II provides for the management of prisons, Part III for personnel, Part IV for treatment objectives and regimes and finally Part V lays down additional rules for special categories of prisoners. These include untried prisoners, civil prisoners and insane and mentally abnormal prisoners.

The Inter-American Convention to Prevent and Punish Torture

This instrument, adopted by the General Assembly of the Organization of American States on 9 December 1985 is in a way a regional reflection of the United Nations Convention against Torture and Other Cruel, Inhuman or Degrading Treatment or Punishment. The objective of the Convention is spelled out in Article 1 as the prevention and punishment of torture in accordance with the terms of the Convention.

Although the instrument is not restricted to prisoners, like its United Nations counterpart it was formulated and drafted with prisoners and detainees mainly in mind. This is reflected in Article 5, which provides *inter alia*, that:

> Neither the dangerous character of the detainee or prisoner, nor the lack of security of the prison establishment or penitentiary shall justify torture (UN Convention against Torture and Other Cruel, Inhuman or Degrading Treatment or Punishment, Article 5, 1985).

Other regional instruments

Other regional instruments relating to human rights norms for prisoners include the Draft European Convention on the Protection of Detainees from Torture and from Cruel, Inhuman or Degrading Treatment or Punishment whose aim is to supplement the remedies provided for in the European Convention on Human Rights by creating a procedure for the protection of detainees from torture and other forms of ill-treatment (Parliamentary Assembly of the Council of Europe, Recommendation 971, 1983). They also include a number of resolutions and recommendations. One of these relates to the custody and treatment of dangerous prisoners. It recommends that governments should as far as possible apply ordinary prison regulations to dangerous prisoners, and that extra security measures should only be applied to the extent to which they are necessary and in such a way that respects the prisoners' dignity and rights.

A resolution from the Committee of Ministers of the Council of Europe dealing with prison labor sets down a number of measures regarding the use thereof. Another resolution deals with electoral, civil and social rights of prisoners. It contains a number of important recommendations concerning the electoral, civil and social rights of prisoners. The basis of these recommendations is that the mere fact of imprisonment does not necessarily prohibit prisoners from exercising their civil rights. Finally, a recommendation dealing with prison leave stipulates that prison leave should be granted to the greatest possible extent on medical, educational, occupational, family and other social grounds. Certain factors should always be taken into consideration including the nature and seriousness of the offence, length of sentence, period of detention completed, personality and behavior of the prisoner, risk to society, family and social situation of prisoner, purpose of leave, its duration and its terms and conditions (Strydom, Pretorius, Klink, p. 158).

No specific instrument relating to prisoners' rights or prison conditions has been formulated under the African regional system. This is mainly because in comparison to the other regional systems, the African system is the newest, the least developed, the least effective, the most distinctive and the most controversial (Steiner and Alison, 1996, p. 689). Steiner and Alison say:

> For these reasons the African system has not yielded anywhere near the same amount of information and "output" of recommendations or decisions - states reports and reactions thereto, communications (complaints) from individuals and state responses thereto .... as have the other two regional regimes, let alone the United Nations system (ibid.).

WHICH WAY SOUTH AFRICA?

Over the last decade South Africa has undergone nothing short of a constitutional revolution. This revolution was a result of a series of events which culminated in a new political order and a new constitutional dispensation. The two main constitutional developments of this period were the interim Constitution and its successor the 1996 Constitution. The latter contains a Bill of Rights substantially carried over from the former. This Bill of Rights proclaims itself as "a cornerstone of democracy in South Africa [which] enshrines the rights of all people in our country and affirms the democratic values of human dignity, equality and freedom" (South African Constitution, Sec. 7(1), 1996). It is presumed that the phrase 'all people' automatically includes prisoners.

In addition to this general protection, specific provision is made under section 35 of the Constitution for the rights of arrested, detained and accused persons. Section 35(1) provides for the right of an arrested person to remain silent and to be promptly informed of that right and of the consequences of not remaining silent. It also provides for the right of the arrested person not to be compelled to make any confession or admission that could be used in evidence against him or her. Provision is also made for the right of an arrested person to be brought to court as soon as reasonably possible, to be charged at the first court appearance or to be released from detention if the interests of justice permit. Under section 35(2) a provision is made for the right of a detainee to be informed promptly of the reason for being detained, the right to legal representation, the right to challenge the lawfulness of the detention and the right to conditions of detention that are consistent with human dignity. Such conditions should include exercise, adequate accommodation and nutrition, reading material and medical treatment. Provision is also made for the right to communicate and be visited.

Section 35(3) provides for the right to a fair trial which includes the right to be informed of the charge with sufficient detail to answer it, the right to have adequate time and facilities to prepare a defense, the right to a public trial before an ordinary court and the right to a speedy trial. It also includes the right to be present when being tried, the right to legal representation, presumption of innocence, the right to adduce and challenge evidence and the right not to be compelled to give self-incriminating evidence. Also included is the right to be tried in a language that the accused understands or if that is not practicable to have the benefit of an interpreter. Other rights under that section include the right of appeal or review, the right not to be convicted for an act or omission that was not an offence under the law at the time it was committed or omitted and the right not to be tried for an offence in respect of an act or omission for which the person has been either acquitted or convicted.

In addition to the rights of arrested, detained and accused persons listed in section 35 of the Constitution, there are a number of other provisions in the Bill of Rights that have an impact on prisoners and prisoners' rights. These include the right to equality, human dignity, freedom and security of the person, and the right to life. They also include the right to privacy, political rights, children's rights, access to information and just administrative action. Also applicable is the limitation clause and the provision on legal standing (*locus standi*) (South African Constitution, 1996).

A detailed discussion of the rights enumerated above is beyond the scope of this chapter. Suffice it to say that most of the rights of prisoners envisaged under international human rights law are incorporated into the South African Bill of Rights. Of particular significance in this context is section 39 of the Constitution which provides for the interpretation of the Bill of Rights. Section 39(1) obliges any court interpreting the Bill of Rights to promote the values that underlie an open and democratic society based on human dignity, equality and freedom. International law must be considered while foreign law may also be considered. In *S v Makwanyane* the Constitutional Court endorsed the use of public international law and foreign law in the interpretation of the Bill of Rights. The Court made specific reference to the jurisprudence of the United Nations Committee on Human Rights, the Inter-American Commission on Human Rights and the European Court of Human Rights.

In the context of prisoners' rights section 39 is of great importance in the sense that there is a wide range of international jurisprudence to draw upon. In that respect it should be noted that by the use of the mandatory 'must' the court is obliged by section 39(1) to apply international law. On the other hand the use of the discretionary 'may' only requires the court to apply foreign law as and when it sees fit. It will also be remembered that according to *Makwanyane's case* the court is not required to use only binding international law. Both binding and non-binding international law may be applied in the interpretation of the Bill of Rights. The relevance of this is that the fact the South Africa is not party to some international human rights instruments (including those on prisoners' rights) does not preclude the courts from applying them in interpretation.

Finally, mention ought to be made of the 1998 Correctional Services Act. According to its preamble, the statute was enacted to give effect to the Bill of Rights, and in particular its provisions with regard to prisoners. Again, a detailed discussion of the Correctional Services Act is beyond the scope of this article. Suffice it to say that Chapter III of the Act provides for the custody of all prisoners under conditions of human dignity. Furthermore, the Act establishes certain institutional mechanisms that will enhance the realization of prisoners' rights. These include parole boards, the judicial inspectorate of prisons and independent prison visitors.

CONCLUSION

International law plays an important role in the protection of prisoners' rights. This role has to be understood in the light of the problems inherent in the enforcement of human rights standards through international mechanisms. The UN Standard Minimum Rules for the Treatment of Prisoners has gained remarkable importance in recent years. The same can be said of the Body of Principles for the Treatment of Prisoners. Several other instruments are offshoots of these two. As international human rights norms evolve, so too do human rights applicable to prisoners. The reports of the UN Human Rights Committee, the judgments of the European Court and the reports of the European Commission have slowly, but surely, given effect to changing attitudes towards detainees and evolving standards of international human rights law applicable to them. The African system under the African Charter has been pretty ineffectual, to say the least. South Africa has mapped its way forward by incorporating most international human rights applicable to prisoners into a colorful and just Bill of Rights. The extent to which this constitutional protection translates into actual enjoyment of the rights is, unfortunately, another story. It can however be authoritatively stated that according to research, the favorable legal climate established by the Bill of Rights does not translate into reality on the ground.

Notes

Another version of this chapter has been previously published in the *South African Yearbook of International Law* 87, 2001: 87-113.

References

African Charter of Human and Peoples' Rights and the United Nations Convention against Torture and Other Cruel, Inhuman or Degrading Treatment or Punishment, Article 5. 1984.

Committee of Ministers of the Council of Europe, Recommendation No R(82) 17.

_____. Resolution 75(25).

_____. Resolution 62(2).

_____. Recommendation No R(82) 16.

ECOSOC Res. 663 C(XXIV) of 31 July 1957 and ECOSOC Res. 2076 (LXII) of 13 May 1977.

European Convention on Human Rights, Article 3.

Naldi, G.J. 1992. Prisoners' rights as recently interpreted by the Supreme Court of Zimbabwe: A Comparative Study with International Human Rights, *African Journal of International and Comparative Law* 4.

Parliamentary Assembly of the Council of Europe in 1983, Recommendation 971. 1983.

Steiner, H J and P. Alison. 1996. International Human Rights in Context. Oxford: Oxford University Press.

Strydom , H A, J L Pretorius, and M E Klinck. 1997. *International Human Rights Standards*, Vol. 1.

The South African Constitution, 1996.

Universal Declaration of Human Rights, Article 5.

United Nations General Assembly Resolution 3452 (XXX) of 1975.

_____. 37/194 of 1982.

_____. 39/46 of 1984.

_____. 40/32 of 1985.

_____. 40/33 of 1985.

_____. 43/173 of 1988.

_____. 45/111 of 1990.

_____. 45/113 of 1990.

_____. 46/119 of 1991.

UN No 65 XIV2. 1962. Study of the Right of Everyone to be Free from Arbitrary Arrest, Detention and Exile.

Van Zyl Smit, Dirk. 1992. *South African Prison Law and Practice* Durban: Butterworths.

15

THE PRISON INDUSTRIAL COMPLEX GOES TO AFRICA AND BEYOND: BRANCH PLANT OR APARTHEID PLANT?[1]

William G. Martin

The writing of this essay was triggered by a small article in the US press in 2000, announcing a new US overseas investment: the building of the first US private prison in Africa. Since majority rule in 1994, the South African state had assiduously courted foreign direct investment, faithfully adhering to the neo-liberal principles and policies required by the IMF, World Bank, and international capital (see Bond, 2000). On August 11, 2000 the Minister of Correctional Services, Ben Skosana, announced that a Rand 1.7 billion ($230 million at the time) contract for the building and running of one of the world's largest prisons in a small South African town. South Africa's business press and daily newspapers hailed the deal as a step forward in the commitment to free markets and the state's unrelenting war on crime. This was also news for North Americans, for the central contractor was the Wackenhut Corporation, the US firm with the biggest international prison holdings. A new foreign frontier for prison profits was, it seemed, about to open up for US prison firms.

The prospect of privatizing prisons outside wealthy white states is a bit startling: how many states in Africa, South Asia or Latin America can pay the $25-40 per prison per day rates that have generated profits for private firms in the US and elsewhere? The South African case thus bears some attention: does it prefigure an outwards spread of the US prison industrial complex, with US and European firms setting up branch plant operations across the planet?

Our answer—to jump ahead—is no. Yet the alternatives this analysis points to are equally disturbing, for they outline a movement towards a global carceral system suited to a neo-liberal world-economy, with private prison and security firms manning critical control points segregated by race and place.

PRIVATIZING PRISONS: THE SOUTH AFRICAN CASE

Wackenhut's South African operation was neither the first nor the biggest private prison in South Africa. The European security firm Group 4 Falck, the product of a succession of mergers and acquisitions in Europe in 1999-2000, had won an earlier contract for what would become South Africa's largest prison, a 2,928-bed maximum-security prison in Bloemfontein. At its opening in May 25, 2001 Skosana hailed the "progressive entrepreneurs" who founded Group 4 and had made it into "world's second-largest security services group" (Skosana, 2001). Group 4's South African operation was assuredly profitable too: in return for a minimal investment, Group 4 and its partners would own the prison for 25 years, receiving a guaranteed stream of payments from the government.

This model set the stage for Wackenhut's successful bid to build an even larger prison in the small, northern town of Louis Trichardt. In return for an apparent investment of only $3.5 million of its own funds, Wackenhut secured a $230 million contract to build, design, and run the prison with its 50/50 local empowerment (Black) partners: three women who had no experience at all in prison management. Little foreign investment was actually involved: the majority of financing was to come from local South African financial houses. As is the case for most private prisons in the US, the site is far from the major cities where most inmates come from, and sits on land donated by the local town. A rising incarceration rate, moreover, is predicated on tougher sentencing laws passed in 1998, as well as a steady rise in awaiting-trial prisoners staying for long periods, even years, in jails—including many poor who cannot afford even the smallest amounts of bail.

What was not announced by Skosana were the actual costs that the South African state would pay for its new private prisons: here silence reigned. Despite legislation calling for more transparency in government, requests for the details of private prison contracts, such as payments to Wackenhut for "available prisoner places," were rigorously rebuffed as they have been elsewhere in the world. State prisons are run cheaply: the Department of Correction Services estimates the daily cost of incarcerating a prisoner is Rand 84 (or round $10 at late 2001 exchange rates) per day, less than one-sixth of prevailing US rates (Stephan, 2001). How Wackenhut would turn a profit while delivering lower costs than state prisons thus puzzled observers at the time. As one private South African study concluded, "for the private company to make a profit while simultaneously cutting costs, there will have to be controversial reductions in the staffing of such prisons" (Oppler, 1998). Or the payments would have to be much higher than state rates to sustain high profits.

WACKENHUT: FROM LOCAL SECURITY TO GLOBAL PRISONS

For Wackenhut Corrections, founded as a division of Wackenhut Corporation in 1984 and a separately traded subsidiary since 1988, the launch of a South African operation was but one part of an unrelenting expansion overseas. Number 2 in private prisons in the US by the turn of the new millennium, Wackenhut was the #1 US firm operating overseas, with "global integrated service solutions" in 56 countries on six continents. As its web page proudly advertised, Wackenhut was

- "an industry leader and pioneer in the privatization of correctional facilities throughout the world," offering

- "a comprehensive range of prison services to federal, state, local and overseas government agencies," making it
- "the largest publicly traded company engaged solely in the business of managing correctional and detention facilities." (http://www.wackenhut.com/fr-wcc.htm)

By the end of 2000 Wackenhut was running 55 correctional/detention facilities with a total of over 40,000 beds in the United States, England, Scotland, Wales, Puerto Rico, South Africa, New Zealand, Curaçao, Australia, and Canada.

Wackenhut's prison operations are relatively new. Wackenhut began life as security firm, founded in 1954 by an ex-FBI agent. For the first forty years of its existence it depended on close connections to US government, offering regular and lucrative appointments to retired members of military, security, and intelligence agencies—including Generals Mark Clark, Paul X. Kelley, Thomas Stafford, and Julius W. Becton, Jr., former FBI director Clarence Kelley, former CIA director William Casey, former CIA deputy director Frank Carlucci, former Admiral and deputy CIA director Bobby Ray Iman, former Attorney General Benjamin R. Civiletti, Ralph E. Davis of the John Birch Society, and Jorge Mas Canosa of Cuban American National Foundation—among others.

As could be expected from this list, Wackenhut early on had an interest in national security as defined by the government; indeed it ran a parallel intelligence system of its own, collecting reportedly millions of dossiers on private US citizens. Far more lucrative has been providing protection for military, nuclear, and intelligence facilities. Recent contracts include security services, for example, for 26 nuclear power plants in 14 states; US government nuclear research labs, including paramilitary teams for nuclear weapons facilities in South Carolina and Nevada; the headquarters of the Nuclear Regulatory Commission and the Department of Energy; armed security for multiple army ammunition depots; Cape Canaveral and shuttle landing sites in Africa; at least 20 US embassies across the world, and even facilities run by an enterprise that one would think could protect its own, the US Department of Defense. Indeed the Department of Defense in 2001 awarded Wackenhut its James S. Cogwheel Award for Outstanding Industrial Security Achievement. Corporate clients number well over 1,000, from GM plants in Latin America to the offices of Nike, Campbells Soup, and Levi's.

In the late 1980s Wackenhut belatedly moved into the private prison business; its first prison opened only in 1989. This was seizing the chance with a vengeance: watching rising prison populations, Wackenhut and its competitors, including the better-known Corrections Corporation of America, avidly pursued state contracts for prison services. The contradictions between promises of lower costs and higher profits soon became evident: as their prison operations expanded, so too did abuses, escapes, local protests and media exposés. In New Mexico, a 500 page legislative report specifically attacked two prisons run by Wackenhut—including one that had a riot in August 1999 that left one inmate and guard dead—revealing understaffing at minimum wages. In Texas

Wackenhut was stripped of a $12 million-a-year contract in September 1999 and fined $625,000; twelve former guards were indicted for having sex with female inmates—as occurred in another Florida Wackenhut facility. Perhaps the most notorious case of abuse took place at Wackenhut's juvenile prison in Louisiana (McNair, 2000), leading the US Justice Department to sue Wackenhut in order to protect imprisoned boys from indoor tear gas attacks, pepper spray, and a lack of basic items including underwear, blankets, medical treatment and food. In September 2000 the State of Louisiana agreed in Federal Court to end its experiments with privately-run juvenile prisons, and was specifically prohibited from placing any more inmates in Wackenhut's Jena facility. In mid-2001 Wackenhut reported nearly $1.3 million in losses due to the closure, with the empty Louisiana facility continuing to cost $200,000 (Aneiros, 2001).

Wall Street was not amused by such problems: the share prices of both the Wackenhut Corrections and its parent company Wackenhut Corporation fell by half over 1995-2000.[2] Yet even as short-term profits in the US dissipated, Wackenhut's long-term gross revenues from all sources continued to grow, rising from $2.15 billion in 1999 to $2.50 billion in 2000—with expansion especially notable in its global security services. The future, it seemed, was indeed a global one.

THE PRISON INDUSTRIAL COMPLEX GOES GLOBAL? LATE 20TH CENTURY PROJECTIONS

Given the failures of privatized prisons in the US—not the least of which is the rise of an organized movement against private prisons and mandatory sentencing—might not US and European prison and security multinationals do what their manufacturing brothers have done, and outsource the bulk of their operations overseas?

One path towards this end is foreclosed, since it is not, *yet*, plausible to outsource the bulk of prisoners who are US citizens, i.e. to ship US prisoners out of the country to take advantage of cheaper labor, locations, and conditions (although this is now being done for "illegal" immigrants and refugees worldwide). It is however possible for US and European firms to replicate their private prison model in other rich, wealthy and white states. In this sense a simple branch plant model is moving ahead. As can be seen from a map of Wackenhut or Group 4's overseas operations, almost all are located in Europe, North America, or Australia/New Zealand. These are limited but highly rich pickings. Of the world's prison population of about 8.6 million at the turn of the century, half is accounted for by the US (1.85m), Russia (1.05m), and China (1.4m) (Walmsley, 2000, p.1). It is unlikely, however, that either China or Russia, wary as they are of the US and protective as they are of state power, will invite in US or even European prison firms.

Leaving aside expansion in the US, the most profitable areas for expansion thus remain Australia and Western Europe (Austria, Belgium, France, Germany, Greece, Italy, Liechtenstein, Luxembourg, Monaco, Netherlands, Portugal, Spain, Switzerland), which had a total prison population of about 425,000 in the late 1990s (Walmsley, 2000, p. 5). Table 1 illustrates the situation as of 1999 (Walmsley, 2000, p.1):

Table 1: Core Prison States and Rates, circa 1999

	Prison Population	Prison Population Rate (per 100,000 of national population)
United States	1,860,520	680
Canada	32,970	110
Japan	52,715	40
Western Europe	285,326	95
United Kingdom	73,195	125
France	53,948	90
Germany	79,666	95
Netherlands	14,057	90
Portugal	13,086	130
Spain	44,197	110
Australia	20,656	110

Growth rates of imprisonment in most of these states in the 1990s century were impressive, reaching and even surpassing almost the 60% rise in the US. Figuring prominently among these are the Netherlands 89%, Italy 53%, Portugal 46%, Germany 40%, the UK 40%, and Australia 51% (Walmsley, 2001, p.16). Declining crime rates in the US have not, moreover, resulted in parallel declines in public or private imprisonment. Continued expansion in these rich states is likely to occur under three conditions.

First, as long as balanced budget policies are matched by economic stagnation (or recession), pressures to privatize state prison expenditures are likely to hold or even rise. The expansion of sub-contracting of health and other services *within* state-run prisons also offers a new path of prison privatization even in states that are committed to owning their own prisons. Privately-run health care within state-owned prisons, given aging prison populations, is a prime example.

Second, politicians, public policy makers, and the media show little sign of relenting in their "wars on crime." Indeed, there are good reasons to fear the broadening and deepening of this process, as economic stagnation accelerates growing inequality between centers of wealth on the one hand, and poor households, neighborhoods, and youth on the other.

Third, new groups are also likely to be criminalized, particularly people of color from the Middle East and Africa. The passage of new laws against immigrants and non-citizens is but one sign of this trend—and is evident not just in the United States but in recent events and public debates in Canada, Australia and Western Europe. Even prior to 9/11, some of Wackenhut's most profitable and operations were immigration "detention" facilities in the United

States, England, and Australia. And the potential for growth here is significant. In the US, between 1990 and 1999 the number of Federal inmates held for immigration offenses grew by 488%, faster than even the 124% increase for drug offenders; by the end of 2000 more persons were in Federal prisons for immigration convictions than for robbery (Beck, 2001, p. 12). This includes, one must notice, only convicted immigrants (even before the Patriot Act and related actions came into effect, the Federal government had been imprisoning immigrants for months and years without trial). In a similar fashion, the Australian government has long been expanding detention centers for Asian refugees; by 2001 Wackenhut was already operating six detention centers, housing 3,500 detainees for the Australian government (Wackenhut Corrections, 2001). And in May 2001 Wackenhut announced it had won a contract to run a new detention center in Scotland.

These observations suggest that neither of the dominant paradigms of prison history and privatization fully hold. On the one hand, there is little evidence that there is a universal replication of the US (or European) pattern of national prison development. While wealthy white states share several key medium-run trends that are often attached to the term "Prison Industrial Complex," the rise of newly criminalized populations tied to transnational fears and wars suggests new, global processes at play. On the other hand, a simple spread of private prison models by the multinational corporations' branch plant operations seems both limited in evidence and explanatory power; many new carceral operations fall outside the explanatory power of capital. While many phenomena can thus be fitted within these paradigms, current patterns, such as the ring of prison and detention facilities encircling the centers of the world's wealth, suggest global processes and inequalities at work. These cannot be explained by national models or local forces alone.

GLOBAL CARCERAL GEOGRAPHY: BRANCH PLANT OR COLONIAL PLANT?

The prospect of expanding prison privatization in Africa and the rest of the world suggests another front in the globalization of punishment and imprisonment. But how likely is this possibility? As one moves beyond the borders of Europe and rich settler states a key limitation is obvious: in the vast majority of states not only are imprisonment rates far lower than in the rich North, but spending on prisoners and prisons is generally also quite meager by comparison. As already noted, some of the largest countries, moreover, have states firmly committed to keeping repressive power in their hands and under their direct control, and this includes two of the very largest prison states, China and Russia.

In the face of these factors, what states might be targeted by private prison corporations? One might first look at states with public funds to divert to private hands via privatization, namely countries that the World Bank terms "middle income states"—those with average gross national income per capita [GNIPC][3] incomes ranging from roughly $1000-5,000 (the US and Japan are

$34,000 per capital by comparison). This includes at the lower end of the range the Philippines ($1,040) and South Africa ($3,000), to Chile ($4600) and Mexico ($5,000) at the upper end.[4]

A second factor enters however: not all these states have significant numbers of prisoners; prison populations and imprisonment rates vary widely across Africa, Asia, Eastern and Central Europe, and Latin America. Small national populations or low imprisonment rates would rule out almost all of West, East and North Africa, and most of South Asia. Richer states, and particularly those with a settler heritage, do however stand out as the country list in Table 2 illustrates. The countries here are only a selection, for illustrative purposes, of those states with either sizable prison populations, incarceration rates, and/or relatively high levels of state expenditure and national income:

Table 2: Wealth and Prisoners? Target African, Asian, Latin American States, Circa 1999

	Prison Population*	Prison Population Rate*	GNIPC US$ 1999***	National Population (million) **
World	8,600,000	140	4,990	5,980
Africa				
Egypt	80,000	120	1,380	63
Kenya	41,064	140	360	29
Lesotho	2,552	120	570	2
Botswana	6,413	400	3,040	2
South Africa	161,163	400	3,160	42
Zimbabwe	19,256	170	530	12
Asia				
China	1,408,860	110	780	1,254
Taiwan	31,000	150	.	21
Kazakhstan	82,945	495	1,290	15
Kyrgyzstan	19,857	440	300	5
Korea	6,414	245	8,480	47
India	381,147	40	440	998
Indonesia	55,026	25	580	207
Philippines	21,287	30	1,060	75
Singapore	11,858	340	21,190	4
Uzbekistan	60,000	260	640	24
Eastern Europe-Middle East				
Azerbaijan	24,881	325	560	8
Belarus	58,879	575	2,550	10
Israel	9,337	150	16,310	6
Russian Federation	1,060,085	730	1,750	146

Turkey	64,907	100	2,880	64
Czech Republic	23,060	225	5,000	10
Ukraine	217,400	430	770	50
Latin America & Caribbean				
Brazil	194,074	115	3,880	168
Chile	30,852	205	4,600	15
Jamaica	4,288	170	2,400	3
Mexico	139,707	145	4,440	97
Peru	27,452	75	2,130	25
Puerto Rico	16,524	435	..	4
Venezuela	23,147	100	3,730	24

Sources: *Walmsley 2000; **World Bank 2001; GNIPC figures for Taiwan and Puerto Rico absent from World Bank tables (since they are not recognized as independent states).

The most recent cases of the spread of the prison industrial complex beyond the borders of the US and Europe indicate, however, that it is not only state strength and the size of a country's prison establishment that determines the target states for private prison corporations. In some areas the international war on drugs is an important factor in promoting imprisonment; as Walmsley (2001) argues, high imprisonment rates in Belarus, Kazakhstan, and Central America are primarily attributable to the imprisonment of non-nationals on drug charges. The establishment of private prisons seems, however, more tightly constrained to middle income states and especially those with recent dictatorships—as indicated by the discussions of prison expansion and privatization in Brazil, Chile, Israel, South Korea, and Thailand.

As in South Africa, many of these states have recently undergone regime change. This opens the door to the reconstruction of the national prison system, particularly the "demilitarization" of prison administration and staff as has taken place in South Africa. Such transitions can also propel forward the adoption of the latest international innovations and so-called "best practice," including private-public prison partnerships. These can set off in turn similar moves in neighboring states, as in Group 4's negotiations to build a central prison for all of prisoners of Lesotho, the small state encircled by South Africa. Lesotho is clearly an outlier here, with a population of only 2 million, a gross national income per capita of only $540, and a total prison population of 2,552 prisoners (although a moderately high incarceration rate of 120).

CONVERGING LOCAL AND GLOBAL FACTORS

As these examples suggest, it takes the intersection of local and global forces to perceive and explain the pattern of private prison expansion beyond the US and Europe. Our analysis pinpoints four general, global tendencies underlining the expansion of private imprisonment at home and the movement of prison multinationals abroad:

1. Growing inequality world-wide, and the corresponding development of a global security system designed to protect the rich, predominantly white, and wealthy;
2. Attempts by prison corporations to evade constraints on US and European operations—including actions of resistance—and generate new profit centers by moving abroad;
3. Pressures by the IMF, World Bank, US and European Union on African, Asian and Latin American states to (a) cut government spending to meet structural adjustment targets, and (b) open their doors to foreign multinationals; and
4. The privatization of state enterprises—including health, education, and prison functions—to the advantage of foreign capital and local ruling classes.

Private prisons are most likely to arise where these global processes are particularly strong and intersect specific, local forces and histories. Among these local factors I would highlight four:

1. A government possessing the administrative and financial authority to generate long-term payments to private capital (our "middle income" states above);
2. The replacement of a repressive regime that leave behind a strong imprisonment culture and military-police infrastructure (as in Russia, Eastern Europe, Chile, Brazil, South Africa);
3. The existence of a state that denies substantive citizenship to, and thus often criminalizes and racializes a significant proportion of its population, most notably settler states with indigenous populations or peoples of color; and
4. High levels of inequality within national and across regional boundaries, particularly the existence of high levels of regional inequality fostering migration across national territorial boundaries and xenophobia.

Taken together, these global processes and local factors provide a framework to understand both the forces behind privatization and where multinationals may target new populations for their operations.

THE POST-LIBERAL, GLOBAL CARCERAL SYSTEM

As the intersection of these processes suggests, emerging imprisonment patterns mark far more than simply the spread of the US private prison model on a world-scale, with multinationals replicating their operations via branch plants.

The duplication of national US conditions is found in relatively few states outside the UK and a few white settler states. The emerging global pattern suggests something more unsettling that is not constrained to private firms and national criminal justice systems: a post-liberal and global carceral regime that targets and criminalizes select populations at the key dividing lines between areas of the rich and poor, white and colored, and settler and indigenous populations.

This is a very different scenario that simply replicating branch plant prisons wherever there is a surplus of state funding and high levels of imprisonment. It is also a quite different understanding than those derived from Foucault's argument that prisons develop as national institutions of control for the citizens of modern, advanced capitalist states (Foucault, 1977). This argument, as inspirational as it is for Europe and the United States, presumes a rupture and linear development of autonomous modern states, economies, and prisons—and then the possible diffusion of this Euro-American model wherever modern states and economies emerge. Such a perspective diverts us from any understanding of the colonial and racial underpinnings of the rise of the West, including not just the interdependent rise of wealth and poverty world-wide, but also the transnational and racialized basis of Western ideologies and institutions of justice and imprisonment (as suggested in Agozino, 2003).

Nor is the world beyond the borders of Europe and the United States awaiting incorporation into a modern prison-industrial complex as a reliance upon a branch plant or a Foucauldian model might suggest. It is far more accurate to see punishment and imprisonment as a long-term, global process, indeed as a single system that produces, protects, and reproduces wealth and racial privilege across the world. In this respect existing historical and theoretical models fail us in either projecting universal models or proclaiming only unique local ones. What is needed instead is a fuller understanding of how the development of prisons in North American and Europe were part of the emergence of a historical world of punishment and prisons, and how this complex has changed over the last 500 years. Such a perspective was suggested long ago in Fanon's and others analyses of colonialism, which began to trace dynamics of under/development, repression and resistance as they operated across the divides of colonizer/colonized, Europe/Africa, rich white/poor black, settler/native (Fanon, 1968, pp. 35-106).

Developing these insights would suggest that the current acceleration of global inequality, neo-liberal policies, and multicultural racism is remaking the world division of imprisonment, with high-tech prisons and detention centers guarding the rich white North—and new forms of punishment, including private prisons for the first time, guarding sub-imperial centers standing between the South and North. Everywhere transnational determinants of national patterns are obvious, from the racialization, criminalization, and incarceration of African and Arab peoples, to rich state's increasingly narrow definition of citizenship and community. This global, post-liberal carceral world, akin to emergent conceptions of a global apartheid system, fits the contemporary data and historical evidence outlined above far better than extensions of the nation-ally-autonomous and replicable models, whether developed from Foucault, the political economy of branch plant operations, or even, in large part, Wacquant's dramatic model of the spread of the US model of the "prisonized ghetto" and the "ghettoized prison" to social-democratic Western Europe (Wacquant, 2001).

Approaching current imprisonment patterns from a world-historical standpoint would also allow us to grasp more fully the centrality of the world prison and security complex to the maintenance of hegemony, including the rise and fall of the US-led, post-World War II regime. As US hegemony is increasingly reduced to pure repressive power, moreover, escalating struggles may be expected to take place over punishment and the private imprisonment complex. Local anti-prison and anti-racist campaigns may increasingly be linked to successful campaigns all across the world against structural adjustment, debt, the privatization of state services, and the promotion of war and violence.

POSTSCRIPT: ASSESSING PREDICTIONS AND PARADIGMS SINCE 9/11

Much in the world of repression and prisons has changed since the above argument was presented and written in late 2001—and much has not. Two world-level developments are especially notable. First, the concentration of global security firms proceeds: in May 2002 Group 4 Falck (the result of a merger in 2000 of Group 4 and Falck), headquartered in Copenhagen, took over Wackenhut International, which in turn had controlled Wackenhut Corrections Corporation. Group 4 Falck, with operations in over 80 countries, desired Wackenhut's US and worldwide security operations in particular; in 2003 Wackenhut Corrections purchased Group 4 Falck's 57 percent holding of Wackenhut Corrections for $132 million. Wackenhut then emerged as an independent firm, under a new name: The GEO Group. In 2004 Group 4 Falck merged with Securicor to form an even larger firm, Group 4 Securicor.

Second, new global forms of regulating unruly populations have emerged in the wake of the US and allied states' pursuit of a global surveillance and incarceration system, from Australia and South Africa's intensive drive to imprison and export "illegal" immigrants, to the now infamous prison complex propagated under Bush's "war against terror." While the abuses in the Abu Ghraib prison have received the most attention, a set of alliances has clearly been developed to construct a control-and-imprisonment system that stretches from the US, across Western and Eastern Europe, to Iraq, Afghanistan, Pakistan and beyond.

These developments have offered private corporations valuable new profit centers especially in the face of stable prison populations, falling official crime rates, and the increasingly publicized failures and costs of prison privatization in their home regions. Providing security services after 9/11 has thus emerged as the central arena for expanding corporate operations and profits. US and European security and prison firms quickly engaged in security and prison operations in Iraq after its conquest by the US (Public Services International Research Unit

2003) and, more importantly, expect significant world-wide growth in immigration detention centers, anti-terrorist security work, and federal and central state prisons in the US and Europe.

Continued expansion of the US prison complex at the local state level remains uneven. Here the patterns and predictions laid out above for late 2001 still hold in 2005: the massive surge of prison growth and privatization in the 1990s has clearly slowed in core areas of the world-economy, and been concentrated and stabilized outside the core. Expansion in semiperipheral states with a history of imprisonment, repression and privatization continues, as evidenced by privatization initiatives in Korea, Chile, Peru, Costa Rica, Mexico and Israel among others.[5]

Yet not all is rosy for prison firms as the costs of private prisons are revealed. In South Africa the revelation of the extremely high costs of the private prisons and allegations of corruption in the awarding of contracts has helped squash any new private prison plans (Sloth-Nielsen, 2003, pp. 24-26). Continued rumors of Group 4 Falck's discussions with Lesotho in the opening years of the new millennium over building a large, private, central prison have remained just that: rumors. In both South Africa and Lesotho ministerial officials have opposed private prisons for quite clear reasons: they dictate not only the loss of state employment and control, but their high costs siphon off funding for existing prisons and other state services. In the case of South Africa, reportedly 50-75% of the entire prison budget went to the two private prison contracts which housed less than 5% of the total prison population (Public Services International Research Unit 2002:50; Sloth-Nelson, 2003). While the two private prisons get high marks by inspectors (Tapscott, 2005), the state prison system has been left grossly underfunded and overcrowded.

One factor was clearly underestimated in our earlier argument: the impact of the burgeoning global justice and movement, which is turning back the rush towards the privatization of social services, and calling instead for the public provision of basic social services and needs. This in turn has changed the climate within which anti-imprisonment and human rights groups operate. Although "alterglobalization" movements are stronger in Latin America than Africa, South Africa's anti-privatization movements, focused upon state services such as water, health, housing and electricity, have nevertheless fostered an unfavorable climate for the high costs and corruption associated with private prisons and public-private partnerships. Of the four new prisons built recently, none have been contracted to the private sector. The search for new models of prison transformation has clearly turned against prison privatization (e.g. Giffard, 2002, *Tract Two*, 2002).

As these locally-active and globally-networked movements push forward alternative practices they will raise the possibility of radically transforming not only private but public prison practices. This prospect only reinforces our call to abandon models based on US and European national systems in favor of an understanding imprisonment as a long-term, world-wide, process. As I have argued above, there are substantive signs that the highly-differentiated yet integrated global system is undergoing significant transformation. Governments in the United States and Europe have set the stage for not simply the acceleration and privatization of imprisonment, but for new, post-liberal systems of control over unruly populations at home, population movements across imposed territorial borders, and access to basic citizenship and human rights everywhere.

The novel contours and outcomes of these processes are suggested by the gulag archipelago at the heart of the United States' new terrorist war, which, when coupled to the imprisonment of poor people of color at home, reveals the collapse of the liberal social compact and a central pillar of the emerging, post-liberal world order. On the other side of the Atlantic a parallel revelation of this process can be seen in the rise of fortress Europe, with new legislation, prisons, and detention centers targeting persons of African and Middle Eastern descent (see Wacquant, 1999). Against these developments stand popular calls for social justice and basic human needs. If we are to imagine and construct alternative forms of social justice, recent evidence suggests they will emerge not from core or even semiperipheral states, but from the activities of new movements pushing against the now generation-old, neo-liberal project.

Notes

1. Suggestions from conference participants and Michael West are gratefully acknowledged.
2. Wackenhut Corrections stock traded as high as $45 per share in 1996, but fell below $20 by the end of that year and has been below $10 for most of 2000; on September 21, 2001 it closed at $13.51. Wackenhut Corporation, the mother firm which owns a majority of the shares of Wackenhut Corrections, saw its own shares reach a peak in 1996 of $45, only to fall sharply in mid-1999 to below $15 per share, where prices have remained in 2000/2001 (WHC closed at $20.25 on September 21, 2001, but by October 26 had fallen to $13.73).
3. Figures on the Gross National Product (GNP per capita) are at market rates (World Bank Atlas method) for the year 2000, from World Bank 2001. Low-income states would range from roughly $100-200 (Ethiopia, Congo-Mozambique, Nigeria, Cambodia) to $400-900) India ($460) and China ($840); obviously these figures are only rough indicators of vast disparities between states, and hide internal inequalities which are vast.
4. In most of these states, the Philippines, South Africa, Chile, and Mexico, however the profits from guarding wealthy corporations and individuals far exceeds possible prison revenues; the global security business is estimated to be worth at least $100 billion/year. Group 4, which like Wackenhut is grounded in the security business, has long been pursuing expansion in Central and Eastern Europe, including the Baltic states, the Czech Republic, Hungary, Poland, and Slovakia; the group's reach also extends as well to India, Singapore, Hong Kong, Indonesia, Morocco, and of course South Africa where the firm just purchased the local guard firm Callguard Security Service and its 3,600 employees. Wackenhut for its part has similar, largely security operations, from Chile to Greece to Columbia.

5.   The best source to track such developments in South Korea, Chile, Peru, Costa Rica, Mexico, Thailand, Israel and related states is the Prison Privatization Report International newsletter published by the by Public Services International Research Unit at www.psiru.org/justice/. For these states see for example newsletters #55 (May 2003) for South Korea; # 61 (March 2004) and #45 (Jan. 2002) for Chile; #54 (April 2003) for Peru; #68 (May/June 2005) and #52 (December 2002/2003) for Costa Rica; #49 (August/September 2002) for Mexico; #70 (Sept.-Nov. 2005), #68 (May/June 2005) and #56 (June 2003) for Israel; and #70 (Sept.-Nov. 2005) and #67 (March 2005) for Thailand. See also for Israel *Globes Online* 2003 and for South Korea, *Korea Times* 2003.

References

Agozino, Biko. 2003. *Counter-Colonial Criminology: A Critique of Imperialist Reason.* London: Pluto Press.

Aneiros, Fabian. 2001, June 15. Wackenhut looks beyond troubled year and tight labor market. *South Florida Business Journal.* September 19, 2001, http://southflorida. bcentral.com/southflorida/stories/2001/06/18/focus9.html.

Beck, Allen. 2001. *Prisoners in 2000.* Bureau of Justice, Statistics Bulletin, August. September 22, 2001, www.ojp.usdoj.gov/bjs/pub/pdf/p00.pdf.

Stephan, James J. *State Prison Expenditures, 2001.* Bureau of Justice Special Report, June. www.ojp.usdoj.gov/bjs/pub/pdf/spe01.pdf

Bond, Patrick. 2000. *Elite Transition: From Apartheid to Neoliberalism in South Africa.* London: Pluto Press.

Fanon, Frantz. 1968. *Wretched of the Earth.* New York: Grove.

Foucault, Michel. 1977. *Discipline and Punish: the Birth of the Prison.* New York: Pantheon.

Giffard, Chris. 2002. Restorative Justice: An Option for South Africa? *Track Two* 11, 2, April: 34-38.

Globes Online. 2003, December 8. Yediot Ahronot: Gov't approves privately owned prisons. January 8, 2004, from www.globes.co.il.

The Korea Herald. 2001, August 30. S. Korea to introduce Asia's first privately run prison. September 18, 2001, from Lexis-Nexus.

Korea Times. February 10, 2003. Private Prison to Open in 2005. Retrieved January 9, 2004, from Lexis-Nexus.

McNair, James. 2000. Wackenhut a Prisoner of Its Own Problems. *Miami Herald,* April 15, 2000. September 18, 2001, from Lexis-Nexus.

Oppler, Sarah. 1998. *Correcting Corrections: Prospects for South Africa's Prisons.* Institute for Security Studies monograph 29, October 1998. September 17, 2001, www.iss. co.za/Pubs/Monographs/No29/Crisis.html.

Public Services International Research Unit (Various). Prison Privatisation Report International. Newsletter. London: PSIRU, University of Greenwich. Retrieved from www.psiru.org/justice/

_____. October 2003. Iraq. Prison Privatisation Report International, No. 58. January 8, 2004, www.psiru.org/justic/PPRI58.asp#IRAQ.

Sloth-Nielsen, Julia. 2003. *Overview of Policy Developments in South African Correctional Services 1994-2002.* CSPRI Research Paper Series, No. 1, July. Cape Town: Civil Society Prison Reform Initiative.

South Africa. Ministry of Correctional Services. May 25, 2001. Skosana: Site visit of Mangaung Maximum Security Prison, Bloemfontein Free State Province. September 18, 2001, wwwdcs.pwv.gov.za/Speeches/Minister/28AMay2001.html.

Tapscott, Chris. 2005. *A Study in Best Practice in Prison Governance.* University of the Western Cape (South Africa): CSPRI Research Paper Series, No. 9.

Track Two. 2002. *Special Issue: Towards Prison Transformation in South Africa.* Vol. 11, No. 2, April. Cape Town: Centre for Conflict Resolution.

Wackenhut Corrections. 2001, September 18. Wackenhut Corrections' Australian Subsidiary in Negotiations to Develop Three New Immigration Detention Centres Totaling 3,000 Beds. Wackenhut press release. September 20, 2001, http://www.wackenhut.com.

Wacquant, Loïc. 1999. Suitable Enemies. *Punishment and Society,* 1: 215-222.

_____ 2001. Deadly Symbiosis: When Ghetto and Prison Meet and Mesh." *Punishment and Society* 3: 95-133.

Walmsley, Roy. 2000. *Research Findings No. 116: World Prison Population List (second edition).* United Kingdom, Home Office Research, Development and Statistics Directorate. September 18, 2001, http://www.homeoffice.gov.uk/rds/pdfs/r116.pdf.

_____. 2001. *An Overview of World Imprisonment: Global Prison Populations, Trends, and Solution.* Paper presented at the United Nations Programme Network Institute Technical Assistance Workshop, Vienna, Austria.

World Bank. 2001. *2001 World Development Indicators database 7/16/01.* September 27, 2001, www.worldbank.org/data/databytopic/GNPPC.pdf.

PART IV

Alternative Visions on Prisons and Punishment

16

BRIDGING THE GULF: REBUILDING BURNT BRIDGES BETWEEN PRISONERS AND COMMUNITIES

Ishka JoJo Alpern

My name is Ishka JoJo Alpern. My friends and family call me JoJo. I'm from Ithaca. For the past eight years and counting I've been incarcerated in the New York Department of Correctional Services for assaulting several civilians and police officers during a drunken rage that, even after all these years, leaves me stunned. At the time of my arrest I was 23 years young and had been struggling with drug and alcohol addiction my entire adolescence. Although my crimes cannot be justified by the above circumstances, they were certainly a foreseeable outcome; all the warning signs were present. Somehow, however, I failed to heed those warnings. The courts, which had dealt with my escalating patterns of criminality and addiction, were ineffective in their intervention. My family and friends, whom I had pushed away while moving ever further into the street life, were not an influence, and the community, being largely unaware, was silent.

I provide this information simply as a contextual backdrop against which my thoughts can be explored and judged. Obviously I am a convicted felon, but I have also spent the last eight years committed to change.

I was lucky enough to find out about this conference[1] in April, with plenty of time to work out a presentation. I drew up a reasonably good outline using bridge architecture and construction as a controlling metaphor. That was early in May. Then: nothing. My inclination towards procrastination took over. I was uninspired even though the issues I wished to present were pressing and relevant to the seminar. And, although the paper lingered in my consciousness, something held me back.

All that changed on September 11th. Exactly 99 months from the culmination of my own petty infamy, the morning skies filled with terror beyond any this generation has known. To place my own criminality in contrast to the bombing of the World Trade Center is not some sick vision of grandiosity, but an attempt at building a set of analogies inherently American. A syllogism based on the fact that every man, woman, and child is a reflection of societal mores and that government and institutions are sources of moral and ethical standards; therefore, deficiencies in the individual result from deficiencies in the government and our institutions, and they must recognize these deficiencies and change accordingly.

I was socialized, as many Americans are, to equate physical domination with respect and power. In my home, school, and on television I learned that physical channels were appropriate and effective forms of expression. I turned my body into a weapon. My fists spoke the words of pain and frustration I could not articulate. That would have been acceptable if I had joined the Army, police department or had become an athlete. And I did do some of those things and was praised highly with trophies and commendations. But when I took it to the streets, my behavior became taboo, and I paid a five to 15 year price.

When I entered the system in 1993 one of the things intimated was that my black ass could get lost in here, that I would be crippled or killed if I tried to flex against the system. What I learned quickly was that the criminal justice system is a huge economy that is held accountable not by the communities or judges that send felons to its confines, but by a few administrative types in Albany. I was immediately struck by the fact that although it was my community that demanded retribution for my criminal behavior, they would have little if any say in the meting out of my punishment. Once the sentence was proclaimed, they were shut out from the process by the very nature of prison architecture and the inherent conditions of confinement: isolation and control. I imagined my situation in terms of a series of circles starting with my self along with my family, community, and our society among humanity. But instead of a series of concentric circles starting in the center and moving outward so that each circle was embraced by another, I envisioned a sort of Venn diagram with very little intersecting area within.

Almost immediately I began to struggle against the separation I felt. I made an instinctive, partially subconscious decision that in order for me to heal emotionally and spiritually, I needed to reconnect my people. I wrote to family and loved ones, friends, and even to members of the community that I knew only superficially. I informed them of my need to change and of my attempts to do so. And in this way I began to draw together the disparate circles, creating a much larger intersecting area of interaction and experience. I can now see that my endeavor was to not only draw my circles closer together, but to set them concentric to one another in a way that would enable me to explore more fully my spirit: that little circle of light in us that connects us to all else. This exploration led me to see beyond sets of circles encompassing and nourishing one another to a vision of spherical interaction in which energy flowed through Earth, humanity, community, family and me, to light—the light connecting back to all the individual circles dynamically creating a spherical cocoon in which I could grow and develop.

You may be asking, "How are the above revelations relevant to this conference?" Well, I believe their relevance begins in the prisoner's ability to see her or himself emotionally and spiritually in relationship to the larger whole. Only then, once this foundational cornerstone has been set, is he able to take concrete steps toward habilitation. (The use of habilitation replaces rehabilitation because one must be habilitated in order to be rehabilitated.) So what is habilitation in this context? First, the ability of prisoners to live at peace with themselves as individuals while exploring their intellect, talents and spirit; then, to live within the prison micro-community similarly; and ultimately, to cohabitate successfully upon release in a healthy and fruitful manner.

To facilitate habilitation, certain resources must be made available to prisoners. Of course, drug and alcohol abuse programming must be available, something the Department of Corrections does mandate for a six-month period for most prisoners. Further, spiritual guidance and services should be encouraged, something the Department does very well. Also, job skills and vocations must be a priority, and from my experience many of the vocational classes are often well fitted if sometimes less well taught. Sadly, education, the one resource essential above those stated already, is poorly provided. What makes this oversight so glaring is the fact that education has been the only proven method of habilitation. The more education a prisoner gets while incarcerated, the less likely he will recidivate. The lower recidivism rates are, the less crime there is. Isn't this the intent of our prison system? How can we afford to miss this essential truth? More education, less crime!

In 1995 when then President Clinton and Governor Pataki collectively eliminated funding for college programs in New York State prisons, I had already earned 36 credits with an excellent G.P.A. That experience resounded within me, providing a track record of success and a springboard into other areas of endeavor. From that, I have learned to think critically and analyze my own experience and relationships with others and institutions from an informed perspective. This single tool empowered me so viscerally I can say that much of what I accomplished over these last eight years is due to that first academic success.

Presently, New York State requires prisoners to attend educational classes only up to the ninth grade level. This is absurd! How many ninth graders do you know that own the skills necessary to provide for themselves and their families? How can we expect a person that has already displayed an inability to reason morally to somehow miraculously change their thinking without giving them the tools to do so? I certainly don't expect success from such a scenario, so how can the government? I'm not sure that they do-and that is particularly frightening.

This brings us back to our earlier syllogism. If our government and institutions are foundations of moral and ethical thought and behavior, and we find that the average prisoner reads at a sixth grade level, there must be change. If violence continues to plague our nation from within and without, we must analyze our domestic and foreign policies to find the catalyst. As bombs begin to drop in Afghanistan and we demand the complicity of other nations with naked threats of retribution, the incubator of individual violent behavior is not hard to find.

The problem I see is this: Although we look to our government and institutions for guidance and service, they are behemoth in size and unable to recognize our individual needs. So it becomes our responsibility as individuals and communities to reach up, restructuring as needed. This sound idealistic, I know, but let me walk through an example. As stated earlier, the New York State

Department of Corrections is a massive beast. It's composed of over 70 facilities, and includes more than 65,000 prisoners. There are at least 25,000 employees, not including people that work closely with the Department providing criminal justice services. This is only on the state level. There are also several dozen county jails as well as a few federal penitentiaries. The state cannot possibly service the individual needs of each prisoner except in the most generic sense. When a community decides that a member's activities are unacceptable, they ultimately end up sending that person to this particular government.

Note

1. "Thinking about Prisons: Theory and Practice." Conference held at SUNY Cortland, N.Y., October 26-28, 2001.

17

NO MORE PROGRAMS!
A RADICAL CRITIQUE OF PRISON
PROGRAMS AND ALTERNATIVES

Howard S. Davidson

If our aim is abolitionism, our immediate struggle is to create means that most directly abolish the institutions and productive relations creating injustice and destroying caring social relationships *worldwide*.[1] In order to abolish the social and economic disparities causing a vast polarization of wealth and misery, imprisonment as a form of social control must also be abolished. We understand that if you struggle against the prison, you struggle against the wider productive and social relations in which prisons are embedded. Jeffery Reiman and others have shown convincingly that the criminal justice system is a racist, homophobic, authoritarian institution reserved for the poor, especially poor people of colour (Reiman, 1990; Christie, 1994; Parenti, 2000).

Since the 1970s it has become increasingly clear that prisons do not fail society; indeed, they endure relatively well as a principle form of state-sponsored repression. Prisons use harsh punishment to enforce a particular definition of crime as harm done to particular persons, and only in certain ways, and harm done to things belonging to some folks. Other harmful acts operate freely in the market place (e.g., owning and operating sweatshops, forcing the poorest of the poor to pay debt to the richest of the rich).

The politics and experience of imprisonment also plays a defining role in transforming a particular "dangerous class" into a "delinquent class." Therefore, the abolitionist struggle against the depoliticalization of criminality and punishment must be intimately connected to and supportive of a struggle for the politicalization of prisoners and against their domestication (Apple, 2000; Collins, 1991; Freire, 1996).

I can put the problem differently. As abolitionists do we demand more prison programs? If so, why; what do we hope to achieve? Is it to ameliorate immediate suffering by providing prisoners with intellectual and emotional relief while they live under cruel, discriminatory conditions kept in place by authoritarian, arguably fascist bureaucrats and guards? Is it to transform prisoners: to rehabilitate, regulate, reintegrate, or politicise them; or is it something more dialogical, reciprocal, and dialectical?

What is achieved by a particular program is not always clear; indeed, the multiple consequences of any activity as complex as educational or therapeutic programs operating in a prison setting are likely to be contradictory. For example, officially sanctioned schooling enjoys considerable support among prisoners. At the same time, prison authorities and their associations support schooling as a more or less effective form of population management (i.e., as a form of control).

The very idea of corrections depends on profound assumptions about socially acceptable values, norms, regulations and laws, as well as presuppositions about "being a good citizen."[2] The ideal of corrections—the espoused purpose of officially sanctioned prison programs—is an internalised discipline and obedience (i.e., domestication). In contrast to security, programs do not teach with physical restraint, fear, and pain; rather, anger management, life skills, cognitive thinking skills, and literacy and higher education programs teach self-governance, self-regulation, and self-control.

But schooling was also introduced as a humanitarian reform to ameliorate the hardships of incarceration. Prisoners report that some programs, especially adult basic and higher education programs, have made a significant difference in how the incarcerated poor live with others and with themselves. Tiyo Attallah Salah El, a leading voice on abolition from "inside", writes:

> In pragmatic terms, we must analyze existing "prison programs" meagre though they may be, to assess precisely how they work, while forming ourselves into political organizations to structure recommendations. We need to gather and duplicate whatever is valuable and bring [into prisons] persons to impart and interpret information and share experiences (Attallah Salah-El, 1992, p. 47).

Abolitionists are well advised by this comment. The rest of this paper is about analysing "how they work" and examining ways in which prisoners have organized themselves in educational activities. I think there are at least two major issues here: (1) the contradictory functions of prison programs and (2) a tendency to accept official definitions of what constitutes prison programs, a definition that prevents a critical consideration of prisoner organized activities.

THE CONTRADICTIONS

In 1989 the American Correctional Association produced a pamphlet on the advantages of literacy education programs. It informed wardens that once

> offenders become accustomed to functioning in the more structured environment of the classroom, they are often more amenable to engaging in more structured activities.... [Although the] immediate benefit of improved literacy levels of ...offenders may have little impact on overall institution operations, *the net effect of education ...is to enhance supervision and security in the correctional environment* (my emphasis, American Correctional Association, 1989, p. 6-7).

Controlling "idleness" is a stated objectives in Federal Bureau of Prisons policy documents on mandatory educational programs. A survey of 823 wardens in U. S. state prisons in 1995 led researchers to conclude that programs "soak up otherwise uncommitted time within the prison week...and thus serve a critical control function within the prison" (Johnson, et al, 1997, p. 38).

The instrumental use of programs to "soak up...time" is not new. There are direct relationships among the growth of corporate capitalism, the exploitation of cheap immigrant labour, and the growth of prison programs during periods of extreme prison overcrowding that coincided with severe economic depressions.

In the 1915 depression, New York's state prisons were overcrowded by 500%. There was nothing for prisoners to do. Wardens spoke freely of a control crisis, just as they do today (Davidson, 1991; Tewksbury & Edwards, 1996). Under pressure from trade unions and a liberal corporate class eager to moralize against the evils of prison industries and the connections to political patronage, state legislation in the North began to restrict the use of prison labour as early as the late 19th century. Wardens hotly protested. The lost patronage limited their political influence and curtailed the one practice they used most to manage the overcrowded population: work. Without work, what would the overcrowded prisoners do?

Wardens, editors of leading periodicals, liberal politicians, and radicals thought a lot about alternative systems of social control in the midst of considerable labour unrest. Famous prison reforms of the day used various types of programs (e.g. prisoner self-government, literacy education, military drill, and after the war, psychological therapy) to control "idleness and moral decay." Reformers celebrated the ability of their programs to keep order and avoid reliance on labour and corporal punishment (Schlossman and Spilane, 1992). By mid-century a professionalised staff, made up of psychologists, educators, and social workers, were documenting prisoners' deficits, devising corrective programs, and showing correlations between program attendance and rehabilitation. In the mid-1970s quantitative evaluations of social engineering began to affect policy making, or at least, that is what the evaluators hoped it would do. But evaluation results backfired. Correlations between programs and reintegration, measured by reduced recidivism rates, were at best marginally significant.

While this evidence created an ideological crisis amongst treatment staff, criminologists have shown that such evidence had minimal influence on departments of correction. Data compiled by the conservative criminologist John DiIulio shows that managers evaluated programs "not mainly in terms of what they do to reduce the likelihood of recidivism or otherwise affect inmates' post-release behaviour but as institutional management tools" (DiIulio, 1991, p. 114). For example, between 1973 and 1983, while program evaluations indicated "nothing works" (Duguid, 2001), the number of on-site prison higher education programs actually increased from 182 to 350 (Silva, 1994, p. 28).

Prison activists and prisoners have shown considerable support for prison programs, especially education. Several academic studies and prisoners' articles celebrate the benefits. The schools are described as cloisters of relative sanity and humanity. People learn to read and write and are able to correspond with family and friends and read books. Educators and prisoners argue that education, especially higher education programs, promote autonomy, self-actualisation, moral development, and dramatically alter individuals' worldviews (*Weltanschauung*) (Collins and Neim, 1989; Faith, 1995; Jones, 1992; Heberle & Rose, 1994).

In an article titled "On Prison Education and Hope," David Lynes captures programming's mixed agenda:

> Unfortunately, despite achieving, at least, a modest academic success, my overall experience with prison university programs, or what passes for them in the Prairies' Region [Canada], prompts me to conclude that my accomplishments were realized in spite of, rather than because of, the various 'curricula'(Lynes, 1992, p. 53).

Pressed by humanitarian concerns, abolitionists have tended to support officially sanctioned prison programs and ignore their control function. This support is more defensible if abolitionists refuse to adopt an instrumental standard in evaluating program merits. *Education is a human right not a correctional strategy or some kind of humanitarian means to occupy prisoners' time.* A left critique of education might argue that an acceptable aim of education is to meet genuine human needs in the most profound and basic sense. It is certainly not an abolitionist position that programs are valid because they reduce recidivism or meet other outcome measures that serve penal interests.

DOING OTHER THINGS WITH YOUR TIME: PRISONER ORGA-NIZED PROGRAMS

The contradictions of prison programs from an abolitionist position do not evaporate the moment we consider prisoner organized educational activities, but the possibilities for politicalization become much greater; indeed, it would seem that politicalization is *a sine qua non* of prisoner organization. This may be an exaggeration; yet a schematic view of their histories suggests that such programs do not exist without some degree of political struggle. Minimally, programs I have examined elsewhere (See Table 1) depended on prisoners carving out a social space through various levels of organized resistance to penal authority (Davidson, 2001). Under severe forms of repression, ingenious methods have been devised to keep programs alive. When the continuous conflict between keeper and kept creates more space for political organization, prisoners' programs have been quick to expand.

The forms that emerge in these struggles are not always progressive. It would be a mistake to romanticize prisoner organized activities by celebrating them simply because they are organized by prisoners. For example, throughout their history at San Quentin prison in California, Nuestra Familia operated oppressive underground economies and enforced through violence self-serving agendas. At times their radical programs were connected to wider political struggles against racism and the state, but these programs were also used for the most instrumental reasons (Cummins, 1994, p. 91). In his account of INSIGHT INC. at Stillwater prison in Minnesota, Robert Weiss describes how the corporate ethos of this well run, institutionally supported prisoner-organized telemarketing business—linked to educational and self-help programs and to a job placements for released convicts—served to maintain a high level of prisoner self-management that coincided with authorities' expectations (Weiss, 1995).

In the current context of a protracted fiscal crisis of the state, official programming budgets have been reduced severely. Meanwhile, by 1996, 21 state prison systems, the Federal Bureau of Prisons, and the Correctional Service of Canada had introduced mandatory program attendance regulations. Linking access to prison jobs, visiting privileges, and parole considerations to program participation records enforces attendance. Those who resist forced programming find themselves housed in the worst cell blocks, unemployed, or sent to Super High Security units.

How do institutions run mandatory programs with very limited budgets? Digitalized capitalism has provided one solution. Computerized programming requires minimal staff supervision and provides effective population management. But prisoner organized educational activities have also been incorporated into the service of fiscal restrains. An example is the Step Toward Education Progress (STEP) program at Angola prison, Louisiana (Myers, 1997). This is one of many peer-learning programs using pre-packaged, functional literacy materials to teach prisoners basic literacy and numeracy skills. Myers writes,

> STEP's strength lies in utilizing untapped resources and its scope is unprecedented at Angola. When conventional methods of education are unavailable, creativity is the key to success. Better educated inmates are used as tutors. Prisoners are the primary and most available resource to make this program effective (Myers, 1997, pp.1-2).

The STEP program operates under the supervision of the prison's education department. At the time Myers wrote, it served over 200 prisoners with 50 tutors. It ran without any cost to the prison by using donated materials and prisoner labour. Yet as much as it served institutional objectives, one must take seriously Myers' view of how it supported prisoners' interests:

> The relationship between student and teacher is a primary reason for STEP's success. Although the program is monitored closely, inmate tutor still teaches inmate student. For a program based on peer education to work successfully, tutors must be credible. Careful testing and screening of tutors [by department of education officials, not other prisoners] provides credibility by ensuring tutors are qualified and matched to the levels they teach (ibid., p. 5).

Programs linked to radical prison politics and political movements on the outside have adopted a more Freirian, participatory perspective toward education that does not presuppose the need for prison authorities to prescribe who is qualified to teach and what should be taught. In 1971 the Black Panthers and Black Guerrilla Family operated "secret Marxist political education groups, which included instruction in basic literacy skills and production of rudimentary textbooks, along with discussion of revolutionary theory" (Cummins, 1994, p. 136). In many cases prisoners' programs have been informal. Even those approved by prison administration that allowed educators from the outside to enter the prison to teach university classes created space for informal activity. Peter Linebaugh describes teaching at Attica prison and how the prison school could be used after hours and between classes as "a place, a situation, where people could get together and talk among themselves. Otherwise, there was no such occasion. We were like the barber shop of old" (Linebaugh, 1995, p. 82).

Prisoner strikes have demanded prisoner operated educational activities in contrast to demands for officially sanctioned programming. We see this expressed eloquently in the manifesto of striking prisoners at Archambault in the late 1970s:

> The Archambault guys demand...that facilities be provided...for writing, producing and editing a paper, which is to be...produced by the prisoners, [and] is to be free of all censorship by the staff of the prison.

> To us, talking about education means talking about the chance to acquire an intellectual and practical formation that increases understanding and decreases alienation from things, from reality and from life. A step toward a liberated spirit.

> The Archambault guys demand...the immediate opening of a special class for illiterate prisoners. Other prisoners will run these classes...[and] there is to be no limit imposed on the number of prisoners who may take these courses (quoted in Gosselin, 1982, pp. 191, 195).

Irish Republican Army political prisoners operated clandestine educational programs during the "blanket protests" of the late 1970s by "shouting to their neighbours through doors, out windows or along water pipes... Without the availability of books, classrooms or even anything but the crudest of writing materials, each man became equally responsible for contributing his own knowledge to the best of his ability" (Dana & McMonagle, 1997, p. 69). Once POW status was won through protests, the IRA's educational programs flourished. An extensive radical library was established. Peer learning—but organized by prisoners and tutors responsible only to each other and their students—taught history, literacy, Gallic, and historical analysis (ibid., p. 72).

SOME FINAL COMMENTS

There is not space in this brief paper to do more than mention a few examples of prisoner organized educational activities. Elsewhere, I have begun to document historical accounts of these activities dating back to the 18th century

(Davidson, 2001). These accounts are very incomplete, hence good conclusions are contingent on further research. Thus, the *Journal of Prisoners on Prisons* prepared a special edition on education in prisons (2004). A major purpose of this issue is to provide an opportunity for prisoners and former prisoners to identify, document, and analyse cases of prisoner-organized education. Other accounts are available through a search of the penal press (Gaucher, 1989; Inmate General Welfare Fund Committee, 2001) and the literature on prison education (e.g., Hammond, 1996; Shand, 1996).

Documenting and analysing these accounts are vitally important projects for abolitionists. From them we can learn a great deal about the dynamics between prisoners' organized efforts and institutional objectives, and how alternative forms of programming can promote prisoner politicalization and resist their domestication. For instance, a view of peer learning literacy councils that was anticipated in the earlier literature (Collins & Niemi, 1989) can be compared against the experiences cited by Myers (1997) and others (e.g., Schlueter, no date).

A crucial question for abolitionists is the relationship between prisoner-organized programs and outside activists. Instead of perpetuating the reformist demand for more state sanctioned programming, advocacy for prisoner organized programs requires abolitionists to dialogue with prisoners in order to work with them in carving out the spaces they need to design and operate programs for themselves. The example of Nuestra Familia and INSIGHT reminds us that not every program should receive support. Clearly a critical engagement is required that must be worked out through praxis. This is already being done, but there is a great deal more to do. For example, abolitionists have collaborated with prisoners to publish prisoners' and former prisoners' research on crime and punishment. In a letter to a member of the *Journal of Prisoners on Prison*'s editorial collective, the prisoner/political activist Lorenzo Stone-Bey comments on this relationship.

> Yes, most prisoners organized education is what Prison officials call a Threat to security, Revolutionary, Gang involvement, etc. and often the response is harassment, transfers from the institution to ... the Super Max and Indefinite Segregation. Yet, we understand the importance of education and political education in particular so we do so without fear of the State Repression. We create our own librarys [sic.] with the books and other material such as you send [i.e., the Journal] and get copies when we can in order to circulate it (Stone-Bey, 9 June 1997).

There are other important examples of engagement in the relationships between prisoner-educators and prison higher education programs (e.g., Faith, 1995).

Confining the analysis of prison programs to those delivered by penal authorities is to do the work of suppressing a much broader conceptualisation. Including prisoner-organized activities in that analysis does not automatically resolve the contradictory relationships between programming and control; however, it substantially alters the borderlines that define what we mean by programs and it is an essential if not sufficient part of an abolitionist strategy for politicalization and against domestication.

I suggest that we set aside demands for more programs operated to manage idleness and rationalized as rehabilitation. Instead I suggest that we position ourselves to critically engage prisoners' activities. Doing so we will not in itself abolish imprisonment and the social relations prisons help to protect and serve, but such engagement will create a collaborative relationship that may help to sustain those cases of prisoner organized activities that strive to be democratic and to resist the depoliticalization of crime and punishment, a resistance that is central to disguising the repressive hegemony we strive to abolish.

Notes

1. I emphasise worldwide because state terrorism has been going on nationally and internationally for some time (Parenti, 2000; Peltier, 1999). There is no genuine peace when justice and caring are assured only for the very rich and middle classes living in nation-states that protect the great wealth of the transnational corporations (Bauman, 1998 Robinson & Harris, 2000; Hutton & Giddens, 2000; Robinson, 1996).

2. The recidivism/rehabilitationist argument perpetuates a dangerous myth: that the root problem with prisons—and the capitalist state hegemony prisons help reproduce—is not imprisonment and the productive and social relations imprisonment serves, but authoritarian or corrupt individuals and bureaucracies, budget considerations, and politicians' interest in votes. Abolitionists who take the latter position end up supporting reform as an end in itself. Released prisoners turn up on the wrong side of recidivism figures not because they fail to be properly rehabilitated. Violations of parole conditions and arrest and reconviction for new crimes are far more likely to result in returning to prison if you are aboriginal, black, Latino(a), living in a low income, overly policed part of the city, too poor to hire a lawyer and unable to negotiate in a literate world than if you are white living in a middle class district. If you are black in urban America and England you are 8 to 10 times more likely to be stopped by the police than if you are white. Therefore, you are far more likely to get charged for an offence. The colour of your skin, your ability to get and keep a decent job are statistically far more significant factors determining successful reintegration than the amount of time attending prison school, higher education, or any other prison program (Duguid, 2001; Harer, 1995).

References

American Correctional Association Program Committee 1989. *Literacy: A Concept for All Seasons*. Washington D.C.: American Correctional Association.

Apple, M. 2000. *Official Knowledge: Democratic Education in a Conservative Age*. Second edition. London: Routledge.

Attallah Salah-El, T. 1992. Attaining Education in Prison Equals Prisoner Power. *Journal of Prisoners on Prison*, 4(1), 45 - 52.

Bauman, Z. 1998. *Globalization: The Human Consequences*. New York: Columbia University Press. SHELF.

Christie, N. 1994. *Crime Control as Industry: Towards Gulags Western Style*. London: Routledge.

Collins, M. 1991. *Adult Education as Vocation*. New York: Routledge & Kegan Paul.

Collins, M. & Niemi, J. A. 1989. Advanced Adult Basic Education in Prisons: The Recruitment, Selection and Training of Inmate Tutors. In S. Duguid (Ed.). *Yearbook of Correctional Education 1989* (pp. 193 - 208). Burnaby BC: Institute for the Humanities Simon Fraser University.

Cummins, E. 1994. *The Rise and Fall of California's Radical Prison Movement*. Stanford: Stanford University Press.

Dana, J., & McMonagle, S. 1997. Deconstructing "Criminalisation": The Politics of Collective Education in the H-blocks, *Journal of Prisoners on Prisons* 8 (1&2), 67 - 74.

Davidson, H. S. 2001. Possibilities for Participatory Education Through Prisoners' Own Educational Practices. *Participatory Practices in Adult Education* (pp.237 - 265). Mahwah, NJ: Lawrence Erlbaum Associates.

——. 1991. *Moral Education and Social Relations: The Case of Prisoner Self-government Reform, New York (1895-1923)* P. Campbell & B. Burnaby (Eds.). Unpublished doctoral dissertation. University of Toronto.

Duguid, S. 2001. *Can Prisons Work?* Toronto: University of Toronto Press.

DiIulio, J. J., Jr. 1991. *No Escape: The Future of American Corrections*. New York, NY: Basic Books, 1991.

Faith, K. 1995. The Santa Cruz Women's Prison Project, 1972-1976. *Schooling in a "Total Institution": Critical Perspectives on Prison Education* (pp. 173 - 192) H. S. Davidson (Ed.). Westport: Begin & Garvey.

Freire, P. 1996. *Pedagogy of Hope*. New York: Continuum.

Gaucher, R. 1989. The Canadian Penal Press: A Documentation and Analysis. *Journal of Prisoners on Prisons* 2(1): 3 - 24.

Gaucher, R. 1988. The Prisoner as Ethnographer: The Journal of Prisoners on Prisons. *Journal of Prisoners on Prisons* 1(1): 49 -61.

Gosselin, L. 1982. *Prisons in Canada*. Montreal: Black Rose.

Hammond, J. L. 1996. Organization and Education Among Salvadoran Political Prisoners. *Crime, Law & Social Change* 25(1): 17 - 41.

Harer, M. D. 1995. Recidivism Among Federal Prisoners Released in 1987. *Journal of Correctional Education* 46(3): 98 - 128.

Heberle, R., & Rose, W. 1994. Teaching Within the Contradictions of Prison Education. *Higher Education in Prisons: A Contradiction in Terms?* (pp. 97 - 106). M. Williford (Ed.). Phoenix AZ: Onyx Press.

Hutton, W., & Giddens, A. (Eds). 2000. *Global Capitalism*. New York: The New Press.

Inmate General Welfare Fund Committee. 2001. *N-side voice SCI Dallas*. SCI Dallas, PA: Inmate General Welfare Fund.

Johnson, W. W., Bennett, K., and Flanagan, T. J. 1997. Getting Tough on Prisoners: Results from the National Corrections Executive Survey, 1995." *Crime and Delinquency* 43(1): 24-41.

Jones, R. 1992. A Coincidence of Interests: Prison Higher Education in Massachusetts. *Journal of Prisoners on Prisons* 4(1): 3 - 20.

Linebaugh, P. 1995. Freeing Birds, Erasing Images, Burning Lamps: How I Learned to Teach in Prison. *Schooling in a "total institution": Critical Perspectives on Prison Education* (pp. 65 - 90). H. S. Davidson (Ed.). Westport: Begin & Garvey.

Lynes, D. 1992. On Prison Education and Hope. *Journal of Prisoners on Prisons* 4(1): 53 - 55.

Myers, K. 1997. A First Step. *The Angolite*, March/April, 1977.

Parenti, C. 2000. *Lockdown America: Police and Prisons in the Age of Crisis*. London & New York: Verso.

Peltier, L. 1999. *Prison writings: My Life Is My Sun Dance*. New York: St. Martin's Press.

Reiman, J. 1990. *The Rich Get Richer and the Poor Get Prison* (3rd ed.). New York: Macmillan.

Robinson, W. I., & Harris, J. 2000. Towards a Global Ruling Class? Globalization and the Transnational Capitalist Class. *Science and Society*, 64(1): 11 - 54.

Robinson, W. I. 1996. Globalisation: Nine Theses on our Epoch. *Race and Class* 38(2): 13 - 31.

Schlossman, S., & Spillane, J. 1992. Bright Hopes, Dim Realities: Vocational Innovation in American Correctional Education. *RAND Notes*. Santa Monica, CA: RAND. National Center for Research in Vocational Education.

Schlueter. P. (no date). SCI Dallas Literacy Council. Unpublished Manuscript.

Shand, R. A. S. 1996. Pre-Release/Transition: Inmate Programs and Support Upon Entry, During Incarceration, and After Release. *Journal of Correctional Education* 1996, 47(1): 20-40.

Stone-Bey, L. June 9, 1997. Personal Communication to Howard Davidson.

Silva, W. 1994. A Brief History of Prison Higher Education in the United States." *Higher Education in Prison: A Contradiction in Terms?* M. Williford (Ed.). Phoenix, AZ: Oryx Press.

Tewksbury, R, & Edwards, T. D. 1996. Legal Issues Regarding Mandatory Prison-Based Education Programs. *The State of Corrections: Proceedings American Correctional Association Annual Conferences 1995* (pp. 45 - 53). Lanham, MD: American Correctional Association.

Weiss, R. 1995. Prisoner Higher Education and the American Dream. *Schooling in a "Total Institution": Critical Perspectives on Prison Education* (pp. 123 - 140). H. S. Davidson (Ed.). Westport: Begin & Garvey.

18

A CALL FOR THE ABOLITION OF PRISONS*

Tiyo Attallah Salah-El

In the history of philosophy, there is perhaps no more powerful image than the "cave" described by Socrates in Plato's *Republic*. This deep, dark, hole, we are told, is inhabited by "prisoners" bound in such a way that all they can see is the play of shadows on an interior wall, fleeting shapes that they mistake for reality. For above these hapless souls, outside their underground dwelling, is the dazzling light of the sun—a sight reached only after an arduous journey upward.

For over a quarter of a century, I have been making that arduous journey, striving and struggling to reach that dazzling light of freedom and justice, not just for myself but also for the other two million women and men presently housed in that cave. During that journey, I gained new insight regarding the pain of prisons and the devastation and brutalization of people by capitalism and imperialism. From that painful experience, I have become an abolitionist of the present prison system.

I may never be able to fully describe the complex dynamic process of how to organize and bring about the abolition of prisons. However, it is my hope that the views and information presented here will help others to further develop their own reasons why they would be willing to undertake the struggle to help abolish prisons. The strength of my vision depended in great measure on what I learned about prison during the twenty-five years of my incarceration and how much I am willing to continue learning. This type of learning requires a lifelong commitment to continual inquiry and knowledge in order to arrive at new levels of understanding and insight.

To sustain my commitment, I think it is important to develop my own personal vision of the abolition of prisons to guide me in my efforts of the value of charting such an unusual course in my life. I have learned that there are many different ways of looking at my current situation. I continue to learn as I live within the rotten, corrupt core of the criminal justice system. This prison has been a teacher for me. It reflects my own mind. Nevertheless, the prison has not changed. It is my mind that has changed.

When one's mind changes, new possibilities begin to arise. This can be a profoundly liberating experience. It has taken me beyond my limited preoccupations with myself. It has certainly changed the way I relate to prisons and the criminal justice system. If we have to be mindful of the ruts our thinking gets us into, then we have to learn to see and approach things differently.

Facing our problems is usually the only way to get past them. There is an art to facing difficulties in ways that lead to effective solutions. We can, by exercising imagination, intuition and creativity in our own work, use the pressure of the problems themselves to propel us through it. It is incumbent upon us to find new ways to break into the cycle of violence, which characterizes so much of the present corrections and criminal justice system in this country.

The least controversial observation that one can make about the American criminal justice today is that it is remarkably ineffective, absurdly expensive, grossly inhumane and riddled with ruthlessness and racism. In my view and views of a growing number of people, it seems clear that the hypotheses that prisons are institutions for control of people of color is a far more viable one than the notion that prisons are an effort to prevent crime. All serious analyses of the history of incarceration reveal the same historical thrust: prisons and other systems of punishment are for social control, not crime control.

The criminal justice system is a huge, multibillion dollar industry, and also very subversive of democratic principles. The establishment has built itself up fantastically over the last decade. And its repressive power has mostly been concentrated on the black community. The system is a very expensive, unaccountable bureaucracy. There is no more unaccountable system than a correction system. The corporate media usually frames the debate over the criminal justice system and that arcane realm of the government contract think tanks, where civilians answerable to no elected official formulate policies and concoct plans that reek havoc on the poor and minorities, especially on black women and men.

Certainly crime has become the most racially divisive issue for American society today. There has been a turning away of looking at the social factors and social issues that create crime. Most people do not want to talk about things like adequate income, employment and anti-poverty programs; all of these are now passé. For that matter, the people are left with the idea that criminals must somehow be simply wicked persons, quite unlike them and if they can genetically define these criminals, it is will make life easier for the 'free' society. It is an easy way out. Then one does not have to feel any guilt for what goes on in one's society. The general public wants its pound of flesh. Does the dominant culture want to prove a point with blacks, and are the politicians going to do it with the criminal justice system?

Race is the big, ugly secret that lies at the heart of U.S. crime policy. The criminal justice system is a system run on sound bites and throwaway lines. The system is not interested in anything that would lower the crime rate, much less in anything decent or human that is going to advance society. It is just a terribly corrupt system. And of course, when one is talking about crime and criminals, it is very, very easy to fall into the acts of demonizing and stereotyping. Not only will most people accept it, one can build a political career around it.

There is a need to unwind; there is a need to find options, a lot of options, especially for the lesser offenders who have drug problems but who are now being sent to prison. There is a need to decarcerate. We must go further than merely condemning prisoners and building more prisons. We have to point the direction in which the solution lies. We must focus upon alternatives to prisons, and whether what we demand or propose will really eliminate crimes. We have to create and offer a well thought out program for accomplishing the change and propose a specific form of alternative with which to replace the present system. These are critical questions that demand workable and acceptable solutions. For example, how would society function if it abolished prisons? What can be done with the dangerous few? Who would benefit? Who would be in charge of the new system?

This is why we, abolitionists, must be clear about our tactics, and above all, we must be armed with a workable program that will enable us to reach our goal. We cannot ignore the lessons that history has already taught us. We must create and project a powerful program for reaching our revolutionary goal of abolishing prisons. I strongly suggest we begin a new way of thinking about abolition.

The problems caused by prisons, crime and the criminal justice system suggest that we may need to take a broader view of certain problems if we hope to solve them. This approach involves asking ourselves what the extent of the problem actually is and discerning the relationship between the various isolated parts of the problem and the problem as a whole. If we do not identify the system correctly in its entirety, we will never be able to come to a satisfactory solution of the problem because a key domain will always be missing, the domain of the whole.

Such experiences can lead to feelings of frustrations, inadequacy and insecurity. When self-confidence becomes eroded, it just makes it harder to solve any other problems that come along. Our doubts about our own abilities to solve the prison problem become self-fulfilling prophecies. They can come to dominate our lives. In these ways, we effectively make our own limits by our own thoughts processes. Then, too often, we forget that we have created these boundaries ourselves. Consequently, we get stuck and feel we cannot get beyond them. Therefore, when someone comes forth with the idea of abolishing prisons, most people react and respond with all sorts of self-imposed boundaries. Some will even turn a deaf ear to the words calling for the abolition of prisons.

I took on the challenge and the risks of facing the full attack from the criminal justice system when I came out as an abolitionist. I lost all my privileges and had many of my possessions destroyed by angry guards. I surprised others and myself with my newfound courage and clarity. I refused to be a slave of the system, I refused to work for the system to continue to function smoothly. In the process, I discovered my limits receding, and I found myself capable of doing things that I never thought I can do. The point is that we do not always know what our true limits are.

Prison abolition, like the abolition of slavery, is a long range goal. Abolition is not simply a moment in time, but a protracted process. Prison abolitionism should not now be considered a pipe dream but an abolitionist approach demands a solid critical analysis of crime that is juxtaposed with social structures, plus anti-crime strategies that focus on the provision of social resources. We must educate the public that prisons need to be abolished as the sole way of attempting to resolve social problems that are better solved by other more human ways and means. Prison abolition is itself a deeper and broader critique of society.

Abolition and revolution are not new. History is replete with stories of the struggle of people on the bottom of the social ladder banding together and organizing to bring radical change for the better in their lives and the lives of future generations. Some struggles succeeded, some failed and others are ongoing. I do not know how long it will take to abolish prisons. That is akin to asking me how much air is in the universe. Therein is the real challenge—our search for answers must be incessant.

Shouldn't we ask ourselves how we can build new systems from below? How can we create a new common language to define injustice and to imagine a society without prisons? What is being done to create the new from within the old? Does such a movement have a chance of surviving and creating change? Survival and victory depend on coordinated action. We must learn how to cooperate quickly and effectively so as to intensify, broaden and deepen our struggles. We need stronger networks of communication and support. We must develop a process of dialogue and organization unprecedented in the history of America.

Let us strive to give hope to many that a new kind of thinking about the abolition of prisons is in the making, one capable of inspiring people to come together, speaking to each other about abolition and revolution. *We must strengthen the hope and dreams of freedom, abolition and revolution.*

Subcommandante Marcos writes:

> Here we are, the dead of all time, dying once again, only now with the object of living. You have to get out of your self to save yourselves. What we seek, what we need and want is that all those people without a party and organization make agreements about what they want and do not want and become organized in order to achieve it (preferably through civil and peaceful means), not to take power, but to exercise it.[1]

Below are some suggestions for beginning the abolition process:

1. Accepting the fact that no one person or organization can keep up even in a cursory manner with all the aspects of struggle, sharing that work through political organizations is necessary, as is developing supportive and cooporative relations among many organizations. Therefore, we should consider supporting, listening, learning and exchanging knowledge (not just "information") with anti-death penalty organizations in their efforts to first bring about a moratorium of the death penalty and the eventual abolition of the death penalty. When such a goal is achieved, we can build upon that

success by inviting them to take the next revolutionary step and buttress our struggle to work toward abolishing prisons. We would then have a much broader base of well seasoned activists, supporters, networks, knowledge, communications, information and funding.

2. It would not be productive to set out with the idea to tear down prisons, but to promote and transform the present prisons into Healing and Caring Centers. The infrastructure is already in place for all the basic needs such as food, clothing, shelter, medications, transportation and recreation. Re-training of prison staff toward becoming in-house teachers, paid at the same pay scale as they are presently being paid. Such a strategy will help placate the various guard unions and other misguided pro-prison advocates.

    Present day prisons could eventually become Healing and Caring Centers for the homeless, shelters for abused and battered women and children, meaningful an productive drug and alcohol treatment centers, meaningful education and vocation programs for families living in abject poverty. Bring new leadership roles into prisons to work along with most treatment personnel.

3. To the best of my knowledge, there has been little if any mention, much less, serious discussion among abolitionists about what to do with the dangerous few. I think we can all agree that for the over all well being and safety of society at large, detention is and may always be required for the small group of people who cause harm to others. This question must first be acknowledged, studied, discussed and revolved by not only abolitionists, but also among broad-based groups of doctors, judges, community organizations, corrections personnel, psychologists, legislators and others on the local, state and federal levels. The general public should and must be invited to take part in these open discussions. This issue will test the resolve of not just abolitionists, but of all involved. Now is the time to begin thinking and planning tactics and strategies regarding this important and sensitive issue. Creating a new way of "Thinking About Prisons" requires the best efforts, ideas and experiences, and honest, careful, sharp, and critical reflection from all who are willing to take on this daring and daunting task. We could and must construct the groundwork for future generations to build a world that is safe and just. Let us begin working at the edges of what is possible. Let us strive toward a new possibility. Let us fight with the weapon of intelligence. I invite you to join us.

Notes

*   Another version of this chapter has been published in *The New Abolitionists: (Neo) Slave Narratives and Contemporary Prison Writings*, (J. James, ed.) SUNY Press, 2002. State University of New York. All rights reserved.

1. To learn about the Coalition for the Abolition of Prisons (CAP), see http://noprisons.org. I am deeply indebted to Monty Neill and the Midnight Collective for sending me the great book, *Auroras of the Zapatistas*, Autonomedia Press, Brooklyn, NY, USA.

19

CONTRADICTIONS AND CHAL-LENGES: CAN COMMUNITY JUSTICE INITIATIVES AVOID CO-OPTATION?

Marsha Weissman and Alan Rosenthal

In city after city community justice initiatives have sprung up purporting to offer new models of justice that bring together community residents, organizations and governmental partners. The goals of community justice models are described in terms of community building, empowerment and restoration. However, many of these initiatives—specialized courts, restorative justice models, and community "partnerships," have fallen far short of these visionary goals and instead fall prey to co-optation. Without a well organized community that is informed on criminal justice issues, and prepared to fight for the integrity of the program, such initiatives are unlikely to have the strength to survive, let alone thrive.

This chapter explores the barriers to implementing community justice initiatives in ways that allow for community empowerment. An example of one such partnership and how it was undermined is discussed. The chapter concludes with recommendations that might help other communities and justice activists avoid the co-optation of community justice programs.

COMMUNITY JUSTICE: HISTORY AND CONTEXT

Community justice programs are linked to a history rooted in social change movements, especially those that flourished in the 1960s. During the heyday of this community organizing, efforts focused on housing, welfare, school governance, civil rights but not courts, corrections or police: the justice system has been largely immune to opening itself up to greater community involvement. Thus, community justice is a phenomenon of the 1990s, encompassing community policing, drug courts, community courts and community collaborations to address such issues as youth violence, drug use and quality of life crimes (Karp & Clear, 2000).

Community justice initiatives are also informed by alternative sentencing and community corrections initiatives that grew up in the 1980s as a response to the over reliance on incarceration. As is now widely understood, the United States has the highest incarceration rates in the developed world, with dramatically disparate impacts on communities of color, especially African Americans. There are now more than 2 million people in U.S. jails prisons and the incarceration rate for the population as a whole is 699 per 100,000. The racial disparities are evident by differences in incarceration rates for white males in federal or state prisons at 449 per 100,000 compared to that of African Americans males, an astonishing 3,457 per 100,000 (Beck & Harrison, 2001).

The antecedents of community justice models are community corrections programs and approaches that were embraced by reformist groups seeking to challenge the growth of imprisonment. Initially these programs were used to present creative sentencing options to judges (Immarigeon, 1999) but were not readily endorsed by "mainstream" criminal justice system players. Nonetheless, over a twenty year period, alternative-to-incarceration (ATI) programs and community corrections became an increasingly accepted, albeit a marginal part of the criminal justice system. For example, New York City has an array of respected ATI programs. Nonetheless, these programs receive less than 10 million dollars a year, monies that are but a drop in the bucket when compared to New York City and New York State correctional costs at $843,591,000 and $2,220,586,000 respectively (New York City Department of Correction 2001; Stephan, 1999).

Interest in community justice approaches took off in 1992, with the arrival of Janet Reno as the U.S. Attorney General. Reno, whose prior experience included a stint as prosecutor for the first "drug court" in Miami Florida, promoted this concept on a national level. Drug courts purport to use the authority of the court to motivate and monitor drug treatment and seek to bring the "community" into the rehabilitative and reintegrative process. Ten key components have been developed for these courts: Key component 10 explicitly states "Forging partnerships among drug courts, public agencies and community-based organizations generates local support and enhances drug court program effectiveness" (National Association of Drug Court Professionals Drug Courts Standards Committee, 1997, p. 34).

Simultaneous to the national "roll out" of drug courts and other community justice models (e.g., community policing), the criminal justice system was hitting new lows in terms of public trust and confidence. The system had multiple critics—the right wing that continued to promote a get tough on crime agenda and continued its rhetoric against "soft on crime" judges and others, clashed with large segments of the African American and progressive communities who took on police brutality, racial profiling, racist drug laws, the death penalty and the general over reliance on incarceration. Crime and justice issues had become polarizing forces in the American polity (Tonry, 1995). Levels of trust in the criminal justice system vary considerably among different segments of the population and questions about the fairness of the justice system have certainly divided Americans along racial grounds (Lasley, 1994; Jones-Brown, 2000; Cole, 1999). The extent of this divide has come to the attention of social science research with some, like Hagan and Peterson (1995) asserting that "a legacy of suspicion and distrust of the justice system in America....is one of the most corrosive and consequential features of crime in this society" (p.17).

The erosion of faith in the criminal justice system has contributed to the growth of community justice initiatives as policymakers seek new ways to reestablish the credibility of the system. Community justice models have expanded beyond drug courts to include other specialized courts (e.g., domestic violence courts, community or "quality of life courts", and family treatment courts), and community coalitions or partnerships to reduce juvenile violent crime, wage the war on drugs, and address domestic violence. Most of these criminal justice initiatives were piloted by the federal government that sets program goals and objectives, recommends strategies and provides the funding for planning and implementation. While requiring the participation, if not leadership, of government (e.g., the courts, the police, district attorneys, local government representatives) they also require extensive community involvement, i.e., "partnerships" among community organizations and institutions including grassroots groups.

PURPOSES OF COMMUNITY INVOLVEMENT

There is a common conceptual framework that undergirds the involvement of community in shaping and implementing public policy, whether the focus is changing welfare (Piven & Cloward, 1972), revitalizing housing (Kingsley, McNeely & Gibson, 1997) reducing health risks (Minkler, Thompson, Bell & Rose, 2001) or addressing crime (Travis, 1996). The framework is built upon a concept of community empowerment that expects community residents to define the problem, identify strategies and interventions that will solve or ameliorate the problem, plan the program design, implement the plan through community action and exercise power to hold public officials accountable for supporting and institutionalizing program efforts.

The literature on empowerment defines it as a process by which individuals and communities gain authority and control over key dimensions of their social and political lives. There are three critical preconditions for empowerment—critical awareness, participation, and control (Zimmerman, 2000). Empowerment presupposes a "change agent" purpose, a restructuring of power relations and social, political and/or economic conditions, rather than acceptance of or adjustment to those conditions and problems. Empowerment as a process involves strengthening the capacity of individuals and communities by skill building, experiential learning and access to resources. It requires the building of an organizational structure that can take up change agent tasks. The outcome of the empowerment process is success in achieving the desired change, ensuring that the empowered community has an ongoing role in policy development and long term sustenance through effective resource development.

DEFINING COMMUNITY JUSTICE INITIATIVES

The rhetoric surrounding community justice initiatives suggests that these efforts represent a paradigm shift—a new way of thinking about the criminal justice system (Barajas, 1996). The theoretical justification for community justice models goes as follows: Community justice may be the only means for the criminal justice system to regain its credibility; community justice offers meaningful benefits to victims, offenders and the larger community (restitution, safety, improvements in quality of life) and community justice models incorporate efforts already underway by community residents and justice agency line staff (Karp & Clear, 1999).

Community justice initiatives are part of a strategy to reduce and prevent crime that requires partnerships between community-based organizations and institutions and community residents and governmental institutions, especially the police and the courts. There is a strong assumption that the community should be involved in the design of the initiative, and be an active participant at all stages of program implementation. The models speak about a focus on problem solving and addressing specific community concerns. For example, the Midtown Community Court was designed to reduce quality of life crimes— unlicenced street corner vendoring and prostitution—that were interfering with neighborhood businesses and larger commercial concerns (Feinblatt, Berman & Sviridoff, 1998). Most community justice initiatives incorporate elements of restorative justice—the aim is ostensibly more than punishing offenders, but rather giving back to individual victims and communities harmed by crime and reintegrating the offender into the community. The goals of these efforts are often stated in terms that go beyond achieving public safety to the building of a healthy community.

These theoretical justifications notwithstanding, there has been little if any information regarding the extent to which community justice models adequately and effectively involve the community and little concern regarding the extent to which the "community" is adequately prepared and empowered to actually take on the tasks and responsibilities required of equal partnership. Community justice explicitly focuses on neighborhoods, problem solving, decentralization of and accountability from authority, community quality of life, and citizen participation (Karp & Clear, 1999). These elements have not been the focus of the traditional criminal justice system and thus hold the potential for conflict among the partners. Preliminary studies suggest that the implementation of community justice models such as community policing or prosecution have not altered traditional objectives, but rather have simply involved the community in expanding tough law enforcement practices (Kurki, 1999) or have used community participation as window dressing to legitimate these practices.

Given the multiple and often contradictory aims of community justice models, it is important to examine the barriers to effective community participation and unintended consequences that distort the "change agent" purposes envisioned by reformers. The purpose of this paper then is to raise some red flags about the dangers and pitfalls of community justice initiatives, and offer suggestions for ways to avoid the co-optation of community justice initiatives and foster more effective involvement of community members in justice programming. A brief case history of a community justice project is presented to illustrate the difficulties of community organizing in a justice context.

BARRIERS

The barriers to achieving community justice initiatives that require partnerships with government fall into three broad categories: (1) different purposes, goals and objectives underlying government partnerships; (2) differential power and resources and (3) different understanding of the role of community assets, deficits and causes of community crime.

(1) Divergent Purposes and Methods: The Whys and Hows of Partnerships

In order for partnerships to work, there has to be a commonality of purpose. The government's motivation for partnering may be quite different than that of the community. Federal, state and local justice agencies seek to restore the legitimacy of criminal law and to rebuild public confidence in the criminal justice system. (Robinson, 1998; Bucqueroux, 1996) In contrast, the community is less concerned about restoring legitimacy and more interested in the restoration of communities that have been "doubly ravaged by crime and the criminal justice system" (Cole, 1999 p.13). In fact, many community activists believe that the criticisms of the present system are well-founded and look to the community justice initiatives to significantly change the paradigm governing American criminal justice policy. While both government and the community have interest in crime prevention, traditional criminal justice practice defines this largely in terms of apprehension, prosecution and incarceration. Community definitions are broader, incorporating visions of a healthy community as a foundation for community safety. Finally, progressive community interest in justice programming calls for a rejection of the devastating policy of mass incarceration and dramatic changes in policies that maintain a racially unequal criminal justice system. In short, there is a fundamental contradiction between the importance of reinforcing traditional control vs. community empowerment (Crawford, 1997; Jurik, Blumenthal, Smith & Portillos, 2000).

The extent to which community justice initiatives incorporate goals that seek to undo U.S. policy of mass incarceration appears to be a key point of divergence between government and community partners. There is little to no evidence that government partners are even willing to dialogue on the question of mass incarceration: as Garland (2001(a)) notes "For all of our philosophizing about the *purpose* of imprisonment, we have scarcely begun to research the question of its *extent*. We have libraries of criminological research about the impact of imprisonment upon the individual offender but scarcely anything on its *social* impact upon communities and neighbourhoods" (p.6). Governmental institutions and representatives focus on the ability of partnership efforts to reduce the sense of community alienation from criminal justice institutions and policies with little discussion or attention paid to the reasons that such distrust exists.

A second but related difference between the community and government partners is the method by which crime is to be reduced. In particular, community participants often emphasize prevention, positive intervention, treatment and restoration over suppression and punishment. For the most part, government partners remain advocates of traditional criminal justice policy that has as its core a punishment agenda and punishment as the overriding sanctioning philosophy (Kurki, 1999). Government partners (e.g. police and prosecutors) are unlikely to endorse reform of draconian drug laws or reform of sentencing guidelines that would reduce the use of incarceration.

(2) Divergence in Power and Authority: Community Empowerment or Co-optation

In principle, community justice initiatives, be they drug courts, community policing or community partnerships, represent a watershed because they allow the community an opportunity to hold public institutions and their representatives accountable (Bucqueroux, 1996). Despite the expectation that community justice initiatives bring residents and organizations to the table, community members are often at a disadvantage when compared to government representatives and others who have professional responsibilities working in the criminal justice system. Community residents are not typically experts on the criminal justice system, and are unfamiliar with the complex and technical workings of the system. This inequality in information leaves community members less prepared to contribute to "problem solving" in a way that puts community solutions at the center. (Johnstone, 2000; Connor, 1998). The uneven power and access to information and resources leaves community members vulnerable to co-optation into law enforcement strategies that may actually exacerbate community problems. For example, using so-called community policing as a means to increase contact between minority youth and the police over minor crimes may actually exacerbate already tense police-community relations.

The limited public knowledge about criminal justice issues and community justice initiatives is a formidable obstacle to power sharing and collaboration between community citizens and organizations and criminal justice agencies. A community that is not familiar with the basic tenets of community justice is not in a position to hold accountable their powerful government "partners"—the courts, the police, prosecutors—when they deviate from the community justice model.

Differential knowledge and access to information and data are part of the larger power differences that exist between the community and governmental agencies. Yet power sharing is critical to community justice initiatives. Empowering the community to have a real say in how justice policies are formulated and implemented are at the core of community justice. Karp and Clear (1999) have described community justice as an ethic that transforms the aim of the justice system into enhancing community life or sustaining community. To achieve that aim, the community partners and the justice system must share responsibility for social control. Similarly, Kurki (1999) points out that the theory underlying restorative justice requires the government to "surrender its monopoly over responses to crime to those most directly affected—the victim, the offender, the community" (p.1) Unfortunately, there is little evidence that those in power are serious about power sharing and all the "messy" consequences that accompany new community roles. The high passions that characterize community participation is the antithesis of the culture of governmental agencies that tend to be impersonal, specialized, professionalized and routinized. Government finds it difficult to support new initiatives without stifling the spontaneity, creativity and grassroots ties that are the strength of community involvement. It is also far from clear that the existing power structure has any real interest in the empowerment of those who are disempowered. A partner who is unwilling to share power will, of necessity, seek to co-opt the other partner.

There are some clear warning signs that indicate when a community justice program is driven by agendas other than community empowerment. The public is often informed of these initiatives after the fact and has not been part of the design of the program. Government officials may invite community members in, but only after establishing "nonnegotiable" rules for those initiatives and often handpicking the individuals to represent the community. It appears that community justice partnerships are used by governmental authorities as a means to develop more personal relationships with select community leaders, and, in some cases, coopt these leaders with personal rewards including jobs, contracts and the like.

If these are in fact irreconcilable differences, i.e. a community justice model that allows for community voices to be heard unimpeded and as equals at the table, vs. traditional criminal justice that relies on hierarchy and characterized by retribution, the more dominant system is likely to co-opt the hoped for reforms of the other. Kurki (1999) worries that traditional criminal justice agencies may add new community or restorative justice components to be fashionable without fundamentally rethinking their mission. To date, there has been little evidence to suggest that community residents have been effectively involved in community justice initiatives, whether defined as restorative justice, crime prevention or community building (Kurki & Pranis, 2000).

(3) Divergence in Perception of Community: Assets or Deficits

Community perceptions of the consequences of many criminal justice policies (e.g. zero tolerance, mandated sentences, locking up non-violent offenders, etc.) on communities, particularly communities of politically and economically impoverished people, are increasingly understood to be destructive to their social and political viability. These communities have a major stake in reversing the deleterious effects of current policies.

Current criminal justice policies, notably the incredibly high rates of incarceration in these very communities, further depletes the community of social capital (Travis, 2000; Petersilia, 2000). When such a wide net is cast to exile those who commit crimes, particularly non-violent crimes, there is a serious disruption of positive social ties and networks that sustain positive normative institutions in the community. Moreover, a criminal record further diminishes the likelihood that individuals who are released to the community will be able to integrate and sustain themselves in legal and constructive ways.

It is likely that incarceration at some point, undermines and plays a criminogenic role in community functioning (Rose & Clea, 1998; Sabol & Lynch, 1997). High rates of incarceration, while removing the few serious, destructive and dangerous individuals from the community, also removes many who are much less of a threat. The absence of these nonviolent, less serious offenders removes important human capital from already struggling communities, removes fathers, mothers, spouses, and siblings from families, and removes employees, and even employers, thereby undermining the stability of social networks upon which community, economic, and ultimately political health depends. When the net of social control gets as wide as it has in recent years, ensnaring two million people in prison, more than criminality is being removed from the social, political and economic life of communities.

The best of community justice initiatives recognize that crime and responses to crime do not occur in a vacuum. Several community justice efforts explicitly reference community building activities. For example, Weed and Seed, a federally funded community justice "strategy" in place in over 200 communities across the United States, involves enhanced and focused law enforcement efforts ("weeding") and social services ("seeding") (Dunworth & Mills, 1999 (a)). Weed and Seed includes a community building component: "to enable residents in the target area to improve their community morale, their neighborhood's physical appearance (buildings, parks, streets, lighting, and so forth), and local economic and business conditions" (Dunworth & Mills, 1999 (b) p.9). Community coalitions, such as those promoted to reduce juvenile gun violence, require positive opportunities, i.e. such as after school activities, and mentoring (Office of Juvenile Justice and Delinquency Prevention, 1996). Even drug courts have reached out beyond treatment resources to bring in employment and housing services.

Despite these efforts, it remains a major challenge to create positive opportunities within a justice context that continues to use traditional criminal justice responses. Proponents of restorative justice speak of its reintegration potential. But the question remains—reintegration into what: neighborhoods with astoundingly high unemployment rates, poor housing stock, non functioning schools (Wilson, 1998)? In New York State for example, the nine communities from which most inmates come, are precisely those neighborhoods that have demographics reflective of a third world country (Abramsky, 2001).

In implementing community justice programs, government agencies fail to take into account how the structural and economic conditions of a neighborhood are essential to its transformation and instead focus only on the "correctional" elements of restorative justice. The community building aspect never includes the kinds of massive redistribution of resources that will be needed to shore up existing institutions and develop new opportunities. Even those "positive opportunities" that are included in community justice models often take a back seat to the "suppression" elements and are introduced in large part as a means to co-opt community support rather than considered concern about significant investment in the socio-economic foundation of the community (Dunworth &Mills, 1999 (a)).

USURPING COMMUNITY INVOLVEMENT: AN EXAMPLE OF A WELL-INTENTIONED IDEA GONE AWRY

An example of how community justice programs fail to achieve progressive goals and objectives is chronicled through an initiative introduced by the Center for Community Alternatives (CCA).

CCA, a community-based organization whose mission is to reduce reliance on incarceration through direct services, research, training and technical assistance, received federal funding to implement a "Partnership to Reduce Juvenile Gun Violence." The program began in 1996 in a mid-sized city in upstate New York. Central to the partnership effort was community mobilization, empowerment or "grassroots community involvement" (OJJDP; CCA). CCA convened more than 60 community organizations, agencies and individuals from the community that was experiencing the highest level of juvenile gun violence. The targeted community was an inner city neighborhood in a city that was becoming increasingly poor and non-white, surrounded by somewhat more prosperous, white suburbs governed by separate towns and villages. The city and the suburbs were all part of an increasing powerful county government that traditionally neglected the city's interests: the economic and race differences between the city and county were exacerbated by partisan differences, with the city largely Democratic and the county overwhelmingly Republican.

The target community in particular faced a myriad of social, economic and political challenges. It is an impoverished community, predominantly comprised of people of color, with the highest incidence of health problems, under education, child poverty, poor governmental services and unemployment (Dunton & Leon, 1995; Community Benchmarks Program, 1998). Governmental partners included the county District Attorney's office and city police department. The Partnership's governing structures were a Community Management Team (CMT) and a Steering Committee. The CMT was open to any community member or organization within the target community interested in efforts to reduce juvenile gun violence. The CMT was responsible for the overall direction of the Partnership, budget review and for providing a forum for discussion of new ideas, issues, improving activities, and strategies. The Steering Committee was selected by the CMT and responsible for implementation of CMT program recommendations, detailed budget development and hiring of Partnership staff. The Steering Committee members were consistent, active members of the CMT: both the Steering Committee and CMT were culturally, ethnically and professionally diverse. CCA was the administrative director of the program for its initial year and one-half. During this time, the CMT-designed strategy emphasized prevention and early intervention, and focused on mobilizing additional community interests through forums and other public events, outreach to out of school, "gang-involved" and alienated youth and development of more after school activities. The CMT focused less on law enforcement initiatives and defined such strategies in terms of community policing in ways that would alleviate tense community-police relations and the apprehension of large scale gun dealers reflecting the communities interest in prosecuting those who would profit from the sale of guns to neighborhood youth.

Discussions at CMT meetings revealed consensus on a complicated set of issues: the desire for community safety; a sense that youth had few opportunities other than crime; a sense of responsibility on the part of the adults in the community that they had not done enough to reach out to "their" children; a sense that the community rated second class law enforcement attention; a sense that the police were ill equipped to sort out serious criminals from the general population of youth and that their response was often misdirected and brutal. Perhaps most important was a sense that efforts to reduce (youth) crime had to attend to the structural conditions that breed crime—poverty, racism, unemployment and the abandonment of inner city neighborhoods. The major activities during this time focused on large scale community mobilization to bring attention to the problem of youth violence.

Extensive community participation was not matched by active involvement of government partners. There was limited participation by the police and District Attorney's office, nominal interest on the part of city government and no involvement of county officials. While this lack of interest limited the prospect of co-optation, it also indicated that the Partnership was not taken seriously by public officials. The lack of engagement by local government was also a significant concern to federal funders and program evaluators who were concerned about how such inactivity would impair Partnership efforts to make the investments in new programming and the ability to sustain the initiative in the long run.

After considerable public attention (media and well attended public forums) to Partnership efforts and as the Partnership's key strategy was being introduced—community outreach—to reach out to youth involved in "street crew" violence, county government officials unilaterally approached the federal funder and offered to make a major investment to "take the Partnership to the next level" through the contribution of financial and political investment. This was of interest to the federal funder, given limited governmental participation in Partnership activities to date. Visions of major local government involvement obscured key questions such as the jurisdictional and turf issues over resource allocation, policing authority, partisan differences, and limited representation of people of color in governmental positions. Also, as recognized by Jurik et al. (2000), there can be multiple agendas of partnerships—"progressive, reactionary or some combination of the two" (p. 294). CCA had long been identified as an organization with a progressive change agenda that contradicted and challenged the more conservative county agenda. Thus, there was county interest in limiting CCA's role in the Partnership.

Transfer of the Partnership to governmental administration resulted in a dramatic change in the Partnership structure. The CMT was disbanded through attrition; governmental partners found community meetings to be disruptive and characterized them as "venting sessions." The composition and role of the steering committee was also drastically altered. Most grassroots members were not invited to participate in the "reconstituted" steering committee and were replaced by hand picked directors of more mainstream social service agencies, more representatives from law enforcement and other local elites (larger business and foundations). Data collection ceased once the Partnership was transferred to governmental control and the federally-funded evaluators were unable to complete their work. The involvement of community elites did result in local funding investment in the Partnership. Modest financial contributions were made by the city and county to match a local foundation contribution.

Somewhat surprising this co-optation did not result in a significant shift to the "suppression" strategy. Rather the co-optation took the form of containing community mobilization, marginalizing a progressive criminal justice agency and agenda and allowing for the Republican-dominated county government to make inroads into the increasingly politically important but Democratically-inclined African American community.

SOLUTIONS: A JUSTICE STRATEGIES APPROACH

While partnering with government and criminal justice agencies may be fraught with barriers and unintended consequences, there may still be benefits to the community to prepare for and engage in such efforts. The most important of these benefits is driven by data that shows the horrific consequences of traditional criminal justice policy on poor communities, especially communities of color. Crime and responses to crime sap the community of vital resources. Despite the danger of co-optation, community responses remain critical to preventing youth from becoming involved in crime, helping reintegrate persons returning from prison, and advocating for changes in criminal justice policy. The challenge then is to develop approaches that better prepare "community partners" to resist co-optation.

Community justice failures can inform future efforts (Jurik, et al. 2000). Both community empowerment literature and the above-described experience underscore that capacity building must be the first order of business in engaging disempowered communities. Capacity building will allow communities to create solutions that reduce crime without increasing the negative collateral consequences of the criminal justice system on their neighborhoods and their families. Key to capacity building is information that ensures community understanding of the operations and consequences of the current criminal justice system.

A self critical examination of the Partnership from a progressive perspective reveals that at the outset, CCA did not sufficiently attend to training and leadership development. Focus groups convened subsequent to the demise of the Partnership (at least with regard to grassroots community participation) revealed that community residents need basic information and data about a range of criminal justice issues. These focus groups confirm a number of public opinion polls and surveys that found that the public is misinformed about crime trends, sentencing and correctional practices (Sentencing Project). The need for basic information and education does not reflect a lack of ability, but rather a recognition that professionals and governmental officials whose job it is to run various criminal justice system programs will undoubtedly be better prepared than community residents who are not professionally involved in the field. The sources of information most often accessed by those engaged in criminal justice reform—think tank policy pieces, supportive editorials in newspapers, conferences and forums—are not necessarily the venues used by, or accessible to, people who are not focused on criminal justice as a "professional."

Mindful of the shortcomings of its "community justice partnership" experience, CCA (2001) is in the process of developing a training program entitled "Just Power" to prepare community members to participate in and lead community justice work. Just Power addresses a concern raised by Karp and Clear (2000)that in order to be a "meaningful vision" community justice work must include "strategies for enhancing community capacity" to take up this work (p. 330). Absent this capacity building effort, "community volunteers are at technical and political disadvantage against professional criminal justice system staff" (Karp and Clear, 2000, p. 343).

The Just Power curriculum is in many respects self-evident and easily adaptable to individual localities. There are four elements of the curriculum: a description of components of the criminal justice system; how the system "works" from arrest to reentry; race and the criminal justice system; and a review of community justice "models." National, state and local data on incarceration rates and reasons for incarceration (general, by race and gender) are included. CCA is currently working on developing training modules on community organizing and leadership within community justice system contexts.

It will of course be extremely difficult to reverse the structure and consequences of the American criminal justice system. Economic and political agendas add additional forces that would perpetuate the policies that underlie mass incarceration and collateral consequences of mass incarceration—political and economic disenfranchisement, destruction of social capital, prisonization of the community. These are formidable forces to overcome (Garland, 2001(b)). For those committed to overcoming these forces, community justice work must be defined primarily as community organizing and leadership and capacity building. Only when communities begin to understand that the current criminal justice system contributes to crime and the destruction of neighborhoods will those most impacted by these policies mobilize to demand a change in policy and practice.

References

Abramsky, Sasha. July 10, 2001. "Breeding Violence". *Mother Jones*.

Beck, Allen, J. and Harrison, Paige, M. 2001. Prisoners in 2000. Washington, DC: Bureau of Justice Statistics, U.S. Department of Justice.

Bucqueroux, Bonnie. Community Criminal Justice: Building on the Lessons that Community Policing Teaches. in *Community Justice: Striving for Safe, Secure and Just Communities*. Louisville, CO: National Institute of Corrections, U.S. Department of Justice.

Barajas, Eduardo. 1996. Moving Toward Community Justice. *Community Justice: Striving for Safe, Secure and Just Communities*. Louisville, CO: National Institute of Corrections, U.S. Department of Justice.

Center for Community Alternatives. 1996. Partnership to Reduce Juvenile Gun Violence: Proposal to the Office of Juvenile Justice and Delinquency Prevention. Syracuse, NY.

Center for Community Alternatives. 2001. Website. http://www.communityalternatives.org.

Community Benchmarks Program. 1998. Selected Government Performance Outcomes for the City of Syracuse: Comparisons of the Six Residential TNT Sectors in the Areas of Crime, Fire, Streets, Trash and Parks, Syracuse, NY: Maxwell School of Citizenship and Public Affairs.

Cole, David. 1999. *No Equal Justice: Race and Class in the American Criminal Justice System*. New York: The New Press.

Connor, Roger, L. 1998. Lawyers meet Community. Neighbors go to School. Tough meets Love: Promising Approaches to Neighborhood Safety, Community Revitalization, and Crime Control. *What the Federal Government can do to Decrease Crime and Revitalize Communities. Research Forum*. Washington, D.C.: National Institute of Justice, U.S. Department of Justice.

Crawford, Adam. 1997. *The Local Governance of Crime. Appeals to Community and Partnerships*. New York: Oxford University Press.

Dunton, Nancy and Scott Leon. 1995. KIDS COUNT 1995 Data Book: Albany, NY: New York State Division for Youth.

Dunworth, Terence and Mills Gregory. 1999a. National Evaluation of Weed and Seed. Research in Brief. Washington, D.C.: U.S. Department of Justice, National Institute of Justice.

Dunworth, Terence and Mills Gregory. 1999b. National Evaluation of Weed and Seed: Salt Lake City Case Study. Washington, D.C.: U.S. Department of Justice, National Institute of Justice.

Feinblatt, John, Berman, Greg and Sviridoff, Mildred. 1998. Neighborhood Justice: Lessons from the Midtown Community Court. New York: Center for Court Innovation.

Garland, David. 2001a. Introduction: The Meaning of Mass Imprisonment. *Punishment & Society*. 3: 5-7.

Garland, David. 2001b. Epilogue: The New Iron Cage. *Punishment & Society* 3: 197-199.

Hagan, John and Peterson, Ruth D. 1995. Criminal Inequality in America: Patterns and Consequences. *Crime and Inequality* (John Hagan and Ruth D. Peterson eds.) Stanford, CA: Stanford University Press.

Immarigeon, Russ. 1999. Sentence Planning Service: A Key to Reducing the Use of Incarceration. *NASA Notes*. Washington DC: National Association of Sentencing Advocates. Http://www.sentencingproject.org/nasa/sentadvart.htm accessed on December 26, 2001.

Johnstone, Gerry. 2000. Penal Policy Making: Elitist, Populist or Participatory. *Punishment & Society* 2: 161 -180.

Jones-Brown, Delores, D. 2000. Debunking the Myth of Officer Friendly: How African American Males Experience Community Policing. *Journal of Contemporary Criminal Justice*. 16: 209-229.

Jurik, Nancy C., Blumenthal, Joel, Smith, Brian, and Portillos, Edwardo, L. 2000. Organizational Cooptation or Social Change? A Critical Perspective on Community-Criminal Justice Partnerships. *Journal of Contemporary Criminal Justice* 16: 293-320.

Karp, David and Clear, Todd. 1999. *The Community Justice Ideal: Preventing Crime and Achieving Justice*. Boulder CO: Westview Press.

Karp, David and Clear, Todd. 2000. Community Justice: A Conceptual Framework. in *Boundary Changes in Criminal Justice Organizations. Criminal Justice 2000* 2 (pp. 323-368). Washington, DC: National Institute of Justice, U.S. Department of Justice.

Kingsley, G. Thomas, McNeely, Joseph, B. and Gibson, James O. 1997. Community Building: Coming of Age. Washington, D.C.: Urban Institute.

Kurki, Leena. 1999. Incorporating Restorative and Community Justice into American Sentencing and Corrections. Research in Brief: Sentencing and Corrections for the 21st Century. Washington, DC: National Institute of Justice, U.S. Department of Justice.

Kurki, Leena and Pranis Kay. 2000. Restorative Justice as Direct Democracy and Community Building. online, accessed December 28, 2001.

Lasley, J. 1994. The Impact of Rodney King Incident on Citizen Attitudes toward Police. *Policing and Society* 3: 245 -255.

Minkler, Meredith, Thompson, Mildren, Bell, Judith and Rose, Kalima. 2001. Contributions of Community Involvement to Organizational-level Empowerment: The Federal Healthy Start Experience. *Health, Education & Behavior* 28: 783 -807.

National Association of Drug Courts Professionals Drug Courts Standards Committee. 1997. Defining Drug Courts: The Key Components. Washington DC: Office of Drug Court Programs, Department of Justice.

New York City Department of Correction. 2001. General Facts and Figures. http://www.ci.nyc.ny.us/html/doc/html/gnlstats.html, accessed on December 26, 2002.

Office of Juvenile Justice and Delinquency Prevention. 1996. Partnerships to Reduce Juvenile Gun Violence. Discretionary Competitive Program Announcements and Application Kits. Washington DC: U.S. Department of Justice.

Petersilia, Joan. 2000. When Prisoners Return to the Community: Political, Economic, and Social Consequences. *Series: Research in Brief--Sentencing and Corrections: Issues for the 21st Century. Sentencing and Corrections Issues for the 21st Century*

Research in Brief Papers from the Executive Sessions on Sentencing and Corrections No. 9. Washington, DC: National Institute of Justice, U.S. Department of Justice.

Piven, Francis Fox and Cloward Richard. 1972. *Regulating the Poor.* New York: Vintage

Robinson, Laurie. 1998. OJP Bureaus and Program Offices, Fiscal year 1998 Program Plan. http://www.ojp.usdoj.gov/plan/progp198.pdf.

Rose, Dina, R. and Clear Todd. R. 1998. Incarceration, Social Capital and Crime: Implications for Social Disorganization Theory. *Criminology* 36: 441-479.

Sabol and Lynch.1997 *Crime Policy Report: Did Getting Tough on Crime Pay?* Urban Institute http://urban.org/crime/crime htm.

Sentencing Project. Crime, Punishment and Public Opinion: A Summary of Recent Studies and their Implications for Sentencing Policy. Washington DC: Author http://www.sentencingproject.org accessed on December 27, 2001.

Stephan, James, J. 1999. State Prison Expenditures 1996. Washington DC: Bureau of Justice Statistics, U.S. Department of Justice.

Tonry, Michael. 1995. *Malign Neglect: Race, Crime and Punishment in America.* New York: Oxford University Press.

Travis, Jeremy. 1996. Lessons for the Criminal Justice System from Twenty Years of Policing Reform. Keynote Address. New Beginnings: The First Annual Conference of the New York Campaign for Effective Crime Policy.

Travis, Jeremy. 2000. But They All Come Back: Rethinking Prisoner Reentry. *Series: Sentencing and Corrections: Issues for the 21st Century (Research in Brief) Sentencing & Corrections: Papers From the Executive Sessions on Sentencing and Corrections No. 7.* Washington DC: National Institute of Justice, U.S. Department of Justice.

Wilson, Cicero. 1998. Economic Shifts that will Impact Crime Control and Economic Revitalization. *What the Federal Government Can Do about Reducing Crime. Panel Papers.* Washington DC: Executive Office for Weed and Seed, National Institute of Justice, U.S. Department of Justice.

Zimmerman, M.A. 2000. Empowerment theory: Psychological, organizational and community levels of analysis. *Handbook of Community Psychology* (J. Rappaport and E. Seidman, eds.) New York: Plenum.

About the Editors

Seth N. Asumah is Professor of Political Science and Chairperson of the African American Studies Department at SUNY Cortland. His most recent books are *Diversity, Multiculturalism and Social Justice* (co-authored with Ibipo Johnston-Anumonwo, 2002), *The Africana Human Conditions and Global Dimension* (co-edited with Johnston-Anumonwo and John Marah, 2002), *Educating the Black Child in the Black Independent School* (co-authored with Valencia Perkins, 2001) and *Issues in Africa and the African Diaspora in the 21ˢᵗ Century* (co-edited with Ibipo Johnston-Anumonwo, 2001). He is a 1999 winner of the Rozanne Brooks Award for Dedication and Teaching Excellence, and a 2002 recipient of "Excellence In Teaching" Award, State University of New York College at Cortland.

Mechthild Nagel teaches in the Social Philosophy Department at SUNY Cortland and is a Senior Visiting Fellow at the Institute for African Development, Cornell University. She is author of *Masking the Abject: A Genealogy of Play* (Lexington, 2002) and co-editor of *Race, Class, and Community Identity* (Humanities, 2000). She has taught college courses in maximum security prisons for men. Her current research is on African prison intellectuals and African approaches to restorative justice.

About the Contributors

Ishka JoJo Alpern has pursued work with youth programs for open source software programming. Currently, he is pursuing a study of prison literature and advocates non-conformism and alternativeprograms to prisons. He completed his undergraduate work while in prison through Marist College until the Omnibus Crime Bill which cut off all funding for college programs. Afterwards, he continued his studies through correspondence courses. Mr. Alpern obtained a certificate in Ministry and Human Services from New York Theological Seminary. He has published several articles and editorials concerning the prison industrial complex.

Diane Antonio earned her doctorate in Philosophy at SUNY Stonybrook, and her Master of Arts in Liberal Studies at Queens College CUNY. Her published work includes: *Of Wolves and Women* (Animals and Women, 1995), *The Flesh of All That Is: Merleau-Ponty, Irigaray, and Julian's 'Showings'* (Sophia, 2001), and "Virgin Queen, Iron Lady, Queen of Hearts: The Embodiment of Feminine Power in a Male Social Imaginary" (Politicos, 2003).

Seth N. Asumah is Professor of Political Science and Chairperson of the African American Studies Department at SUNY Cortland. His most recent books are *Diversity, Multiculturalism and Social Justice* (co-authored with Ibipo Johnston- Anumonwo, 2002), *The Africana Human Conditions and Global Dimension* (co-edited with Johnston-Anumonwo and John Marah, 2002), *Educating the Black Child in the Black Independent School* (co-authored with Valencia Perkins, 2001) and *Issues in Africa and the African Diaspora in the 21st Century* (co-edited with Ibipo Johnston-Anumonwo, 2001). He is a 1999 winner of the Rozanne Brooks Award for Dedication and Teaching Excellence, and a 2002 recipient of "Excellence In Teaching" Award, State University of New York College at Cortland.

Mary Barr: Combining personal experience with statistical analysis, Ms. Barr's insights on substance abuse and related health and justice system issues have been featured in media, conferences and universities internationally. Her innovative self-empowerment series has been featured in various correctional facilities, for which she is the only private citizen to receive the STEP Medal of Honor. She was instrumental in the historic development of the first transitional program in the Former Soviet Union and was invited to Colombia, South America to research counternarcotics issues. What makes these accomplishments even more remarkable is Ms. Barr has overcome abuse, addictions, homelessness, and numerous incarcerations.

Howard S. Davidson is Associate Professor of Continuing Education at the University of Manitoba. He is the founding editor of the *Journal of Prisoners on Prisons*, a journal which provides prisoners and former prisoners a forum to publish their perspectives on the criminal justice system.

Jill Soffiyah Elijah serves as Deputy Director of the Criminal Justice Institute (CJI) at Harvard Law School (HLS). Ms. Elijah practiced law through various avenues before transitioning into the clinical practice of academia. She was a Supervising Attorney at the Neighborhood Defender Service of Harlem (NDS), where she defended indigent members of the Harlem, New York community. Prof. Elijah has authored several articles and publications based on her research of the U.S. criminal justice and prison systems.

Somjen Frazer received her B.A. with honors from Cornell University. A Presidential Research Scholar (1999-2003), she also received a Bartels Action Research Fellowship (2001-02) and was a John Kenneth Galbraith Scholar in Inequality and Social Policy at Harvard University's Kennedy School of Government (2001). She received an MLitt in sociology as a Rhodes Scholar at Oxford University, where her dissertation focused on homophobic hate crimes. Somjen Frazer is a research associate at the Center for Court Innovation and an evaluator for the TEACH program, which helps teens learn to educate other teens about HIV/AIDS and substance abuse.

Michael Nieto Garcia is a doctoral candidate in the Department of English at Cornell University, where he is completing a dissertation on the ethnic self in Richard Wright and Richard Rodriguez.

Ed Kinane has long been a persistent critic of the U.S. Army's School of the Americas at Ft. Benning, GA. In the late nineties this led to 14 months in federal prisons. He has also been jailed numerous times for his nonviolent civil disobedience. In 2003 Ed spent five months in Iraq with Voices in the Wilderness— an unprosecuted act of protracted civil disobedience. Ed has a masters in anthropology from the New School for Social Research.

Drew Leder, M.D., Ph.D., is a professor of Western and Eastern Philosophy at Loyola College in Maryland. He is the author of many books, including *Sparks of the Divine: Finding Inspiration in Our Everyday World* (Sorin/Ave Maria Press,

2004), *Spiritual Passages: Embracing Life's Sacred Journey* (Tarcher/Putnam, 1997), and *The Absent Body* (U. of Chicago Press, 1990). Dr. Leder has worked extensively with prisoners in a maximum security environment, exploring with them the nature of violence, incarceration, and self-transformation. The results of this work are found in *The Soul Knows No Bars: Inmates Reflect on Life, Death, and Hope* (preface by Cornel West; Rowman and Littlefield, 2000). Lately he has been working to support contemplative practices in prison, helping to write and distribute an informational resource guide.

William G. Martin teaches sociology at Binghamton University and volunteers teaching college courses at local prisons. His research and teaching interests include the relationships between Africans and the world-economy, the sociology of knowledge and racial formations, and global social movements, particularly the Black International. His most recent undergraduate courses include courses on Euro-America and African peoples, Introduction to Global Sociology, and Global Black Movements; his most recent publications include essays on the prison industrial complex, the African state, southern Africa and the world-economy, and anti-systemic movements.

Greg Moses is an independent scholar specializing in philosophies of nonviolence and civil rights. For several years, he helped to coordinate an education program at Green Haven prison in upstate New York, under the auspices of George W. Webber and the New York Theological Seminary. He is author of *Revolution of Conscience: Martin Luther King, Jr. and the Philosophy of Nonviolence.*

John C. Mubangizi is a professor in the Faculty of Law at the University of Kwazulu-Natal, Durban, South Africa, where he currently serves as Deputy Dean of the Faculty. He is the author of *The Protection of Human Rights in South Africa: A Legal and Practical Guide* (2004). He has also authored several articles on human rights, both in national and international journals.

Clayton Morgareidge is Professor Emeritus of Philosophy at Lewis & Clark College in Portland Oregon where he taught courses in ethics, social and political philosophy, and the history of modern philosophy. He is currently working on issues in consciousness and free will.

Mechthild Nagel teaches in the Social Philosophy Department at SUNY Cortland and is a Senior Visiting Fellow at the Institute for African Development, Cornell University. She is author of *Masking the Abject: A Genealogy of Play* (Lexington, 2002) and co-editor of *Race, Class, and Community Identity* (Humanities, 2000). She has taught college courses in maximum security prisons for men. Her current research is on African prison intellectuals and African approaches to restorative justice.

Alan Rosenthal is a criminal defense and civil rights attorney, litigating cases involving police misconduct and violations of civil rights in both jails and prisons. He is currently the Director of Justice Strategies, the research, training and policy initiative of the Center for Community Alternatives. He has drafted legislation on "Racial Profiling and Data Collection," and "Citizen Review Boards" and authored the CCA publication *Sentencing for Dollars*, a review of the financial consequences of a criminal conviction, and a working paper, *Unlocking the Potential of Reentry and Reintegration*.

Tiyo Attallah Salah-El is a decorated Korean War veteran, a Quaker, a composer and a jazz saxophone player. While serving a life sentence in Pennsylvania, Salah-El founded "the Coalition for the Abolition of Prisons" and edited its newsletter. He also earned a BA in African American history and a MA in Political Science. He continues to be active in prison activist and abolitionist circles, writing articles and finalizing his autobiography.

Rashad Shabazz is completing his doctorate in the History of Consciousness program at the University of California-Santa Cruz. His dissertation is a comparative study of post-World War II prison literature in South Africa and North America. His research is an attempt to think about how prisons became central to the changing landscape of post-war society. Mr Shabazz is also an editor for the *Journal of Prisoners on Prisons* and teaches in philosophy and Black Studies at Laney College in Oakland, CA.

Susan Terrio is an Associate Professor of French and Anthropology at Georgetown University where she holds a joint appointment in the departments of French and Sociology/Anthropology. Her areas of expertise include the cultural anthropology of contemporary France and Western Europe and the social and cultural history of France since the revolution of 1789. Prof. Terrio is the author of *Crafting the Culture and History of French Chocolate* (2000). She is currently a fellow at the Radcliffe Institute for Advanced Study at Harvard University where she is writing a book-length monograph entitled *Judging Mohammed at the Paris Palace of Justice: Juvenile Delinquency, (Im)migration and Exclusion*.

Marsha Weissman is the founder and Executive Director of the Center for Community Alternatives where she has established model programs for youth and adults involved in the juvenile and criminal justice system. She serves on a number of boards including The Sentencing Project. Her publications include "Women's Choices: Case Management for Women Leaving Jails and Prisons" (*The Source*, 2003), "Earning trust from youths with none to spare" (*CHILD WELFARE: Special Issue, Children with Parents in Prison*), and "On the Front Line: Defense Attorneys and Sentencing Advocacy" (*The Defender*, 1997).

Index

Index

James, Joy 4
Jospin, Lionel 119, 121
Journal of Prisoners on Prisons 197, 228
just desert 6
just mercy 85-92
justice 3-9, 13, 27, 32, 34, 35, 38, 40, 43, 45, 47, 50, 67, 70, 77, 78, 85-90, 113, 115, 116, 119-121, 125-127, 130, 132, 133, 142, 160, 161, 165, 172, 178, 180, 181, 188, 190, 191, 201-203, 207-215, 217, 218, 223, 225-228
juveniles 114, 160, 161
rates of arrest of 114

Kampala, Uganda 139
Kant, Immanuel 79
Kathrada, Ahmed 149, 150
Kenyatta, Jomo 8, 143
Kikumura, Yu 17
Kittay, Eva 86
Krantz, Les 132

Labanino-Salazar, Ramon 16
law 2, 3, 6, 7, 14, 24, 25, 27, 34, 35, 40, 77, 79, 85, 86, 88-90, 99, 106, 113, 116-118, 120, 121, 131, 132, 137, 140, 142, 144, 146, 148, 150, 152, 154, 157, 158, 160, 162, 164, 166, 167, 170, 172, 174, 176, 178, 180, 210-212, 214, 216, 217, 226, 227
"law and order" 99
law-referencing vs. life-reverencing 86, 90
Lebranchu, Marylise 121
Lebron, Lolita 14
Leder, Drew 4, 6, 55, 56, 58, 59, 62, 64-67, 70, 226, 227

legislation 7, 35, 40, 89, 95, 98, 99, 102, 103, 115, 116, 128, 170, 181, 193, 228
Lesotho 141, 175, 176, 180
Levinas, Emmanuel 87
Lexington control unit 14
Liberia 141
lived body 56, 64, 66
lived space 60, 62, 63, 66
lived time 57-59, 70
Long Walk to Freedom 149
"Lotería en Babilonia, La"
See "Lottery of Babylon, The"
"Lottery of Babylon, The," 7, 127

Malambo, Johnson Philip 150
Mali 43, 45-49
Mandela, Nelson 149-152
Marx, Karl 79, 154
mass incarceration 7, 211
Mbeki, Govan 149
McKinney, Congresswoman Cynthia 16
media 2, 3, 7, 20, 74, 95, 96, 98, 101-103, 106, 107, 109, 113-115, 117, 118, 120, 121, 142, 171, 173, 202, 216, 225
Memory 57, 59, 67, 68, 87-89, 147
emotional 88
embodied 89
Merleau-Ponty, Maurice 64-66, 70, 225
Miami, Florida 16, 208
Midtown Community Court 210
Military Industrial Complex 2
minimum sentencing guidelines 4
Minkowski, Eugene 58, 70
minority status 114, 115
Mkunqwana, Monhde Colin 150
moral panic(s) 6, 7, 9, 95-97, 99, 101-103, 105, 107, 109, 110